International Yeats Studies

vol. 6

ISBN 978-1-63804-122-1

Published by Clemson University Press in Clemson, South Carolina

To order copies, contact Clemson University Press at 116 Sigma Dr., Clemson, South Carolina, 29634 or order via our website: www.clemson.edu/press.

Contents

Volume 6, Issue 1

Yeats's Stolen Children

Martin Lockerd

Initially published in *The Irish Monthly* (1886), reprinted in the collection *Poems and Ballads of Young Ireland* (1888), and later included in *The Wanderings of Oisin and Other Poems* (1889), "The Stolen Child" quickly established Yeats's early reputation as a poet of the Irish folk, and it has remained one of his most recognizable and beloved lyrics. I confess, though, that as a young college student reading it for the first time, the poem elicited more embarrassment than admiration. It felt cloying and sentimental, hardly worth mentioning in the same breath as the cold, intellectually complex, Modernist poems of his mature period. It was only some years later, after my wife and I suffered the stillbirth of our first daughter, that I found I couldn't read the poem without the threat of tears. I came to understand "The Stolen Child" not as a twee poem about mischievous fairies, but as a poem that deals seriously with trauma and loss—one that combines the artist's desire to express the inexpressible loss of a child with the folk Irish instinct to frame that injury within the logic of fairyland.

This article begins by arguing for "The Stolen Child" as an artistic sublimation and reenactment of the early trauma of Yeats's three-year-old brother's passing, an event that the adult Yeats identified as "My realization of death" (*CW3* 55). The poem, I claim, frames its traumatic content within the context of folklore and extends that content into a surprisingly complex lyric form that has gone unremarked upon by even such groundbreaking formal critics as Helen Vendler. Understanding the poem's successful abreaction of child loss in turn allows for a consideration of a later poem that fails at the same task. Five years after the publication of "The Stolen Child," following the death of Maud Gonne's son Georges, Yeats revisited the trauma of child loss in the unpublished poem "On a Child's Death." There he foregoes the explanatory fictions of folklore in favor of a rawer, and hence unpublishable, lyric of loss. This movement from early success to later failure suggests the problems inherent not only in attempting to process trauma on behalf of someone else, but also in attempting to do so without the aid of deep-seated meaning-making narratives, such as that of fairy abduction in rural Ireland. In this sense, "On a Child's Death" expresses modernity's failure to provide a meaningful alternative to the folk and religious traditions of trauma-framing that were unseated by scientism and cultural pluralism.

Trauma, like so many theoretical paradigms, is notoriously resistant to pithy definition. For the last thirty years critical consensus has generally held that "trauma is that which defies witnessing, cognition, conscious recall and representation."[1] Building on the work of Sigmund Freud and employing the techniques of deconstruction, early trauma theorists such as Cathy Caruth emphasized the impossibility of knowing and articulating trauma to such an extent that they risked evacuating the traumatic event and witness of real meaning. Within this earlier model, according to Richard Crownshaw, the traumatic event effectively cannot be known; therefore, "it engenders through its insistent return a compulsive and repetitive acting out rather than working through."[2] By making all individual experience of trauma an expression of ontic woundedness or absence, Caruth's Freudian model carries with it the universalizing implications that "all of modernity is traumatic," and that all trauma is, at root, structural, transhistorical, and textual (i.e. expressed solely through language's failure of expression).[3] Drawing on the insights of historian Dominick LaCapra, Crownshaw points out that within such a theoretical framework "Historical trauma is reduced to a textual trace, and textual trauma supersedes history."[4] Lucy Bond and Stef Craps summarize the tension between earlier models of structural trauma and more recent, historicized models:

> These different positions are indicative of a tension within trauma theory between those who are primarily concerned with doing justice to traumatic repetition as a sign of survival and those who seek to drive home the point that one needs to heal from trauma if one is to be able to fully reengage with life and work towards a better tomorrow.[5]

Structural trauma results from a Freudian notion of a foundational absence within all human beings and thus cannot be overcome. By contrast, historical trauma relates to a specific instance of loss and carries at least the possibility of being worked through in time. What these divergent models perhaps fail to account for are the myriad ways in which literature reveals how one person may both "work through" a traumatic event, by the process of witnessing that event in art, and yet still continue to feel traces of the psychological wound of that original loss as part and parcel of the universal human encounter with suffering and death.

Yeats's poems about lost children illustrate the potential verity of both historical and structural models of trauma, thus revealing the limitations of both. On the one hand, he is seemingly able to "work through" the trauma of his brother's death by embracing the cultural narrative of the changeling and by aestheticizing his pain within the formal qualities of "The Stolen Child." On the other hand, he fails to articulate a satisfactory response to Gonne's (and by projection his) loss of a son and falls back on a universalized lament about the cruelty and essential senselessness of death. The success of the former and failure of the latter poem, in terms of working through trauma, rest squarely with the larger failure of Yeats's attempt to cope with modernity by moving beyond local, historicized systems of belief and enfolding all human history, religion, and culture into an overarching, trans-historical, cyclical system of occult Gnosticism. This failure in turn reminds us of a central shortcoming of modernity as a whole, namely, the loss of meaningful, shared cultural trauma-framing beliefs and practices. As I write these words in the wake of a global coronavirus pandemic, I am reminded that our era is simultaneously better equipped than ever before to temporarily confound death through medical technology and worse equipped than ever before to meaningfully engage with and make sense of death.

I. A Stolen Child

Robert Corbet Yeats died of croup on March 3, 1873. The condition stems from inflammation in the respiratory system and expresses itself as a harsh, barking cough that would freeze the blood of any parent. Yeats lived a life of some hardship, but few events in that life might be better characterized as traumatic than the death of his infant brother. Roy Foster relates that Willie, nearly eight years old at the time, tried to cope by quickly converting the loss of his brother into art:

> Lily and WBY woke to hear their mother cry "My little son, my little son" and horses' hoofs galloping for the doctor. After the death, the children sat drawing pictures of the ships along the Sligo quay, with flags at half mast. Susan Yeats, who thought she heard the banshee cry before her child died, was probably precipitated by the loss into the depression from which she never really returned. (*Life 1* 21).

She had little chance of return. Three years later, her fifth and youngest child, Jane Grace, succumbed to pneumonia before her first birthday. Deirdre Toomey points out that Yeats's *Autobiographies* neglect to mention his mother's existence until the recounting of Robert's death, some twenty pages in: "Susan Yeats thus enters the narrative with death, again a most unusual presentation in autobiography."[6] Following the deaths of her children, as well as the never-ending displacements and penury caused by J. B. Yeats's failures as husband, father, and painter, Susan Yeats entered a semi-paralytic state for the remainder of her life. She became in her son's mind, Toomey argues, "away"—the euphemism employed by the Irish peasantry for those people taken by the fairies and replaced with a broken substitute.[7] We can see a presentiment of

Yeats's earliest fairy lyric in Robert's death, Susan's retreat from consciousness, and the folk explanations that frame each. We can also see young Willie's attempt to cope with Robert's death by making art that turned his private loss into a cause for public mourning. The boy's need for emotional expression, his need to revisit and work through the experience of his trauma, would later find an appropriate public voice in "The Stolen Child."

As we have seen, Caruth's structural trauma model implies that literature, and language in general, revisit trauma to seek closure that cannot be achieved, since the original, painful experience exceeds full understanding and participates in a universal absence at the heart of the human psyche. Yeats's poem speaks to the partial truth of Caruth's model; he clearly feels compelled to revisit and retell his loss. But, without recognizing the historicity of the original traumatic event and Yeats's eventual artistic response to that event, we risk missing the ways in which the poem not only reenacts but works through the trauma of Robert's death. The particular trauma-framing practices of nineteenth-century Ireland play a strong role in Yeats's process of recovery and recuperation.

"The Stolen Child" draws on Irish folk beliefs about fairies and changelings to create art that revisits trauma in search of closure. Because fairies, to his mind, were not the tiny, playful, sweet creatures of much Victorian literature, Yeats often eschewed even the word fairy. He once explained this policy in a letter to a poet who had attempted to "prettify" and domesticate the fairies: "I myself try to avoid the word 'fairy' because it has associations of prettiness. *Sidhe* or 'gentry' or 'the others' is better. The Irish peasant never thinks of the fairies as pretty. He thinks of them as terrible, or beautiful."[8] As we will see, he regularly opted for the spelling "faery." Belief in the Sidhe began in prehistoric, pagan Ireland. Once incorporated into the metaphysical framework of Christianity, those pagan gods were generally reconceptualized as fallen angels. These bad but not damned angels, according to some, were caught between heaven and hell when the gates of each closed after Lucifer's rebellion.[9] If not immortal, they are, at the very least, extremely long-lived. They spend their lives haunting the countless fairy mounds around Ireland. Part of the terror associated with the Sidhe among the Irish peasantry sprang from the belief that the fairies would spirit away healthy, beautiful mortals and replace them with changelings. These often malformed and sickly creatures were generally the spirits of ancient, decrepit fairies, who could no longer sport and cavort with their own kind. When a loved one took suddenly ill or died, the family would naturally assume that they were "away" and would thus suspect fairy abduction and substitution.

Sometimes this suspicion would lead to acts of violence meant to chase out the changeling and force the Sidhe to return what they had stolen. As late as the 1890s, a father and mother in County Donegal, just north of Sligo, killed their child in an attempt to get the fairies to take back their changeling.[10] Then there is the more notorious incident of Bridget Cleary in 1895. The twenty-six-year-old woman had become willful and mentally disturbed. In an attempt to exorcise the fairy possessing her, Bridget's husband and family members burned her to death.[11] Michael Cleary spent the next three nights waiting beside the local fairy hill for his bride to return. He would eventually be convicted of manslaughter and sentenced to fifteen years of hard labor. The Cleary case is horrifying but exceptional. Toomey notes that Yeats's essays concerning folk beliefs about changelings emphasized "the importance of not injuring the 'substitute'" and saw in this practice both a pact of non-aggression with the Sidhe and an inspiringly humane mode of treating the weak and broken.[12] General belief held that the fairies most desired beautiful newborns and infants. Blaming the Sidhe for infant mortality provided an answer for what might otherwise feel like senseless human suffering.

The devout might seek such answers within the Catholic catechism, but, for many an Irish peasant, even the metaphysically sophisticated Church failed to satisfactorily account for the grief of infant death with either the promise of paradise or the notion of a limbus infantium, that spiritual realm where unbaptized infants spend dumb eternity in neither the pain of Hell nor the ecstasy of Heaven. Belief in fairy abduction provided a more immediate, ancient, and local explanation for loss, while at the same time denying the believer any immediate solace, which is, as the wounded know, the last thing we desire at the moment of bereavement. In the face of his own loss, Yeats found that the various myths surrounding fairy abduction provided a source for artistic abreaction whereby he might, however subtly, express and partially expurgate the trauma of his brother's death. It seems only natural that Yeats chose Sligo as the setting for his poem about a child stolen away by the Sidhe. There he learned about the fairies from country people and the servants in the kitchen of his grandparents' grand home, Merville; and there, he experienced Robert's death. Yeats's need for emotional expression and his need to revisit the experience of his trauma would eventually find a public voice.

The conventional reading of "The Stolen Child" goes something like this. In the first stanza, the fairies describe their "leafy island" on Lough Gill and tempt the child with their song:

Come away, O human child!
To the waters and the wild
With a faery, hand in hand.
For the world's more full of weeping than you can understand.[13]

They go on to describe their dances at Rosses Point, a sandy peninsula north of Sligo, and contrast their carefree "footing" to a human world "full of troubles" and "anxious in its sleep."[14] When not dancing, we are told, the fairies spend their time in the pools below the Glen-Car waterfall whispering to sleeping trout and giving them "unquiet dreams"—a somewhat ominous pastime. In the final stanza, the Sidhe celebrate their successful temptation of a now "solemn-eyed" child. Why "solemn-eyed"? He has, according to the traditional reading, given up the little comforts of a human home: the peaceful song of the kettle heating over the fire, the sight of mice playing around the oatmeal chest. Viewed in this light, the poem describes something more like a seduction than an abduction. The young boy is tempted into leaving behind his family in favor of the promise of a life without pain. "Stolen" by the Sidhe and presumably replaced with a changeling, the child chooses a faery world with familiar Sligo geography but very different playmates and pastimes. Readers all agree that the boy is losing something, giving up his peacefully human world for a threateningly supernatural one. What they miss is that this is a poem as concerned with the carefully concealed poet as it is with either the speakers (the fairies) or the subject (the boy).

This is a surprisingly complex poem. Among other things, it highlights the difference between lyric enunciation and narrative. As Jonathan Culler points out in his *Theory of the Lyric* (2015), this type of poetry cannot be treated like traditional mimetic storytelling even if it contains narrative elements: "In narrative fiction, the question of the relation between *story* and *discourse* or between what is enunciated and the enunciation is generally theorized as one of perspective—from what point of view are events reported (in fictions the priority of event to narration is assumed)." By contrast, in lyric "the present of discourse or articulation cannot be reduced to the narrating of past events; on the contrary, the narrated events seem to be subsumed by, trumped by, the present of lyric enunciation."[15] Reduced to a narrative, the "The Stolen Child" fails to impress and may even threaten to embarrass. Does Yeats literally believe in fairy abduction? Does he wish us to? The only satisfying answer seems to be the paradoxical yes-and-no that characterizes the lyric mode as more performative than didactic. If we try to take the poem seriously, it becomes either parochial, false, or both. If we refuse to take it seriously, it becomes, at best, a parable about the emptiness of utopian fantasy and the pleasures of simple, human life: the kettle on the hob, the mice running round the oatmeal chest. No purely hermeneutic search for meaning can explain its power. Only by exploring the form of the fairies' song can we begin to hear its warning note and, further, the submerged voice of the poet, who laments the boy's decision as he inhabits the perpetual now of loss and grief. At the poem's conclusion, the boy has made his choice; however, the poem's structure rails against that choice and, by so doing, expresses the emotions of neither the fairies nor the child. Instead, it becomes a sublimated expression of the poet's wish that the child would resist—that he would give up on the temptations of another world to stay with his family in this world.

The poet's implicit opposition to the child's abduction extends beyond the content of the poem and into its form. What Culler calls "triangulated address"[16] —that ritual dimension of the lyric whereby the speaking voice of the poem addresses the reader by addressing someone or something else—becomes even more complicated than usual in "The Stolen Child."

Where dips the rocky highland
  Of Sleuth Wood in the lake,
There lies a leafy island
  Where flapping herons wake
The drowsy water rats;
There we've hid our faery vats,
Full of berries
And of reddest stolen cherries.[17]

We, as readers attuned to the lyric "I," assume a singular speaker, and we may well have one. Initially, there is no reason to doubt that our fairy speaker is a singular representative addressing the child of the title on behalf of a group. But the following refrain, always rendered in italics, clearly represents a different kind of speech act, more akin to a chant than a chat:

Come away, O human child!
To the waters and the wild
With a faery, hand in hand.
For the world's more full of weeping than you can understand.[18]

Within the first stanza, the poet juxtaposes two different modes of address. The first is descriptive. It focuses on conveying the nature of fairy life in a manner that the speaker calculates will best entice the child. The second is imperative. It commands the child to follow and warns of the world's many sorrows. These complementary speech acts work toward the same goal for three stanzas. By contrast, the poem's final stanza reconfigures the act:

Away with us he's going,
  The solemn-eyed:
He'll hear no more the lowing
  Of the calves on the warm hillside
Or the kettle on the hob
  Sing peace into his breast,

Or see the brown mice bob
 Round and round the oatmeal chest.[19]

Their abduction complete, the fairies shift their address from the boy to each other, from a monologue to a circular dialogue; nevertheless, we remain the fixed mark of their triangulated address.

Hand in hand with the Sidhe, the child moves into a world without weeping, even as we are left behind to mourn both his loss and what he has lost. The Sidhe do not simply steal the child from us; they steal the child's future and recount his losses for our benefit. What's worse, they do so within a fixed present. The child *is* going. His passage from our world to theirs remains locked in the present progressive tense, but the fairies' self-reflexive dialogue in the final stanza places his losses firmly in an immutable future tense: "He'll hear no more the lowing." This shift from present to future tense is as strange as the speakers' shift in address. The vast majority of lyric poetry does neither. Present tense is the particular province of the lyric, and the stable I/Thou address is equally dominant in the genre. When tense shift does occur, as Culler notes,[20] it usually entails a movement from the past tense into a poetic present, as in Wordsworth's "I Wandered Lonely as a Cloud," in which the speaker pulls an anecdote into the frame of a present reverie. Conversely but similarly, lyric time may slip from present action to future recollection of that action, though this is far less common. Yeats enacts such a temporal shift in a later poem of grand historical trauma, "Leda and the Swan," in which the non-progressive present of the rape ("He holds her helpless") gives way to the interrogatory past tense only at the end ("Did she put on his knowledge with his power…?").[21] The most present moment in "The Stolen Child," perhaps the most present moment in his corpus, is the moment of the child's departure: "Away with us he's going, / The Solemn-eyed." All the child's future losses described thereafter are contained in the progressive present, which (and this is the important point) is the tense of trauma.

"If all time is eternally present," T. S. Eliot tells us in *Burnt Norton*, "All time is unredeemable."[22] Traumatic experience has a date, a time, and a place rooted in the past tense, but its consequences live in the progressive present. Loss, especially the loss of a child, does not happen once; it recurs; it is always happening, just as the child in Yeats's poem is always going away. Thus far, Caruth's Freudian model of structural trauma holds true enough, but, in asserting the perpetual present of "The Stolen Child," I am not interested in suggesting that Yeats *only* iterates structural trauma by illustrating language's inability to encompass the universal human experience of psychic absence. His poem involves both an acting-out and a working-through of the original traumatic event. The formal expression of trauma in the tense of the "The

Stolen Child"—its inherent abreactive quality, its imaginative recreation of a traumatic past experience in the distinct present of the lyric—makes it possible for both to occur at once. Time and speaker, however, represent only two of the lyric dimensions of Yeats's poem about loss. The poet, who functions neither as speaker, nor subject, nor any of the three presumptive audiences (the boy, the fairies themselves, and the reader), makes his presence felt in the poem's formal play with rhyme and rhythm.

Helen Vendler's groundbreaking book *Our Secret Discipline* (2007) draws attention to the fact that Yeats saw his job as a poet as the work of putting ideas into verse form. His obsession with the difficulty of this task finds voice in "Adam's Curse," in which the speaker claims that the work of the poet, who may take hours to write a single line, is more grueling than that of the manual laborer. Although those with experience working on farms or construction sites may demur, once we understand the intensity of Yeats's investment in lyric form as the only mode suitable to the expression of our profoundest ideas, we can also begin to understand better his definition of poetry as an internal struggle: "We make out of the quarrel with others, rhetoric, but of the quarrel with ourselves, poetry."[23] This famous aphorism opens Section V of Per *Amica Silentia Lunae* (1918), Yeats's mostly unsuccessful attempt to lay out the mystical foundations of his poetry in prose for the benefit of his bewildered readers and reviewers. The poet, he tells us, makes poetry not to convince others of a cause or teach a lesson but to pursue a visionary ecstasy that can only come from a disciplined and unflinching encounter with reality.

Yeats immediately connects this artistic escape from self-deception and into ecstasy with one of life's cruelest realities, the death of children:

> An old artist wrote to me of his wanderings by the quays of New York, and how he found there a woman nursing a sick child, and drew her story from her. She spoke, too, of other children who had died: a long tragic story. "I wanted to paint her," he wrote, "if I denied myself any of the pain I could not believe in my own ecstasy."[24]

In "The Stolen Child," Yeats's pursuit of ecstasy and quarrel with the reality and lingering trauma of his brother's death manifests itself in the interplay of content and form. The vast majority of Yeats's poetry, especially his early work, plays with rhythm and rhyme in regular, if not always conventional and predictable, ways: "The Cloak, the Boat, and the Shoes," "The Indian Upon God," "Down by the Salley Gardens," "Who Goes with Fergus?," the rose poems, the ballads, etc. "The Stolen Child" is different in respect to formal regularity. In fact, it is a poem of formal chaos in regard to stanza length, rhyme scheme, and rhythm. Within this chaos, we find again the poet, who implicitly warns both receivers of the poem's triangulated address (i.e. the child and the reader) against following the deceptive Sidhe.

Yeats's fairies are not crass enough to speak in free verse. They seemingly aspire to regularity of traditional lyric form without attaining their end. This chaos playing at order manifests itself most noticeably in the length of the stanzas. Stanzas one and four are each twelve lines, but they bookend middle stanzas of fifteen and fourteen lines respectively. The effect is neither immediately noticeable, nor retrospectively accountable. Yeats easily could have balanced the poem into three, twelve-line stanzas. He chose not to. Likewise, he chose not to establish a regular rhyme scheme in stanza one only to distort it in the proceeding verse paragraphs. The center of the poem is the conventional, predictable abab rhyme scheme (highland/lake/Island/wake) that opens each stanza. That center fails to hold. In stanza one, it gives way to a series of couplets (rats/vats; fairies/cherries), which lead naturally enough into the italicized couplets of the chanted refrain (*child/wild/hand/understand*). That's all well and good. Were this pattern maintained through the rest of the poem, this rhyme scheme would feel conventional enough, a quatrain followed by couplets. We could inventively treat the stanzas as something like truncated hybrid sonnets. But things go awry in the second stanza. The opening abab quatrain (glosses/light/Rosses/night) gives way to the expected cc couplet (dances/glances), followed inexplicably by an extra b rhyme (flight) in the seventh line. Instead of returning to the couplet pattern following this seeming interruption or misstep, the succeeding four lines follow the rhyming logic of a Petrarchan quatrain. The next two stanzas continue this chaotic rhyming by distorting the original pattern from stanza one in new and jarring ways.

Aside from producing this erratic rhyme scheme, Yeats also gives us a poem of unpredictable rhythm. If the iamb is the regulatory rhythm of English speech, the Irish spirits can't seem to pull it off. The very first line ("Where dips the rocky highland") is a truncated iambic tetrameter that ends with an unresolved iamb. The next line ("Of Slewth Wood in the lake") substitutes a trochee in the middle foot ("Wood in"), becoming a syncopated iambic trimeter. This metric reduction finds its epitome in the key line of the final stanza and of the poem as a whole ("The solemn-eyed"). The fairies may be the poem's speakers, but the poet makes their speech a parody of human verse and punctuates the consequence of their theft by highlighting the boy's solemnity with those two iambic feet "The solemn-eyed." But why present the fairies as undisciplined artists in this manner? Since, as we have already learned from Culler, the lyric cannot be thought of in terms of fictive narrative, it must express trauma differently. Yeats's first lyric of loss achieves its sense of woundedness by establishing and then repeatedly violating its own formal pattern. What we have here is form as an extension of trauma.

In a 2013 lecture given at University College Dublin's Humanities Institute on the subject of contemporary trauma studies, Kali Tal remarked that she often describes trauma to her students in terms of narrative.[25] Throughout life, we draw on what she refers to as a "cultural library of coherent narratives"[26] about the past, present, and future of our own lives. Unless already distorted by depression or existential pessimism, our future narratives tend to follow predictable patterns of improvement leading to marginal gains in happiness. Only the deranged person gets married expecting that said marriage will end within five years because of a sudden brain aneurism or, much more likely, a car accident. The very possibility of living functionally in an unknown future demands that we construct more or less comforting narratives about the results of our present endeavors. Such future narratives are especially vulnerable to what Tal conceptualizes as "plot violations." Justifiably, we treat such violations as unbelievable; hence our inevitable resort to denial as a means of coping with sudden grief. "This can't be happening" is the predictable refrain of the traumatized. "When the scripts aren't there," Tal remarks, "and there's nothing to say, that's what trauma is."[27]

The very idea of changeling abduction springs from the unbelievability of infant death. It provides a narrative supplement that offers to redress the traumatic plot violation of infant mortality. However, far from simply providing a superstitious explanation for a natural occurrence, the changeling myth affords access to a deeper, if not readily ameliorating, truth that Yeats saw at the heart of the Celtic imagination; the ancient beliefs that vivify Irish art and lend it its passion and melancholy are based on the assumption that material "reality" presents only one aspect of a larger reality that stretches beyond death and beyond the limits of language. Yeats makes this point clear in "The Celtic Element in Literature" (1903):

> Certainly a thirst for unbounded emotion and a wild melancholy are troublesome things in the world, and do not make its life more easy or orderly, but it may be the arts are founded on the life beyond the world, and that they must cry in the ears of our penury until the world has been consumed and become a vision. [. . .] Matthew Arnold has said that if he were asked "where English got its turn for melancholy and its turn for natural magic," he "would answer with little doubt that it got much of its melancholy from a Celtic source, with no doubt at all that from a Celtic source is got nearly all its natural magic."
>
> I will put this differently and say that literature dwindles to a mere chronicle of circumstance, or passionless phantasies, and passionless meditations, unless it is constantly flooded with the passions and beliefs of ancient times.[28]

Yeats's "Stolen Child" amounts to far more than a "chronicle of circumstance" because it refuses to treat the death of a child as yet another cruel reality of an absurd universe, a position he comes dangerously close to in his later poems about child mortality. This child is lost but not gone. He is with the Sidhe in a world without weeping. Moreover, he is immortalized in the poem itself.

Yeats did not stop thinking and writing about children. His poetic prayers for his children and his famous late poem "Among School Children" ("How can we know the dancer from the dance?") are iconic. However, he never returned to the idea of the changeling. Having corrected the plot violation of Robert's death by wedding it to Sligo folklore and weaving it into his abreactive lyric, Yeats depersonalized an early trauma and made it into lasting art. In one of the critical manifestos of literary Modernism, "Tradition and the Individual Talent" (1919), T. S. Eliot speaks to this process of depersonalization and provocatively calls poetry an escape from emotion. Poetry, Eliot insists, "is not the expression of personality, but an escape from personality. But, of course, only those who have personality and emotions know what it means to want to escape from these things."[29] Yeats made such an escape. He wrote a depersonalized poem informed by the emotions of personal trauma. The solemn child, who drew ships with flags at half-mast when his brother died, grew up. The poet who wrote a poem about a stolen child did too. By the next time Yeats faced the death of a child in verse, he had distanced his poetry somewhat from its earlier folkloric preoccupations in favor of idiosyncratic occult Gnosticism. His next lyric of loss abandoned the historicized trauma-framing narrative of changeling abduction in order to ask the unanswerable questions at the heart of structural trauma. The result was a profound, in both senses of that word, failure.

II. A Dead Child

Just over a year after Yeats's consequential first meeting with Maud Gonne in January of 1889, she gave birth to another man's son and named him Georges. Yeats didn't learn of the boy's existence until after the one-year-old child's death, presumably of meningitis, in August of 1891. Infatuated as he was, the young poet happily accepted Gonne's explanation that Georges was adopted. Strangely enough, Yeats relates in his *Memoirs* that, following Georges's death, Gonne claimed to have adopted the boy "some three years ago" (*Mem* 47). According to Yeats, she related the mathematically untenable story of Georges' birth and the tragedy of his sudden death in a confused letter: "Mixed into her incoherent grief were accounts of the death bird that had pecked at the nursery window the day when it [Georges] was taken ill, and how at sight of the bird she had brought doctor after doctor" (*Mem* 47). It should come as no surprise that Yeats fixates on Gonne's bird omen in relating the story of her loss, nor that he recalls the one-year-old Georges as a three-year-old. Yeats's own brother, Robert, died just weeks before his third birthday. Yeats, whose mother had been so severely scarred by the deaths of two young children, would have had good reason to worry about Gonne. He also had ample reason to identify with her loss and seek to ameliorate it through verse, as he had done for himself in the composition of "The Stolen Child."

When Gonne, dressed in mourning, retuned to Ireland some two months after her letter, she found herself quite accidentally on the boat carrying the body of Charles Stuart Parnell. Contrary to the opinion of many who witnessed her arrival, she did not wear black for the uncrowned King of Ireland, but for her lost child. In Gonne's own mind, she bore the weight of a profounder loss for herself and her nation. Before his death, Gonne had professed a hope that "Georgette" or "Georginet," as she affectionately called the boy, would one day be the king of a free Irish nation.[30] His loss was a blow. "Following her [Gonne's] arrival in Dublin," Yeats relates, "she went over again the details of the death—speech was a relief to her. She was plainly very ill."[31] Aside from having temporarily lost the ability to speak French, a language almost as familiar as English to Gonne, the bereaved mother became addicted to chloroform, without which she could not sleep.

Yeats and AE attempted to comfort her with theosophical theories of the afterlife. One of AE's speculations about potential methods for directing the process of reincarnation supposedly led Gonne, upon returning to her home in France, to attempt to recapture Georges's soul by having sex with the boy's father, Lucien Millevoye, in the mausoleum she had erected for her son's remains. Theoretically, the child produced by this act would become a new container for the dead boy's spirit. The result was Gonne's daughter, Iseult. Yeats's account of Gonne's visit and what we know of her resulting necromantic exploit demonstrate the depth of her trauma and the lengths to which she was willing to go in order to correct the plot violation of Georges's death. These events also underscore the difficulties faced by those who lack the cultural, religious, or folk beliefs that help to bring such unspeakable pain within the circle of expected and, therefore, manageable loss. Notably, neither AE nor Yeats spoke to Gonne about changelings or fairy abductions. By 1891, Yeats was more prone to occult than folk explanations of the inexplicable. Gonne's attempt to reincarnate Georges seems to prove that, far from helping to frame and make sense of traumatic loss, such gnostic wisdom treats grief as something to be erased by magic. It also suggests that Yeats's failure to give artistic voice to Georges's death stemmed at least in part from his alienation from the types of traditional trauma-framing narratives that allowed him to create "The Stolen Child."

Yeats's first attempt to make sense of Gonne's loss for her came immediately on the heels of her visit to Dublin in the form of a poem focused on one of Yeats's favorite subjects, unrequited love. Not long before Georges's death, in what seems in retrospect like a transparent attempt on Gonne's end to demarcate the limits of their relationship, she had related a vision to Yeats. In some past life, they were brother and sister "on the edge of the Arabian desert," and they were sold into slavery (*Mem* 46). Misreading this revelation as a declaration of a special bond, Yeats rushed to do exactly what Gonne must have been trying to prevent; he proposed. She, of course, rejected the proposal, insisting that they must remain special friends, spiritual siblings, but no more.

Reflecting on this event in the aftermath of the death of Gonne's son, and keen to provide some amelioration of her suffering, he composed the poem "Cycles Ago." The speaker of the poem notes Gonne's dejection—"The sad rose colours of autumn with weariness mixed in your face"—and links it to his own loss of her love: "My world was fallen and over, for your dark soft eyes on it shone; A thousand years it had waited and now it is gone, it is gone."[32] By the poem's conclusion, Gonne's grief at the loss of her child has become, at least in the speaker's eyes, intertwined with the larger grief of their recurring history of mingled glances and unrealized love:

> Ah cycles ago did I meet you and mingle my gaze with your gaze,
> They mingled a moment and parted and weariness fell on our days,
> And we went alone on our journeys and envied the grass covered dead
> For Love had gone by us unheeding, a crown of stars on his head.[33]

Yeats's cyclical understanding of history and human fate, as expressed here, is essentially tragic in nature and offers little hope or comfort. Unlike "The Stolen Child," which transmutes loss into first-rate poetry and treats it as an historically rooted trauma that can be worked through with the aid of communally shared trauma-framing narratives, "Cycles Ago" implicitly embraces a structural notion of trauma by making each individual loss part of an essential absence at the heart of human existence. It literally treats trauma as something that cannot be meaningfully addressed because it recurs in ceaseless cycles. If you are torn from your beloved sister and sold into slavery in one life, it is only one manifestation of the essential trauma of human existence that will recur centuries later when your beloved rejects your marriage proposal just before watching her son die. The best we can do at the nadir of each cycle is envy the dead and move forward with the certain knowledge that our wounds will continue to reopen in new and devastating ways.

Yeats continued to play with the tragic notion of cyclical trauma until the end of his career, most notably rehearsing it in his last play, *Purgatory* (1938).

That is not to say that Yeats maintained such a position consistently. In *Yeats and the Poetry of Death*, Jahan Ramazani warns against assuming consistent symmetry between Yeats's avowed beliefs about death and his greatest poems on the subject: "The system's displacement of death onto subsequent lives should not blinker our reading of the poems, since the strongest lyrics seldom ratify its view of death."[34] "Cycles Ago" is not one of Yeats's stronger lyrics in large part because it adheres to Yeats's system by treating all of human existence as, to an extent, an expression of cyclical, structural trauma, with death merely opening the door to yet more of the same. I like to think that Yeats's decision not to publish the poem, after going so far as to prepare the proofs for inclusion in *The Countess Kathleen and Various Legends and Lyrics* (1892), signals that he found this pallid vision ultimately unsatisfactory.

In 1893, almost two years after writing and rejecting "Cycles Ago," Yeats attempted once again to process Gonne's loss in verse. For what Ronald Schuchard calls "obvious personal reasons," Yeats omitted "On a Child's Death" from *Poems* (1895) and never published it (*YA3* 191). Without speculation, we can say that "On a Child's Death" meant a good deal to Yeats. In May of 1899, he inscribed it in a copy of *Poems* (1899), which he gifted to Lady Gregory, the one person with whom he had shared all the vicissitudes of his relationship with Gonne. Schuchard brought the poem to light in 1985; little has been made of it since. Yeats dated the inscription of "On a Child's Death," September 5, 1893, which Schuchard takes as a clear indication that the poem was originally composed to commemorate the second anniversary of Georges's death. The immediate sense of the poem is readily apparent. Yeats indicts the "shadowy armies of the dead" for greedily taking the child when their ranks already swell with kings and poets. Had they not done so, he suggests, "She" (Gonne) might have experienced a love capable of preserving her from the worldly, political tumult that Yeats so often blamed for separating her from his love. Since the poem is not widely known or readily available, I will reproduce it in full here:

> You shadowy armies of the dead
> Why did you take the starlike head
> The faltering feet, the little hand?
> For purple kings are in your band
> And there the hearts of poets beat;
> Why did you take the faltering feet?
> She had much need of some fair thing
> To make love spread his quiet wing
> Above the tumult of her days
> And shut out foolish blame & praise.
> She has her squirrel & her birds
> But these have no sweet human words

And cannot call her by her name:
Their love is but a woodland flames [sic].
You wealthy armies of the dead
Why did you take the starlike head. [sic] (*YA3* 153)

"On a Child's Death" appears to have been somewhat hastily transcribed, but retroactively distinguishing error from artifice can be difficult. The title itself presents a quandary. Yeats clearly wrote it out in lower case letters as "on a child's death." Was the diminutive title a reflection of the subject? Was it an indication that the poem should be treated as an embryonic draft, an unfinished bit of occasional verse? Yeats was, of course, never a particularly good speller or careful penman. For example, the third-to-last line seems to read, "Their love is but a woodland flames"; presumably, the "s" at the end of flames was a mistake. Even more glaring than this is the use of a period instead of a question mark in the poem's final line, though not glaring enough to merit comment by the BBC News, which reprinted the poem with the enigmatic period intact in a 2015 article by Hugh Schofield, salaciously titled "Ireland's heroine who had sex in her baby's tomb."

Questions were essential to Yeats's poetic technique. He ended more of his poems with questions than any of his contemporaries—thirty-nine poems in all if we include "On a Child's Death." Lee Zimmerman explores this tendency in his article "Singing Amid Uncertainty: Yeats's Closing Questions" (1983). Seeking a unifying thread, Zimmerman posits that, unlike the impersonal poetics of Pound and Eliot, Yeats's work consistently sought after deeply personal utterance within the bounds of fixed verse; simultaneously, he warns against assigning a rigid function to the formal practice of questioning:

> Obviously they [closing questions] work in some similar and important ways but since the distinctive effects each achieves in context are equally important, they work in some very different ways as well. "Leda and the Swan," for example, ends with an honest, if hopeless, inquiry, "Among School Children" with a rhetorical question, and "The Second Coming" with something in between.[35]

To be sure, these three poems demonstrate a virtuosity of rhythm and rhyme unapproached by "On a Child's Death," but they can aid in conceptualizing the nature of its closing question. "Why did you take the starlike head?" feels like a literal question, more directly plaintive than the complex interrogatives found in later poems.

Taking up the issue of rhetorical questions in Yeats's "Among School Children," Paul de Man famously argues that any meaning we ascribe to the final lines—rhetorical or literal—is necessarily indeterminate. Although reading the question literally ("Please tell me, how *can* I know the dancer from the dance?") requires far more interpretive gymnastics than we would need if we simply accepted the question as rhetorical; we cannot, de Man maintains, "make a valid decision as to which of the readings can be given priority over the other" because "none can exist in the other's absence."[36] Though we need not accept whole cloth de Man's deconstructive premises and conclusions about "valid" hermeneutic decisions, he is right to highlight the suggestion of ambiguity in the closing question of "Among School Children." "How can we know the dancer from the dance?" Yeats strongly implies that we can't, while simultaneously inviting us to engage in the kind of elaborate counter-reading produced by de Man. Likewise, in "The Second Coming" Yeats refuses to ask a straightforward question. "And what rough beast, its hour come round at last, / Slouches towards Bethlehem to be born?" seems genuine enough until we remember that Yeats begins it by asserting "and now I know," thereby undercutting the supposed uncertainty of the query. As in "Among School Children," this question blurs the boundary between the rhetorical and the literal enough to invite reevaluation. We cannot be entirely sure whether we are being asked or told. What results is the kind of ambiguity we associate with great poetry in general and Yeats's oeuvre in particular.

Conversely, "On a Child's Death" asks an unambiguously literal question: "Why did you take the starlike head?" Why did death claim Gonne's boy? Yeats implies no answer, and his addressee, death, remains characteristically mute. All Yeats can do on Gonne's behalf is thrust forward the predictable question that must follow the "this can't be happening" of traumatic plot violation: "Why did this happen?" I daresay the closing question of "On a Child's Death" ranks among the more weighty in Yeats's corpus, if only because it highlights a particularly modern dilemma. With no mutually shared and believed-in narrative about what comes after death, how can we make sense of it as anything other than a senseless and endlessly recurring species trauma? Of course, the ordinary people of the west of Ireland whom Yeats so admired could have answered this question by relying on the trauma-framing narratives of their culture, both pagan and Catholic. Because he has consciously abjured such answers by subscribing to a trans-historical and trans-cultural occultism, Yeats is left trapped within Caruth's structural trauma, condemned to repeatedly act out instead of working through loss.

The resultant sense of helplessness in the face of universalized trauma extends into the form of "On a Child's Death" in a manner that produces a lyric far different from "The Stolen Child." Following our extended examination of formal chaos and complexity in "The Stolen Child," a poem written several years prior, "On a Child's Death" cannot help appearing less technically mature, or at least less technically daring. Its heroic couplets and monotonous iambic tetrameter even employ the "monosyllabic rhyming-strings" that Vendler equates with Yeats's earliest, immature work.[37] I would argue that the poem's simple, predictable form acts as an appropriate extension of the simple yet profound question at its heart. As if to signal its knowledge of its own simplicity, the poem foregoes a predictable metrical syncopation early on, reserving it for later use. In keeping with the poetic tradition of punning on feet as both human and metrical, we ought to expect the rhetorical question in line six—"Why did you take the faltering feet?"—to contain a faltering foot. It does not. The lines of smooth iambic tetrameter are not broken until line eleven: "She has her squirrel & her birds." The line still follows a rising rhythm, but the last two iambs are compressed into an anapest. Pets, even Gonne's somewhat eccentric ones, are no replacement for a stolen child. The comfort they offer is itself a faltering and incomplete thing because, as Yeats points out, they lack the human capacity for speech (for poetry) and, by extension, love. Functioning as a source of reciprocal love in his mother's life, "Georgette" might have turned her mind from the world of public action to a world of domestic affection—one that would, presumably, have some day included Yeats. A less generous reader might insinuate that Yeats mourns the child as a lost means to an end. Such a cynical reading misses the affection of the poem's earlier lines, in which the poet represents the child via a series of heart-wrenching synecdoche: "the starlike head / The faltering feet, the little hand." In writing this poem Yeats mourned the loss of a child who might have called him father and speaks the question that any father might fling into the void of such loss: why? Why take what was small and weak and full of promise when death has already undone so many of the great? Yeats had implied such a question before but never asked it openly.

This was, we know, not the first time Yeats mourned the death of a young boy in verse. Writing about Georges, he must have felt again the loss of his brother, Robert. In commemorating Robert's death, Yeats had crafted a poem that worked through personal pain and trauma by aestheticizing them within the trauma-framing narrative of local Irish folklore. In doing so, he gave new form to ancient modes of making sense of the inexpressible loss that accompanies the death of a child. Strangely enough, as Yeats's poetic powers waxed, his ability to engage artistically with this particular type of loss waned. We need not accept Schuchard's speculation that Yeats thought the poem too personal for publication. For a poet willing to publish his deepest feeling of self-torturing and sometimes degrading romantic obsession, his fears of physical and sexual impotence, his regrets and shortcomings, his fears about death, Yeats seems the last person who would shy away from publishing personal loss, that is, if he could transmute such loss into meaningful art. The major difference between "The Stolen Child" and "On a Child's Death" is that Yeats's stolen child becomes Gonne's dead child. The earlier poem denies death the last word by placing the child outside of death's domain. This is similar to what Christians do when they bury their dead; they deny death's victory even while recognizing that a death has occurred. "On a Child's Death" makes death the ultimate reality, the void at the heart of human existence. It lacks the traditional meaning-making narratives of Irish religious and folk tradition as well as the "ennobling and heroic vision of death" that Rhamazani identifies in several of Yeats's later elegies.[38] Little wonder that Yeats sensed something wrong, incomplete, unpublishable in "On a Child's Death."

Notes

1 Richard Crownshaw, *The Afterlife of Holocaust Memory in Contemporary Literature and Culture* (Basingstoke: Palgrave Macmillan, 2010), 4.
2 Crownshaw, *Afterlife*, 8.
3 Crownshaw, *Afterlife*, 8.
4 Crownshaw, *Afterlife*, 9.
5 Lucy Bond and Stef Craps, *Trauma: New Critical Idioms* (New York: Routledge, 2020), 73–74.
6 Deirdre Toomey, "Away," in *Yeats and Women*, ed. Deirdre Toomey (New York: St. Martin's Press, 1997), 138.
7 Toomey, "Away," 153.
8 Edward Hirsch, "Wisdom and Power: Yeats and the Commonwealth of Faery," 8, nos. 1–2 (1986), 23.
9 Peter Alderson Smith, *W. B. Yeats and the Tribes of Danu: Three Views of Ireland's Fairies* (Buckinghamshire, UK: Smythe, 1987), 131.
10 Carole G. Silver, *Strange and Secret Peoples: Fairies and Victorian Consciousness* (Oxford: Oxford University Press, 1999), 63.
11 Silver, *Strange and Secret Peoples*, 64.
12 Toomey, "Away," 153.
13 W. B. Yeats, *The Collected Poems of W. B. Yeats*, (New York: MacMillan, 1951), 18.
14 Yeats, *Collected Poems*, 19.
15 Jonathan Culler, *Theory of the Lyric* (Cambridge, MA: Harvard University Press, 2015), 36.
16 Culler, *Theory of the Lyric*, 186.
17 Yeats, *Collected Poems*, 18.
18 Yeats, *Collected Poems*, 18.
19 Yeats, *Collected Poems*, 19.
20 Culler, *Theory of the Lyric*, 285.
21 Yeats, *Collected Poems*, 211–12.
22 T. S. Eliot, *The Complete Poems and Plays: 1909–1950* (New York: Harcourt Brace & Company, 1971), 117.
23 W. B. Yeats, *Per Amica Silentia Lunae* (New York: Macmillan, 1918), 29.
24 Yeats, *Per Amica*, 30–31.

25 Kali Tal, "Kali Tal. Issues in Contemporary Trauma Studies," November 26, 2013, *UCD Humanities Institute Podcast*, podcast audio, 60:00. https://soundcloud.com/ucd-humanities/kali-tal-trauma-studies
26 Kali Tal, "Issues in Contemporary Trauma Studies," 8:38.
27 Kali Tal, "Issues in Contemporary Trauma Studies," 10:15–10:55.
28 W. B. Yeats, "The Celtic Element in Literature," in *Ideas of Good and Evil* (London: A. H. Bullen, 1903), 289–90.
29 T. S. Eliot, *Selected Prose of T. S. Eliot*, ed. Frank Kermode (New York: Farrar, Straus and Giroux, 1975), 43.
30 Conrad A. Balliet, "George Gonne and the Soul of the King of Ireland," *YA9*, ed. Deirdre Toomey, 263–65 (London: Plagrave Macmillan, 1992), 263.
31 Balliet, "George Gonne and the Soul of the King of Ireland," 47–48.
32 W. B. Yeats, "Cycles Ago," in *The Early Poetry, Volume II—"The Wanderings of Oisin" and Other Poems to 1895: Manuscript Materials*, ed. George Bornstein (Ithaca, NY: Cornell University Press, 1994), 487.
33 Yeats, "Cycles Ago," 487.
34 Jahan Ramazani, *Yeats and the Poetry of Death* (New Haven and London: Yale University Press, 1990), 3.
35 Lee Zimmerman, "Singing Amid Uncertainty: Yeats's Closing Questions," *YA2*, ed. Richard J. Finneran, 35–45 (London: Macmillan Press, 1983), 37; 36.
36 Paul de Man, *Allegories of Reading: Figural Language in Rousseau, Nietzsche, Rilke, and Proust* (New Haven and London: Yale University Press, 1979), 12.
37 Helen Vendler, *Our Secret Discipline: Yeats and Lyric Form* (Cambridge, MA: Harvard University Press, 2007), 90.
38 Ramazani, *Yeats and the Poetry of Death*, 205.

Spirits on Stage
Rosicrucian Magic in *The Countless Children*

Sørina Higgins

I. Introduction

Although Yeats's *The Countess Cathleen*,[1] originally published in 1892 and first performed in 1899, is normally associated with the early stages of his career, the play's textual history spans at least a thirty-five-year period, with manuscript fragments and proof corrections existing from 1889 to 1934.[2] It is thus not surprising to find that critical discussions of the play often focus on connections between Yeats's revisions and key transitional moments in his personal and professional life, including everything from his tumultuous relationship with Maud Gonne, to his disillusionment over the nationalist response to the 1899 production, to his forays into more experimental forms of theater. What is surprising, given this extensive body of scholarship, is that critics have heretofore failed to address the relationship between this haunting play and a particular magical ritual that Yeats experienced in 1893—a Golden Dawn initiation rite called the "Ceremony of the Grade 5° = 6° of Adeptus Minor."[3] That experience fundamentally shaped many of the revisions he made to stage choreography, symbolic tableaux, emblems, and characters, as he wrote into *The Countess Cathleen* doctrines and performances lifted directly from the high drama of this secret society.

At a basic level, these changes highlight the degree to which Yeats believed, quite literally, in the magical power of the dramatist. The Adeptus Minor or 5° = 6° initiation teaches the value of humility, enacts self-sacrifice, and dramatizes death and resurrection. The goal of this rite is for the initiate to "apply myself to the Great Work—which is, to purify and exalt my spiritual nature so that with the divine aid I may at length attain to be more than human, and thus gradually raise and unite myself to my higher and divine genius."[4] By illuminating and attending to the direct correspondence between this ritual and the spiritual teachings in *The Countess Cathleen*, I will demonstrate that the play was carefully revised to teach syncretistic doctrines of resurrection, purification, and divinization; to enact the evocative power of the poetic imagination; and to offer enlightenment to the audience. I begin by providing an overview of Yeats's magical interests from the late 1890s through the early 1900s, focusing on several short prose works from the period. I then present a description of the relevant ritual, followed by a substantial analysis of corresponding major revisions to the play. These comparisons reveal that Cathleen is an adept on the road to divinization, that Aleel is an enlightened poet-seer, and that the audience is meant to access their higher selves by participation in this theatrical performance.

II. Yeats and Magic

Magic was of the utmost importance to Yeats. Before joining the Golden Dawn, he had already studied and practiced magic on his own and in various groups, including the Dublin Hermetic Society, the Theosophical Society, and the Esoteric Section of the Theosophical Society. He was initiated into the Hermetic Students of the Golden Dawn (G.˙.D.˙.) in 1890. The G.˙.D.˙. was a secret society structured on a system of hierarchical grades through which initiates moved towards enlightenment and divinization via study, examination, and ritual practices.[5] Its core idea is that everything in the universe has evolved from primal light and that all beings can return to their divine source, becoming one with it.[6] To achieve that divine goal, members studied "the basics of occult science" and "*practical magic*."[7] Initiates travelled through an orderly system of Grades, each marked by high ceremonial rituals, designed to train the aspirant in achieving altered levels of consciousness.[8]

Yeats remained in various permutations of the G.˙.D.˙. longer than nearly any other member.[9] Although he would later turn to his own spiritual visions, Yeats dedicated a great deal of time and energy in the 1890s and early 1900s to mastering the G.˙.D.˙.'s system of magic, participating vigorously in a leadership crisis throughout 1900 and 1901, and emerging as a high-level adept with lecturing and leadership responsibilities. He found the G.˙.D.˙.'s teachings and practices in harmony with his own beliefs that humans are essentially divine, that there exists a kind of universal memory or collective mind called the *Anima Mundi*, that a trained adept can achieve altered states of consciousness to tap into this higher self, and that poets can use literary symbols to communicate spiritual truths to the initiated and uninitiated alike.[10]

Yeats's dedication to magic deepened further in 1893 when he joined the more magical Rosicrucian Inner Order of the Ruby Rose and Golden Cross, which members referred to as the R.R. & A.C. after its Latin name, *Roseae Rubeae et Aureae Crucis*. Rosicrucianism traces its legendary beginnings to a putative founder called Christian Rosenkreutz, who discovered secret wisdom and whose body lay preserved in its tomb for a hundred and twenty years. Combining religion and philosophy, its main tenets include magic, spiritual alchemy, and Qabalah.[11] The Rosicrucian inner order in the G.˙.D.˙. was a new development; before its birth in 1891, the G.˙.D.˙. had been "without magic," but after its introduction, magic quickly became the heart of the Order, at least in part because of Yeats's efforts.[12]

After joining this inner order, Yeats progressed to a high level of adeptship as a practical magician. The lofty rank of Adeptus Minor could not be attained until after several years of intense study and practice of the system of "Outer" rituals, which were "intended as a preparation for the practical work to be performed in the Inner or Second Order."[13] Once through the Portal into the R.R. et A.C., an adept would dedicate a great deal of time to study, meditation on systems of symbolism, visualization techniques, and other internal or psychological disciplines, all designed to achieve unity with the higher, divine self. Many of the ritual practices were intended to give insight into the essence of reality.[14] Magic granted vision into timeless planes of being, which the trained magus could manipulate to create real effects here in the material world.

However, as Yeats progressed in his studies, his primary interest was not in power over external nature. Instead, as Mary Catherine Flannery notes, "magic began to mean [. . .] a kind of control over self which makes possible a control over events."[15] The R.R. et A.C.'s ritual practices were mostly visualization techniques that trained the mind to achieve higher forms of consciousness. Aren Roukema explains that modern "occultists often saw 'magic' as an effect of imagination that produced psychological effects within the self so that magicians themselves, rather than their surroundings, were affected."[16] "The entire object of all magical and alchemical processes," writes Regardie, "is the purification of the natural man, and by working upon his nature to extract the pure gold of spiritual attainment."[17] Modern ceremonial magic was inward-focused and aimed at the spiritual transformation of the practitioner: "the abnegation of the lower self and the union with the higher."[18] In short, modern magic aimed at putting the practitioner in touch with his or her higher, divine self.

III. The Evocation of Spirits

One distinctive feature of the G.'.D.'.'s theories of spiritual evolution that Yeats heartily adopted was the evocation of otherworldly beings. Neophytes (aspirants in the lowest grade) learned "how to attract and come into communication with spiritual and invisible things."[19] Adepts in higher grades were given detailed rituals for making spirits "fully and clearly visible" and compelling them to do the magician's will.[20] The belief in communication with the spirit world is fundamental to Yeats's varieties of religious experience and to his concept of the poet-seer. For example, he often called upon "the spirit of the moon," and he and Maud Gonne regularly "evoke[d] a druid for help on the rites for the Celtic Mystical Order."[21] He frequently invoked Aengus, Lug, or Midir (characters from the Celtic pantheon), sometimes alone, and sometimes together with Gonne or with his uncle George Pollexfen.[22] Later, of course, his wife George performed automatic writing, taking dictation "purporting to be from disembodied communicators from realms of spirit," and that material formed the basis of *A Vision*.[23] He also attended séances, recorded communications with a putative spirit called Leo Africanus, and wrote essays on spiritualism and clairvoyance. He describes a realistic séance in *Words Upon the Window-Pane*, and evocations appear in *Rosa Alchemica*. The existence, immortality, and transformation of souls, as well as ongoing dialogue with them after death, were crucial to him.

The theme of spirit evocation runs through four prose works that Yeats composed between 1895 and 1901, the same period when he was actively revising *The Countess Cathleen* following his admission into the R.R. & A.C. The first, a brief essay entitled "The Moods" that appeared in *The Bookman*,[24] makes no mention of magic *per se*, but it does make bold claims about the revelatory power of poetry and drama. Yeats describes literature as "wrought about a mood... as the body is wrought about an invisible soul,"[25] and he further asserts that these moods "are the labourers and messengers of the Ruler of All"; they are "gods" or "angels."[26] The feeling invoked by a literary work is an otherworldly entity, making its presence or nature felt via the symbols the author has assembled. Yeats's "moods" are thus more than mere conveyors of emotion, atmosphere, or tone. They are revelations that enable the individual to have a "part in eternity."[27] The poet-mage has a particular responsibility in relation to these revelatory moods: "the imaginative artist [. . .] belongs to the invisible life, and delivers its ever new and ever ancient revelation."[28] The artist, Yeats believed, was a kind of prophet-seer, communicating salvific revelation.

His next essay on the theme of evocation, "The Symbolism of Poetry," was published in *The Dome* in April 1900, and it expands the messenger motif.[29] This piece is a rejoinder to those readers who think that poetry does not need to be theorized. On the contrary, Yeats writes, all writers and artists "have had some philosophy," and it "has evoked their most startling inspiration, calling into outer life some portion of the divine life."[30] The words "evoked" and "calling" are clearly intentional, for he literally means the evocation of spirits. The phrase "divine life" refers to unity with the higher self, which was the goal of all modern magic. By referencing the "outer life," he reminds artists of their obligation to share revelations with their audiences. Later in the essay, he makes this claim explicit: "All sounds, all colours, all forms, either because of their preordained energies or because of long association, *evoke* indefinable and yet precise emotions, or, as I prefer to think, call down among us certain disembodied powers"—certain moods, gods, or angels—"whose footsteps over our hearts we call emotions."[31] The word "evoke" here is precise. Yeats, the magical practitioner who recently learned to evoke spirits as part of his R.R. &

A.C. training, believes that the symbolic arrangement of words and images in poetry actually calls down—or calls up—divine spirits. Poetry and drama are magical: they are efficacious for invoking spiritual beings.

The third prose work on this topic is the essay "Magic," written in 1900–01 when the R.R. & A.C. was in the throes of its leadership crisis.[32] He delivered this material as a lecture on May 4, 1901, and it was published in *The Monthly Review* in September 1901, and then again in *Ideas of Good and Evil*.[33] This is his public expression to the uninitiated world at large of his spiritual beliefs. Its opening is designed to startle readers: "I believe in the practice and philosophy of what we have agreed to call magic," and, he further declares, "in what I must call the evocation of spirits."[34] He goes on to say that, while he does not know what these spirits are, he believes in "the power of creating magical illusions, in the visions of truth in the depths of the mind when the eyes are closed."[35] He contends that human minds flow in and out of one another, sharing memories and archetypes in a great *Anima Mundi*, the vast collective unconscious which "can be evoked by symbols."[36] Taken in context with "The Symbolism of Poetry," it becomes clear that this is a reiteration of the doctrine that divine spirits can be called up by words and images—symbols—written on a page, spoken aloud, or performed on a stage.

Yeats's belief in the artistic evocation of spirits is reinforced throughout the essay, suggesting that its real subject is not the initiated magician but the poet. When, for example, he wants to stress that spiritual power resides in the sequence of phonemes—the very vibrations of sound waves—he asks rhetorically, "Have not poetry and music arisen, as it seems, out of the sounds the enchanters made to help their imagination to enchant, to charm, to bind with a spell themselves and the passers-by?"[37] Invocation relies heavily on acoustics, for it is "operated through the harmonious combination of the forces of sound, Colour, Number and Form."[38] Further emphasizing the magical power of the poet, he suggests that "Men who are imaginative writers to-day may well have preferred to influence the imagination of others more directly in past times."[39] In other words, both magicians and writers use their imaginations to influence other people's imaginations: both use symbols to invoke and evoke "invisible beings, far-flung influences."[40] Both the magician and the creative writer can use "spoken words" or "unspoken thought" to call spirits "up, as it were, out of Hell or down out of Heaven."[41] These three essays together make clear that Yeats believed in the literal existence of supernatural beings who could be evoked by words and symbols, either in magical ritual or in creative writing, to share eternal truths with an audience.

While Yeats's public essays on moods, symbolism, and magic contain startling revelations about his occult beliefs, a privately printed pamphlet divulges much more. Written in March 1901 and given to the Adepti in

April 1901 "to warn his colleagues against the danger of fragmentation,"[42] this pamphlet, entitled *Is the Order R.R. & A.C. to remain a Magical Order?*, reveals Yeats's beliefs in the invisible masters of the "Third Order," in the organic vitality of the Order, and in the dangers of calling up evil spirits unintentionally. After a schism divided the G∴D∴'s leadership, splinter groups had begun to form among the remaining Inner Order members. Yeats believed that such divisions were extremely dangerous, and he wrote this pamphlet to urge unity. Yet it is no dry committee report. According to Margaret Mills Harper, this document "represents an early attempt to meld matter with presentation, to speak not as a solitary genius but as a personality joined to the minds of others and linked by correspondence to higher authors on the chain."[43] Its diction, underlying assumptions, obscure references, and goals all assume a like-minded community of adepts highly versed in magical theory and practice. It has far-reaching implications for understanding his work from this period and beyond, as it "represents his most thoughtful philosophical observation about the nature of the universe and of man's relationship to everything outside himself."[44] It is the bridge between his magical endeavors and his theatrical turn.

Yeats begins this essay by reminding his fellow Adepti that they have to decide whether they intend the R.R. & A.C. "to remain a Magical Order at all, in the true sense of the word."[45] But what does "magical" mean here? According to Yeats in 1901, "The central principle of all the Magic of power is that everything we formulate in the imagination, if we formulate it strongly enough, realises itself in the circumstances of life, acting either through our own souls, or through the spirits of nature."[46] Magic, then, is the act of imagining something and, through deep concentration, making it real. It is a process of controlled meditation and visualization that can have an effect either inside the magical practitioner or outside in the phenomenal universe. It is, he states, "a discipline that is essentially symbolic and evocative."[47] Given what we have already seen in the essays on moods, symbolism, and magic, we know that "symbolic" and "evocative" are equivalent for Yeats. The use of words—whether in ritual, poetry, or dramatic performance—to evoke symbols results in the invocation of spirits. Magic, poetry, and drama all involve a master of words conjuring symbols in another's imagination, which activates spiritual forces and effects real change in that person's consciousness.

This pamphlet "in effect concluded the episode" of the Order's leadership crisis, but Yeats's warnings were not heeded.[48] The R.R. & A.C. only lasted another two years. In 1903, the Order split in two: Yeats and the more magically inclined adepts went one way, forming the Amoun Temple of the Stella Matutina branch of the G∴D∴, while the more mystically inclined Christian members went another. He had written that separating into groups creates "centres of death, to this greater life [of the Order]; astral disease sapping up, as it were, its vital fluids."[49] Yeats's pamphlet proved prophetic, and he turned to drama to express his spiritual beliefs.

Many scholars agree that the turn of the century saw Yeats increasingly directing his energies toward the theater. "After 1897–98," writes Flannery, "Yeats turned away from active revolutionary politics and toward the theatre."[50] Terence Brown agrees that "it was upon the enabling powers of drama and mythology, which he had already begun to exploit as an artist in the 1890s, that his imaginative survival would increasingly come to depend in the new century."[51] Yeats himself saw this happening: "His own view, at this juncture," claims R. F. Foster, "was that his future lay in poetic drama" (*Life 1* 218).

His turn toward drama, however, did not mean that he was repudiating magic; rather, he brought his experience with staging magic ritual to his work in theater. He did not decide to be an author instead of a magician, for he saw the two vocations as coterminous, writing in 1900: "I cannot now think symbols less than the greatest of all powers whether they are used consciously by masters of magic, or half unconsciously by their successors, the poet, the musician and the artist."[52] Artists are not merely the successors of magicians: they *are* magicians, working their spells in public rather than in private and on the audience's imagination rather than on the forces of nature. Indeed, the artist-poet-playwright is the greater of the two, for it is "the function of the chosen spirit, the seer, to project his visions in the concrete imagery and symbolism of art [. . .]. The artist has a higher function than the 'magician.' The artist, in effect, goes one step further," bringing salvific eternal knowledge to an audience.[53]

Theater and ritual have long been associated, but in Yeats's plays, they are fused. "Occultism, or [. . .] spiritual ideas, underlie all his early plays" writes Richard Ellmann, while Michael Sidnell and Wayne Chapman observe that magic "pervades" *The Countess Cathleen*; these observations are perfectly true, but do not go far enough to explain the specificity of his occult dramaturgy.[54] Foster comes closer when notes that Yeats believed "the function of art was to invoke spiritual realities" (*Life 1* 210). As we have seen, Yeats quite literally believed that his poetry and plays invoked spiritual realities, even spiritual beings. But it is not merely that Yeats was involved in occult rituals, enjoyed the theatricality of those rites, and used what he learned as an initiate to color his own plays and heighten their drama. He goes much farther than that. Yeats actually *stages* occult rituals in *The Countess Cathleen*, performing before the public the ceremonies he learned in secret.

IV. The Play & the Rite

In particular, *The Countess Cathleen* stages elements of the initiation ceremony into the Grade of Adeptus Minor. Roukema writes that it is "one of the most impactful occultist rituals."[55] Regardie describes it as "the jewel in the crown of the Order ceremonial system" and "the most important as well as the most beautiful of the grade rituals employed by the Golden Dawn."[56] This rite was "an extremely complex ritual in four parts [. . .] quite unlike anything that the candidate had experienced before. It was a second initiation, not a mere progression, and it involved the symbolic death and resurrection of the candidate."[57] The imagery and choreography of this ritual were theatrical, visually impressive, "startling and spectacular," emotionally effecting, and "awe-inspiring."[58] R. A. Gilbert writes that "the effect on candidates must have been overwhelming."[59] Brown writes that it "fed the poet's imagination with a richly profuse symbolism," turned him into a symbolist, and led him to "expect poetry to serve as a handmaiden to magic."[60] An examination of the play Yeats was revising after this time reveals how true these claims are.

The Countess Cathleen is the story of a noblewoman who sells her soul to two demons in exchange for money to feed her starving tenants. She dies of a broken heart, but her soul goes to heaven because her motives were pure. As Yeats revised the text many times, its enactment of Rosicrucian beliefs became less analogical and more literal. *The Countess Cathleen* is "Yeats's most revised work," both in the number of changes and the length of revision period (over thirty years); consequently, it is "the most complex to collate" of all his plays.[61] Five versions were published between 1892 and 1913, and other variations exist in manuscript form and in notes from performances.[62] For the purposes of this article, I am interested in all revisions that occurred after 1893, regardless of when they enter the manuscript record or publication history. I do not pursue the chronology of revision beyond noting whether a variant was present before Yeats's Adeptus Minor initiation or introduced afterwards.[63] The play evolved significantly even in just those first three years. By 1895, "the mood was utterly transformed."[64] The new version had a more lofty, spiritual atmosphere, "an elaborate mythological imagery," and profound "new meanings." Specifically, I assert that those "new meanings"[65] reveal the influence of the Adeptus Minor initiation ceremony in their emphasis on the soul's Christ-like nature and the poet's role as seer. There are eight important revisions Yeats made after his inner-order initiation, which I shall detail below..

1. Cathleen's Charity

The first lesson taught by the Adeptus Minor ritual is the importance of humility and self-sacrifice. At the beginning of the ceremony, the candidate is "warned that not in any vainglorious spirit are the mysteries to be approached."[66] Because the candidate has entered, symbolically at least, in an attitude of pride, the officiant issues a rebuke:

> O Aspirant! It is written that he[67] who exalteth himself shall be abased, but that he who humbleth himself shall be exalted, and that blessed are the poor in spirit for theirs is the Kingdom of Heaven. It is not by proclamation of honours and dignities, great though they may be, that thou canst gain admission to the Tomb of the Adepti of the Rose of Ruby and the Cross of Gold, but only by that humility and purity of spirit that befitteth the aspirant unto higher things.[68]

As an enactment of the aspirant's humility, the leaders strip off his fancy ornaments, "clothe him in the black robe of mourning," and proclaim: "Let his hands be bound behind his back, symbolic of the binding force of his obligations, and put a chain about his neck, the emblem of repentance and humility."[69] The physical enactment of self-deprecation was designed to make a deep impression upon an imaginative candidate.

Although the Countess Cathleen is a model of the virtues of humility, purity of spirit, and selflessness in all versions of the play, the memory of Yeats's own symbolic mortification was likely a key factor in his decision to alter the opening scene so that her charitable spirit is rendered even more obvious. Originally, the setting was a public inn, and Cathleen did not appear. In the revised version, Cathleen, Oona (her old nurse), and the poet Aleel visit the Rua family in their poor cottage, a setting which emphasizes their poverty and thus lends greater force to Cathleen's charity when, in response to their hungry lamentations, she "empties her purse upon the table."[70] The fact that she wishes she had more money to give, having already dispensed the rest to others in need, further highlights her charitable spirit, but, more importantly, it speaks to the primary force of Yeats's revisions—the establishment of Cathleen's role as a humble, self-sacrificial figure and symbolic aspirant.

2. Ceremonial Crucifixion and Burial

In the next part of the Adeptus Minor ritual, there are two scenes enacting death, burial, and resurrection. First, there is a mock crucifixion. An officiant commands: "Let the Aspirant be bound to the Cross of Suffering."[71] The stage directions indicate: "*The aspirant is led to the Cross, and his hands are put through the running nooses and cords are bound about his waist and feet*."[72] Regardie interprets this mock crucifixion as an example of the "'Dying God' formula about which in *The Golden Bough* Frazer has written so eloquently."[73] While he admits that "examples of this are to be found in every mythology and every mystical religion that our world has ever known," Regardie boasts: "I doubt that it has ever attained to a more clarified and definite expression than in this ceremony of the Adeptus Minor grade."[74] Be that as it may, having the aspirant enact the crucifixion is certainly a dramatic means of encountering the "dying god" myth.

After the initiate undergoes the mock crucifixion, an oath of secrecy is administered, and then the ceremony proceeds to burial:

> the candidate is now removed from the cross, and the officers then narrate to him the principal facts in the history of the founder of the Order—Christian Rosenkreutz. [. . .] When the history lecture mentions the discovery of the vault wherein the tomb and body of the illustrious Father were discovered, one of the initiating adepts draws aside a curtain, admitting the candidate to a chamber erected in the midst of the temple.[75]

There is a vault built in an inner room of the space where the ritual is being enacted: an elaborate structure covered with significant symbols. Regardie writes that the revelation of the vault was meaningful and memorable: "As a climax to the very simple temple furniture of the Outer grades, it comes as a psychological spasm and as a highly significant symbol."[76] It appears that in the case of Yeats-as-aspirant, this was certainly true.

A more dramatic moment was yet to come. The ceremony of "the Second Point" is the most theatrical section. The initiate is taken inside the Vault or Tomb, where an altar stands in the middle of the space. At the appropriate moment in the ritual, two of the presiding adepts roll the altar off to one side—revealing a coffin underneath it. The adepts open the lid, and "the candidate, no doubt to his great surprise, beholds the head of the Chief Adept, who is lying with his eyes closed."[77] As the stage directions indicate: "*Chief Adept lies in Pastos on his back to represent C.R.C. [Christian Rosenkreutz]*" and then (quite a while later, so the altar and coffin must have had good ventilation), the Second and Third Adepts "*open lid, disclosing Chief Adept within*."[78] The revelation of the body of their Chief in a coffin is a theatrical, emotionally impressive moment.

3. Staging Cathleen's Body

Yeats revised the ending to imitate the choreography of the buried Chief Adept. At first (in 1892), the stage directions after line 810 read: "*A row of spirits carrying the lifeless body of the COUNTESS KATHLEEN descend slowly from the oratory. [. . .] The spirits lay the body upon the ground with the head upon the knee[s] of OONA.*"[79] Cathleen is dead. Her corpse is carried on stage, her head laid upon the lap of her friend. At first, Yeats had Cathleen die offstage soon after signing away her soul and did not show her on stage again until the presentation of her lifeless body.

However, he later changed the stage directions to these: "*The peasants return. They carry the COUNTESS CATHLEEN and lay her upon the ground before OONA and ALEEL. She lies there as if dead.*"[80] The most important change here is that Cathleen is not dead: "*She lies there as if dead*" (emphasis mine)—but she is still alive. The audience might think she is dead when she is carried in, but then she speaks. This modification enacts the shock an aspirant must have felt when the altar was rolled away, the coffin lid was opened, and the body of the Chief Adept was revealed inside, lying motionless, eyes closed; but then, with relief, the aspirant realized his chief was still alive. Yeats also altered the staging of Cathleen's (still-living) body. It is laid out upon the ground, positioned as if for burial. Her head is not put into Oona's lap; she is at a little distance from the people who love her, her body carefully arranged upon the earth. In other words, her body is choreographed to correspond to that of the Chief Adept's, buried in the earth beneath the altar.

These two changes—keeping Cathleen alive and staging her body as if for burial—are designed to convey the meaning Yeats believed he found in the Adeptus Minor ritual. As is usual in modern magical systems, one symbol represents many things: the entombed Chief represents simultaneously the candidate's higher genius, the legendary founder Christian Rosenkreutz, Osiris, Christ, and all other dying-and-rising-god archetypes—which in turn are all metaphors for the individual soul's potential godhood. The buried body represents "the aspirant's higher Self which is hidden and confined within the personality, itself wandering blindly, lost in the dark wilderness."[81] Similarly, Cathleen has been wandering in a dark wood at the beginning of the play—another post-initiation addition. In the added scene at the Rua family's cottage, she tells them: "I was bid fly the terror of the times," but "I have lost my way."[82] She is in great distress, wandering and lost. But at the end of the play, after she has submitted to a kind of crucifixion—the sacrifice of her soul for the sake of others—she receives a ritual choreography that associates her body with the higher self.

4. Sermon from the Grave

In the Rosicrucian ritual, after the revelation of the Chief Adept's body, the aspirant is treated to a sermon. Lying there in the "pastos" or coffin, "without moving or opening his eyes, the Chief Adept utters a brief discourse" as if from beyond the grave.[83] The aspirant is declared to be:

> Buried with that Light in a mystical death, rising again in a mystical resurrection, cleansed and purified through Him our Master, O brother of the Cross and the Rose. Like Him, O adepts of all ages, have ye toiled. Like Him have ye suffered tribulation. Poverty, torture and death have ye passed through. They have been but the purification of the Gold.[84]

The Chief continues in that alchemical vein: "In the alembic of thine heart, through the athanor of affliction, seek thou the true stone of the Wise."[85] Although the death and resurrection imagery are obvious in this alchemically inflected speech, the dramatic visual presentation would likely have made this point in the ritual especially memorable for the aspirant.

5. Cathleen's Deathbed Speech

That may well have been the case for Yeats, as he revised the ending of *The Countess Cathleen* to include a speech issued from a grave. Lying on the ground as if arrayed for burial, Cathleen, "half-rising," enjoins her attendants:

> Bend down your faces, Oona and Aleel:
> I gaze upon them as the swallow gazes
> Upon the nest under the eave, before
> He wanders the loud waters: do not weep
> Too great a while, for there is many a candle
> On the high altar though one fall. Aleel
> Who sang about the people of the raths,
> That know not the hard burden of the world,
> Having but breath in their kind bodies, farewell!
> And farewell Oona, who spun flax with me
> Soft as their sleep when every dance is done:
> The storm is in my hair and I must go. *[She dies]*[86]

There are many aspects of this speech that are performative of the Adeptus Minor ceremony. The high altar on which the candle-souls are burning is taken directly from the staging of the ritual's Second Point, which includes an altar in the middle of the many-sided vault.[87] Cathleen's command to Oona and Aleel to "bend down" puts them in the posture of the aspirant—standing over the Pastos—and positions her in the role of the apparently dead Chief Adept lying in the Tomb.[88] Her injunction not to "weep / Too great a while" echoes the sermon's statement that tribulation, poverty, torture, and death are all only "the purification of the Gold": in both cases, grief will give way to something better. Both talks promise that sorrow and suffering only last for a short time because of the offered hope of resurrection. In the Rosicrucian sermon, this hope is made explicit. The speech begins with a claim that the aspirant's higher self, like the Chief in the coffin, is "Buried with that Light in a mystical death" and will "ris[e] again in a mystical resurrection."[89] In Cathleen's speech, the only hope of a glorious future is in the subtle hint provided by the little light of candle flames: "there is many a candle / On the high altar though one fall."[90] She does not know, of course, that her soul will be accepted by God and go to heaven; the audience must wait a few more moments to receive the vision that brings such a promise. Peter Ure writes that the new ending "is undoubtedly more effective than the final scene was in the 1892 version" because it "gratifies expectation by giving the Countess a death-bed and not just a funeral,"[91] but equally important, Yeats's revision deepens the spiritual impact of the play by infusing it with Rosicrucian doctrine.

6. Serpent and Lightning/Sword

The next sizable revision is the inclusion of an important symbol that serves as a framing device at the beginning and end of the ceremony: the dual image of the Serpent and the Lightning/Sword. These represent various modes of enlightenment available to the aspirant. At the beginning of the ceremony of the First Point, when the aspirant is told to humble himself, he is stripped of all his ornaments and given a diagram to hold. This diagram depicts "sword and serpent," because—as the Second Adept informs him—"the flaming sword and the serpent of wisdom shall be the symbol which shall procure thee admission" to the vault.[92] According to the Kabbalistic system adapted by modern occultists, there are many paths towards enlightenment. The first, the way of the Serpent, is the most difficult, the slowest, and the most common. As summarized by Kathleen Raine, this first path is "the 'gyring, spiring' way of the Serpent, by which the wandering Fool makes his journey."[93] It is the long, slow path of study, examinations, initiations, and rituals that most aspirants take years to complete.

But the path of the Sword or the Lightning is rare and precious: Raine explains that it occurs when "the descending lightning-flash [. . .] comes down from heaven to earth. It is the descent of inspiration."[94] It is a sudden moment of direct revelation. In that instant, the goal of magical meditation is achieved, "symbolised by the Lightning Flash among the sacred leaves" and by a searing sword-light that "flows downward continually."[95] This rare, direct revelation is sometimes compared to lightning, sometimes to a flaming sword, and sometimes to both at once: "We receive power," writes Yeats, "from those who are above us by permitting the Lightning of the Supreme to descend through our souls and own bodies. The power [. . .] comes to a soul and consumes its mortality because the soul has arisen into the path of the Lightning, among the sacred leaves."[96] A few special persons could be blessed by this instantaneous flash of enlightenment.

In the Third Point of the Adeptus Minor ceremony, one of the officiants goes into more detail about the symbolism of the winding serpent and the sword/lightning. Referring to the aspirant's "Admission Badge of the Sword and Serpent," the officiant explains: "The one is ascending, the other is descending; the one is fixed, the other is volatile; the one unites the Sephiroth, the other the Paths. Furthermore, in the Serpent of Wisdom is shown the ascending Spiral, and in the Sword the rush of the descending White Brilliance [. . .]."[97] Although both serpent and sword represent paths to enlightenment, the sword of lightening, given only to the blessed few, is the most direct. At this moment, the Chief Adept attempts to call upon this rare inspiration on behalf of the initiate. The stage directions state: "*Chief Adept raises his hands, invoking the Divine White Brilliance.*"[98] He pauses. This pause is dramatically designed to give the aspirant time to visualize the flash of white lightning and to give a chance for enlightenment to perhaps occur. After the theatrical, pregnant pause, he says to the Aspirant: "'Arise now as an Adeptus Minor of the Rose of Ruby and the Cross of Gold in the sign of Osiris slain."[99] In order to complete the initiation, "*All rise. Second and Third Adepts raise aspirant, and extend his arms in a cross.*" Then they receive him as a full Adeptus Minor.[100] Thus, the ritual ends where it began: with the desire for a direct, descending lightning-bolt of inspiration.

7. The Storm

The same can be said of play's revised conclusion, in which that flash of enlightenment is symbolized, fittingly enough, by lightening. Whereas the 1892 version contains no mention of a thunderstorm, the version that first appears in the 1895 edition of *Poems* closes in more operatic fashion, as a wild lightning storm bursts into the play.[101] After Cathleen utters her last words, "The storm is in my hair and I must go,"[102] Aleel, in his grief, stands and shrieks a curse against "Time and Fate and Change." The heavens respond with "*A flash of lightning followed by immediate thunder.*"[103] Then, suddenly, Aleel sees the air full of spirits:

> Angels and devils clash in the middle air,
> And brazen swords clang upon brazen helms:
> [*A flash of lightning followed by immediate thunder*]
> Yonder a spear, cast out of a sling,
> Has torn through Balor's eye, and the dark clans
> Fly screaming as they fled Moytura of old.[104]

In his moment of wild anguish, Aleel is granted enlightenment: he is allowed to see the angels with their swords, the spear tearing through the air. But Cathleen had it first, because the storm was in her very hair. And then the *audience*, too, sees the vision of armed angels. The stage directions read:

> *The darkness is broken by a visionary light. [. . .] Half in the light, half in the shadow, stand armed angels. Their armour is old and worn, and their drawn swords dim and dinted. They stand as if upon the air in formation of battle and look downward with stern faces. The peasants cast themselves on the ground.*[105]

Yeats has done something utterly astonishing here. Not only does he claim that Cathleen is an inspired adept with enlightenment in her own body, and not only does he show the poet-bard gaining inspiration at the last, but he also reveals the sword of divine brilliance to the uninitiated audience.

Unfortunately, these hosts of supernatural spirits proved too difficult to stage. One manuscript (a copy of the version that appeared in the 1899 edition of *Poems*) has a typed note with handwritten corrections added in ink by Yeats himself, stating:

> *Owing* [sic] to the limited stage resources of the Irish Literary Theatre the vision [. . .] had to be omitted. Instead a single angel in white armour and with thin white/~~wheit~~ hair came to the door of the cottage Aleel on seeing him said 'An armoured child of God stands by the door, / 'His face all worn/~~pale~~, ~~and~~ his hair all silver pale / With beating down the darkness and by age'/ He then continued as before [. . .][106]

One angel walking on the ground is certainly easier to stage than heavenly hosts floating in the air. In both cases, however, Aleel has a vision in which he can see "Angels and devils clash in the middle air, / And brazen swords clang upon brazen helms."[107] In the simplified staging, the angel still appears and wears armor as metonym for the sword of divine brilliance. In a draft preface for the 1901 *Poems*, Yeats wrote:

> The present version of 'The Countess Cathleen' is not quite the version adopted by the Irish Literary Theatre, a couple of years ago, for our stage and scenery were capable of little, and it may differ still more from any stage version I make in future, for it seems that my people of the waters and my unhappy dead, in the Third Act, cannot keep their supernatural essence but put on too much of our mortality in any ordinary theatre.[108]

These comments reveal that Yeats desired to keep the supernatural essence of these mysterious, semi-divine figures (angels? "people of the waters"? the "unhappy dead"?) and struggled with how to stage something paranormal. But he refused to eliminate the possibility of audience enlightenment. In the 1911 stage version, Yeats made sure to put the sword back on stage, indicating: "A winged angel, carrying a torch and a sword, enters from the Right with eyes fixed upon some distant thing."[109] In other words, he worked hard to stage the sword of enlightenment in a way that would work practically in the theater and still reveal to the audience as much divine truth as they could handle, not being initiates themselves. Aleel compels the angel to speak and learns that God has accepted Cathleen's soul into heaven, which provides the audience with confirmation that her enlightenment was true and real.[110] She is a Rosicrucian adept who has enacted sacrifice and death; the hope of her resurrection lingers after the curtain descends.

8. The Poet-Mage

The last significant revision I will address is the addition of Aleel, the visionary lover and bard. This figure adds a personal dimension to the Rosicrucian revisions of *The Countess Cathleen*, giving Yeats a stand-in who explores the role of the poet-mage.

The 1892 version featured a minor character named Kevin, "a young bard," who was played by Yeats himself.[111] When Kevin tries to sell his soul to the demons, having grown tired of it "because her face, / The face of Countess Kathleen dwells with me. / The sadness of the world upon her brow,"[112] they refuse, knowing that his soul already belongs to another. Yeats's decision to replace Kevin with Aleel in 1895[113] is generally regarded as a crucial change. Ure thinks that "The enlargement of Aleel's role is of course the most striking feature common to all the revised versions,"[114] while Foster writes: "By 1899 the character Aleel had come into focus as a hopeless poet-minstrel attached to a self-sacrificing goddess-figure" (*Life 1* 209). Much of this is true, yet the specific additions involving Aleel also show how Yeats was expanding his concept of the poet/playwright-as-mage in relation to the self-sacrificial adept figure. These additions include: Aleel's presence during a scene that highlights Cathleen's charity; his role as a singer; his status as a lover who idealizes Cathleen as his beloved; and his part in the play's concluding visionary scene.

In the added scene of Cathleen's charity, which I discussed above, Cathleen is lost in the forest, and laments:

> [. . .] the bard Aleel who should know these woods
> For we met him upon their ~~edge~~ border but now
> Wandering & singing like a wave the foam of the sea
> Is so wrapped up in dreams of terrors to come
> That he can give no help.[115]

He too, like Cathleen, is "wandering blindly, lost in the dark wilderness" at the beginning of the play.[116] Yet he tells the cottagers to close the door and keep out the evil things that are haunting the woods. He trusts to the power of music to keep himself and Cathleen safe, "For though the world drift from us like a sigh / Music is master under all the moon."[117] Thus he introduces the power of music, a creative art, against the forces of evil.

The Rua family's squalid cottage is the setting for Aleel's first song. It is addressed to his own "impetuous heart," which he bids to "be still" and never speak about its "sorrowful love." He hides his love underneath his "lonely" music. But then the song shifts in tone and speaks about someone—presumably God—"who could bend all things to ~~h~~His will." This divine being has hidden the door to heaven behind the moon and stars.[118] Aleel is also given two other new songs, "Lift up the white knee" and "Were I but crazy for love's sake," which serve to increase and emphasize his role as a poet. He is hopelessly in love with a woman he cannot have; is wandering in spiritual darkness; is a visionary poet-bard; and believes in spiritual realities that he cannot yet see. In other words, he is like Yeats: a young poet-initiate, in love with Maud Gonne, climbing the ranks of a magical secret society, still spiritually unsatisfied.

The love-theme is greatly expanded in revisions. Kevin only mentions briefly that he feels sad when he looks at Cathleen and that he does not want to live any longer, merely hinting at unrequited love. But then Yeats gives Aleel and Cathleen a love scene—added after Yeats's renewed attempts to woo Gonne—in which their talk is rife with spiritual significance.[119] The Countess welcomes him into her presence, saying that it is only music that can now make her happy. He has come to warn her that she is in danger, claiming divine authority: "They who have sent me walk invisible," and "When I slept at twilight [. . .] / my sleep became a fire. / One walked ~~among~~ in the fire with birds about his head."[120] Cathleen identifies this figure as the Celtic god Aengus, while Aleel is more ambivalent, suggesting that it may be Aengus or perhaps an angel. Moments later, Aleel notes that this figure in the flames "was angelical," but Cathleen contradicts him: "No, not angelical, but of the old gods."[121] This ambiguity recalls Yeats's speculation in "Moods" when he ponders what it is that poetry evokes. Like this dream-apparition, poetry might call either "the gods of ancient days still dwelling on their secret Olympus" or "the angels of more modern days ascending and descending upon their shining ladder."[122] Thus Aleel, the poet-mage, is visited by a mysterious supernatural figure, whether god or angel, that speaks truth.

It is interesting that Aleel, who appears to be a pagan bard, holds the Christian interpretation—angels—while the Countess Cathleen, representative of a presumably Christian landed gentry, insists upon the older, pagan interpretation of this figure. And as Nicholas Meihuizen points out, Cathleen blends Christian and occult imagery in this syncretistic passage:[123]

> This heart shall never waken on earth—I have sworn
> By her whose heart the seven sorrows have pierced
> To pray before this Altar until my heart
> Has grown to Heaven like a tree And there
> Rustled its leaves till Heaven has saved my people.[124]

The woman who was pierced by seven sorrows is the Virgin Mary in Roman Catholic teaching, and, as Meihuizen observes, the tree-and-leaf imagery Cathleen uses is reminiscent of the Kabbalistic Tree of Life or Sephirotic Tree, which was a core image in modern occultism.[125] Such syncretism is characteristic of orders like the G.'.D.'., which freely blended ancient Egyptian religion, medieval Christianity, Jewish mysticism, and neo-paganism. Therefore, Aleel and Cathleen together present the religious mixture Yeats had encountered in the R.R. & A.C.

The scene's evocation of a spiritual blending between a man and woman may well call to mind Yeats's relationship with Maud Gonne, but I want to suggest that Aleel's hopeless love for Cathleen is more than a mere autobiographical allusion to Yeats's infatuation with his ideal beloved. When Cathleen refuses Aleel, she rejects the idea that it is their differing class status that keeps them apart, pointing instead to his spiritual superiority:

> If the old tales are true
> Queens have wed shepherds and kings beggar maids,
> Gods [sic] procreant waters flowing about your mind
> Have made you more than kings or queens; and not you
> But I am the empty pitcher.[126]

It is Aleel's identity as a poet, Cathleen claims, that gives him the higher status. And she specifically calls his artistic ability "God[']s procreant waters flowing about your mind." To Cathleen, as to Yeats, poetic inspiration is divine revelation.

Finally, as we have already seen, Aleel is added to the ending, where he is given a vision of supernatural beings whom he dares to confront. As Ure describes the altered ending: "Scene v in 1892 concludes with Oona's vision of the angelic spirits. In 1895 this was transformed into the far more elaborate war-in-heaven and apotheosis, and these are mediated to us not by Oona but by Aleel."[127] In these alterations, Aleel is the kind of poet-mage Yeats calls for in "The Moods," written in the same year. As we have seen, Yeats believed that the mood at the heart of any work of imaginative literature is a divine messenger and that the imaginative artist's job as a citizen of "the invisible life" is to communicate "ever new and ever ancient revelation."[128] Given this context, it is clear that Aleel's communication of his angelic vision, followed by the *staging* of an angel carrying the symbol of enlightenment, is designed to call down actual spirits into the theater, thereby illuminating the audience and enabling them to have a "part in eternity."[129] Aleel is a microcosm of Yeats's ideas at that time. Giving him some of Yeats's own characteristics emphasizes the important role the poet-mage has to communicate eternal truth. Aleel is a poet, a lover, and a seer, communicating salvific revelation.

V. Conclusion

The question remains as to *why* Yeats staged elements of the Adeptus Minor ritual. This question becomes especially urgent given the fact that he swore an oath never to reveal the Order's secrets to anyone outside the R.R. & A.C. In the "Obligation" section of the Adeptus Minor ritual, the aspirant vows "That I will keep secret all things connected with the Order, and its secret knowledge, from the whole world, equally from him who is a member of the First Order of the Stella Matutina, as from an uninitiated person, and that I will maintain the veil of strict secrecy between the First and Second Orders."[130] Later, the aspirant is warned: "Let thy tongue keep silence on our mysteries."[131] The bold nature of his occult revelations on stage means that he may well have worried, as he does in his essay "Magic," that "I look at what I have written with some alarm, for I have told more of the ancient secret than many among my fellow-students think it right to tell."[132] This raises the question of why he would take the risk of violating his vows and introducing potentially dangerous spiritual forces into the playhouse.

Yeats, I suggest, was willing to take this risk because he believed the potential spiritual benefits outweighed the risks and that mediating hidden truths through symbolism rendered them safe for the uninitiated. Both the play and the ritual teach the same spiritual doctrines: the importance of humility, the necessity of self-sacrifice, the inevitability of suffering, the cycle of death and resurrection, the possibility of enlightenment, the divinity of the soul, and the importance of symbolism for communicating truth. We have seen that Cathleen is an example of the aspiring adept, who in turn is represented by the Chief Adept in the tomb of Osiris/Christ, identifying Cathleen with the feminine soul or anima that will rise again and know its true divine nature. We have seen that Aleel develops from a wandering, confused young bard to a powerful, visionary prophet-poet-seer. "In a real way," writes Brown, Yeats's plays of the 1890s and early 1900s were "transposing the beliefs of the Golden Dawn to a wider arena."[133] This is literally true: Yeats carefully revised the play to teach doctrines of resurrection, purification, divinization, and enlightenment—and to offer a taste of these truths to the audience.

Some hermetic traditions include a requirement that high-level adepts find acceptable ways of spreading truth to the uninitiated public. Later Rosicrucian groups, such as A. E. Waite's Fellowship of the Rosy Cross (FRC), required their high-ranking members to find ways to "communicate the mystical philosophy expressed by the Secret Tradition" to the uninitiated via systems of symbolism; once initiates "absorbed the symbolism of the Secret Tradition," they were "expected to generate it."[134] The creative arts, especially writing, were particularly well suited to the task of creating systems of symbolism in order to convey to an uninitiated audience as much truth as they could safely handle.

While the G.·.D.·. of which Yeats was a member appears to have been stricter about secrecy than the later FRC, it still taught that truth existed throughout all creation and that it was valuable for all humankind. Regardie finds parallels between magical systems and modern psychology, writing: "the Golden Dawn magic, the technique of initiation, is of supreme and inestimable importance to mankind at large. In it the work of academic psychology may find a logical conclusion and fruition, so that it may develop further its own particular contribution to modern life and culture."[135] Whether or not Yeats ever received a command to generate systems of symbolism that could be used to subtly communicate truths to those outside the Order, he at least encountered the principle that initiates were meant to spread the light to the whole world. Like members of the FRC after him, then, he had to maintain a balance between strict secrecy and the dissemination of truth.

The R.R. & A.C. also taught that illumination may sometimes occur even without the recipient's intention. There are moments throughout the Adeptus Minor initiation that speak of the awesome enlightening power of the ceremony above and beyond the aspirant's own efforts. When the initiate swears the Oath of Obligation, "because of the symbolism attached to it and because of the active aspiration which is induced at this juncture, illumination may quite easily occur" writes Regardie.[136] Furthermore, the theatrical nature of ceremonial magic may have an impact all on its own: "Through the admittedly artificial or conventional means of a dramatic projection of these personified principles in a well-ordered ceremony a reaction is induced in consciousness."[137] Theatrical performances and ceremonial magic share conventional means of deploying symbolism, staging, costumes, choreography, lighting, spoken lines, colors, and perhaps music to impact those who observe the spectacle:

> Without the least conscious effort on the part of the aspirant, an involuntary current of sympathy is produced [. . .]. The aesthetic appeal to the imagination [. . .] stirs to renewed activity the life of the inner domain. And the entire

> action of this type of dramatic ritual is that the soul may discover itself exalted to the heights, and during that mystical elevation receive the rushing forth of the Light.[138]

Yeats and Florence Farr (the actress who played Aleel and was an occult playwright herself) shared a belief "that the sound of words can enter into the innermost being" and give, via their very acoustical properties, intimations of "the great truth that heaven and hell and God can be with us here and now.'"[139] This means that the sheer phonetics and acoustics of spoken language, according to Farr and Yeats, can communicate spiritual truths to a listening audience, whether they know it or not, whether they want it or not. Plays, then, were one of Yeats's chief means of subtly communicating esoteric truth to the wider public. The Countess Cathleen, which is "marked by a ritualistic element" in which actors "declaim elevated verse and [. . .] chant their lines in a sacerdotal manner," is a quintessential example of this kind of teaching.[140] In this play as he revised it after his 1893 deeper initiation, Yeats used symbolism, the sounds of words, and staging to call down spirits into the souls of his audience.

NOTES

1 The Countess's name is variously spelled as *Kathleen* or *Cathleen* in different versions; I use the latter throughout for simplicity.

2 See Michael J. Sidnell and Wayne K. Chapman, eds., *The Countess Cathleen: Manuscript Materials* [hereafter *CCMSS*], The Cornell Yeats (Ithaca, NY: Cornell University Press, 1999).

3 Israel Regardie, *The Golden Dawn: The Original Account of the Teachings, Rites, and Ceremonies of the Hermetic Order* [hereafter *GD*], 7th edn, revised and corrected by John Michael Greer (Woodbury, MN: Llewellyn Publications, 2015), 3:288.

4 *GD* 3:301.

5 The use of the "therefore" symbol instead of a period is a Masonic tradition carried on by modern occultists: "Frequently, among English and always among French authors, a Masonic abbreviation is distinguished by three points, ∴, *Albert Gallatin Mackey and William James Hughan, An Encyclopedia of Freemasonry and Its Kindred Sciences: Comprising the Whole Range of Arts, Sciences and Literature as Connected with the Institution* (New York and London: Masonic History Company, 1913), 2.

6 *GD* 6–7.

7 Chic Cicero and Sandra Tabatha Cicero, "Preface to the Seventh Edition," in *GD*, xxix. Italics original.

8 *GD* 12.

9 R. A. Gilbert, *The Golden Dawn Scrapbook: The Rise and Fall of a Magical Order* (York Beach, ME: Samuel Weiser, 1997), 179.

10 George Mills Harper, *Yeats's Golden Dawn* [hereafter YGD] (New York: Barnes & Noble, 1974), 69.

11 There are many variant transliterations of 'Qabalah.' There seems to be some consensus that, "generally speaking, the original Jewish tradition is Kabbalah with a 'K'; Christian Cabala [. . .] starting with a 'C,' while the Western Hermetic tradition spells Qabalah with a 'Q.'" See Mark Horn, "Kabbalah, Cabala or Qabalah: What's up with These Different Spellings?," January 11, 2018, Gates of Light Tarot, https://www.gatesoflighttarot.com/blog/2017/9/3/kabbalah-cabala-or-qabbalah-whats-up-with-all-these-different-spellings; cf. Anthony J. Elia, "An Historical Assessment of the Narrative Uses of the Words 'Kabbalah,' 'Cabala,' and 'Qabala/h': Discerning the Differences for Theological Libraries," *Theological Librarianship: An Online Journal of the American Theological Library Association* 2, no. 2 (December 2009): 11–23. I retain whichever spelling an author uses when relevant and use the more hermetically oriented 'Qabalah' myself.

12 R. A. Gilbert, *The Golden Dawn: Twilight of the Magicians* (San Bernardino, CA: R. Reginald/Borgo Press, 1988), 35.

13 *GD* 39.

14 *YGD* 104.

15 Mary Catherine Flannery, *Yeats and Magic: The Earlier Works* (Gerrards Cross, UK: Colin Smythe, 1977), 53.

16 Aren Roukema, *Esotericism and Narrative: The Occult Fiction of Charles Williams* (Boston: Brill, 2018, 11.

17 *GD* 13.

18 *GD* 38.

19 *GD* 22.

20 *GD* 5:489.

21 Kathleen Raine, *Yeats the Initiate: Essays on Certain Themes in the Work of W. B. Yeats* (Savage, MD: Barnes & Noble Books, 1990), 218–19; John Kelly, *A W. B. Yeats Chronology* (New York: Palgrave Macmillan, 2003), 67.

22 Kelly, *Chronology*, 54–55.

23 Margaret Mills Harper, *Wisdom of Two: The Spiritual and Literary Collaboration of George and W. B. Yeats* (Oxford: Oxford University Press, 2006), 5.

24 Allan Wade, *A Bibliography of the Writings of W. B. Yeats* (London: Rupert Hart-Davis, 1951), 62.

25 W. B. Yeats, "The Moods," in *Essays and Introductions* (New York: Macmillan, 1961), 195.

26 Yeats, "The Moods," 195.

27 Yeats, "The Moods," 195.

28 Yeats, "The Moods," 195.

29 CL II:478 n3; Wade, *Bibliography*, 62. Kelly states that "The Symbolism of Poetry" was published on April 2, 1900; see *Chronology*, 66. That must be an error, as Yeats wrote to Lady Gregory on April 10: "I will send it you when it comes out"; *The Collected Letters of W. B. Yeats: 1886–1900*, ed. Warwick Gould, John Kelly, and Deirdre Toomey, vol. II (Oxford: Clarendon Press, 1986), 512. Perhaps it had already been released, and Yeats was unaware of that fact?

30 W. B. Yeats, "The Symbolism of Poetry" [hereafter SP], in *Essays and Introductions* (New York: Macmillan, 1961), 153–64; 154.

31 SP 156–57, emphasis added.

32 Kelly, *Chronology*, 70, 72, 74.

33 *Life 1* 244; Wade, *Bibliography*, 61; Kelly, *Chronology*, 76.

34 W. B. Yeats, "Magic," in *Essays and Introductions* (New York: Macmillan, 1961), 28–52; 28.

35 Yeats, "Magic," 28.

36 Yeats, "Magic," 28.
37 Yeats, "Magic," 43.
38 "Flying Rolls of the Golden Dawn" (Scribd), 96, accessed December 8, 2020, https://www.scribd.com/document/26946230/6629823-All-the-Flying-Rolls-of-the-Golden-Dawn.
39 Yeats, "Magic," 43.
40 Yeats, "Magic," 41.
41 Yeats, "Magic," 36, 40.
42 *YGD* 76.
43 Harper, *Wisdom of Two*, 71.
44 *YGD* 70.
45 W. B. Yeats, "Is the Order of R. R. & A. C. to Remain a Magical Order?" [hereafter ItO], in *YGD* 259–68; 259.
46 ItO 265.
47 ItO 260.
48 *YGD* 47.
49 ItO 262.
50 Flannery, *Yeats and Magic*, 94.
51 Terence Brown, *The Life of W. B. Yeats* (Oxford: Blackwell, 2001), 104.
52 Yeats, "Magic," 49.
53 *YGD* 104.
54 *CCMSS* xlviii; Richard Ellmann, *Yeats: The Man and the Masks* (New York: Dutton, 1958), 131, http://hdl.handle.net/2027/mdp.39015054028686.
55 Roukema, *Esotericism* 52.
56 *GD*, 26, 1:115; *MRA* 26; Israel Regardie, *My Rosicrucian Adventure: A Contribution to a Recent Phase of the History of Magic, and a Study in the Technique of Theurgy* (Las Vegas: New Falcon Publications, 2017).
57 Gilbert, *Scrapbook*, 64–65.
58 Gilbert, *Twilight*, 36; Gilbert, *Scrapbook*, 66.
59 Gilbert, *Twilight*, 36.
60 Brown, *Life*, 70.
61 *CCMSS* ix; *VPl* 1; Peter Ure, "The Evolution of Yeats's 'The Countess Cathleen,'" *The Modern Language Review* 57, no. 1 (1962): 12–24; 12–13, https://doi.org/10.2307/3721967.
62 *CCMSS* xxxiii–xxxiv.
63 For readers who are curious about the exact details of precisely when a change entered the manuscript record or publication history, I recommend *VPl* 1–179 and *CCMSS*, especially xxix–xxxii (Chronology of Manuscripts), xxxiii – xxxiv (Published Versions), and xxxv–xxxvi (a summary of major changes in each version).
64 *CCMSS* l.
65 *CCMSS* lii.
66 *GD* 31.
67 Some *Golden Dawn* rituals use masculine pronouns; however, men and women were equally eligible for all roles and ranks in the Order.
68 *GD* 3:295.
69 *GD* 3:296.
70 *CCMSS* 383; *VPl* 19.
71 *GD* 3:298.
72 *GD* 3:299.
73 *GD* 32.
74 *GD* 32.
75 *GD* 32–3.

76 *GD* 33.
77 Ellic Howe, *The Magicians of the Golden Dawn: A Documentary History of a Magical Order, 1887–1923* (Wellingborough, UK: Aquarian Press, 1985), 88.
78 *GD* 3:306, 309.
79 *CCMSS* 354; *VPl* 160–62.
80 *CCMS*, 499; *VPl* 159.
81 *GD* 33. Regardie writes that the Adeptus Minor ritual "identifies [the candidate] with the chief officer," so that symbolically the candidate "is slain as though by the destructive force of his lower self. After being symbolically buried, triumphantly he rises from the tomb of Osiris in a glorious resurrection through the descent of the white light of the spirit"; *GD* 14.
82 *CCMSS* 385; *VPl* 21.
83 Howe, *Magicians*, 88.
84 *GD* 3:309.
85 *GD* 3:309.
86 *CCMSS* 501–02; *VPl* 163.
87 *GD* 3:305.
88 The Chief Adept in the tomb simultaneously symbolizes Christian Rosenkreutz, Osiris, Jesus, and "the aspirant's higher self"; both Christian Rosenkreutz and Osiris "may be considered as the type and symbol of the higher and divine genius" (*GD* 3:303). This burial ceremony, then, "depicts the spiritual rebirth or redemption of the candidate, his resurrection from the dark tomb of mortality through the power of the Holy Spirit" (*GD* 3:303).
89 *GD* 3:309.
90 *CCMSS* 501; *VPl* 163.
91 Ure, "Evolution," 20.
92 *GD* 3:296.
93 Raine, *Yeats the Initiate*, 245. The phrase 'gyring, spiring' comes from Yeats's poem "Blood and the Moon," which Raine is discussing in connection with Golden Dawn rituals.
94 Raine, *Yeats the Initiate*, 245.
95 ItO 261, 260.
96 ItO 266.
97 *GD* 3:316.
98 *GD* 3:313.
99 *GD* 3:313.
100 *GD* 3:313.
101 W. B. Yeats, *Poems* (London: T. Fisher Unwin, 1895), 153, http://archive.org/details/poemswilliambutl00yeatrich.
102 *CCMSS* 502; *VPl* 163.
103 *CCMSS* 503; *VPl* 165.
104 *CCMSS* 504; *VPl* 165.
105 *CCMSS* 504–05; *VPl* 167.
106 *CCMSS* 505.
107 *CCMSS* 504; *VPl* 165.
108 *CCMSS* 751.
109 *CCMSS* 738.
110 *CCMSS* 505, 738; *VPl* 167.
111 *CCMSS* 282.
112 *CCMSS* 342; *VPl* 134–36.
113 See *CCMSS* 359.
114 Ure, "Evolution," 20.
115 *CCMSS* 385; *VPl* 21.

116 *GD* 33.
117 *CCMSS* 387; *VPl* 23.
118 *CCMSS* 387; *VPl* 23.
119 *CCMSS* 442–52; *VPl* 81–91; cf. *Life* 1 230.
120 *CCMSS* 443; *VPl* 83.
121 CCMSS *448*; VPl *87*.
122 Yeats, "The Moods," 195.
123 Nicholas Meihuizen, *Yeats and the Drama of Sacred Space* (Amsterdam: Rodopi, 1998), 44.
124 *CCMSS* 449; *VPl* 87.
125 Meihuizen, *Yeats*, 44.
126 *CCMSS* 450; *VPl* 89.
127 Ure, "Evolution," 19.
128 Yeats, "The Moods," 195.
129 Yeats, "The Moods," 195.
130 *GD* 3:300.
131 *GD* 3:306.
132 Yeats, "Magic," 51.
133 Brown, *Life*, 125.
134 Aren Roukema, "A Veil That Reveals: Charles Williams and the Fellowship of the Rosy Cross," *Journal of Inklings Studies* 5, no. 1 (2015): 71, 48.
135 *GD* 30.
136 *GD* 32.
137 *GD* 18.
138 *GD* 18.
139 Brown, *Life*, 125; Florence Farr, *The Music of Speech, Containing the Words of Some Poets, Thinkers and Musicmakers Regarding the Practice of the Bardic Art, Together with Fragments of Verse Set to Its Own Melody by F. Farr* (London: Elkin Mathews, 1909), 18.
140 Terence Brown, "W. B. Yeats and Rituals of Performance," in *The Oxford Handbook of Modern Irish Theatre*, ed. Nicholas Grene and Chris Morash (Oxford University Press, 2016), 5.

Syntax as Experience: On Yeats's "The Fisherman"

Yuki Tanaka

In "A General Introduction for My Work" (1937), W. B. Yeats writes that he needed "not as Wordsworth thought, words in common use, but a powerful and passionate syntax" to match "passionate subject-matter" (*E&I* 521–22). Critical accounts of "passionate syntax" have often rehearsed Yeats's own description: his distorted syntax is meant to convey intense subjectivity and feelings that cannot be expressed in normative sentence structures.[1] But reading Yeats's syntax can be simply confusing, as it requires constant negotiation with what he means. Think of the fifth stanza of "Among School Children," where Yeats maintains a sentence throughout a whole stanza to create what he calls "a complete coincidence between period and stanza" (*E&I* 522):

> What youthful mother, a shape upon her lap
> Honey of generation had betrayed,
> And that must sleep, shriek, struggle to escape
> As recollection or the drug decide,
> Would think her son, did she but see that shape
> With sixty or more winters on its head,
> A compensation for the pang of his birth,
> Or the uncertainty of his setting forth? (*CW1* 220–21)

Reading this stanza, we cannot grasp the structure of the whole sentence at once. The grammatical subject of this interrogative sentence is "what youthful mother." But the predicate "Would think her son [. . .] a compensation" is delayed until four lines later, while Yeats piles up an apposition and three relative clauses. Moreover, as soon as the sentence finds the predicate, it is interrupted by another clause: "Would think her son, did she but see that shape."

Although there has been renewed interest in formalist studies of Yeats's poetry, syntax has played a minor role, overshadowed by considerations of his rhymes, prosody, and stanzaic forms.[2] But more than other formal devices, syntax makes us conscious of reading as a temporal process and could help us arrive at a subtler understanding of Yeats's poetry. Reading syntax is experiential: to make sense of a sentence, we read one word at a time, then move on to the next sentence, in the order the author created. This process is amplified in poetry, where a sentence is broken up into lines, giving us more time to ponder how one syntactic unit connects to the next. As Derek Attridge has argued in a recent book, a poem is "a *formal* event, involving [. . .] shifts in register, allusions to other discourses (literary and non-literary), rhythmic patterning, linking rhymes, movements of syntax, echoing of sounds: all operating in a temporal medium to surprise, lull, intrigue, satisfy."[3] Yeats's passionate syntax creates these modulations of meaning, staging a mind constantly thinking, rethinking, and qualifying thoughts.

By attending to the experience of reading Yeats's syntax word by word, line by line, I will offer a nuanced reading of a poem that has often been read as a straightforward *ars* poetica. Completed in 1914, "The Fisherman" voices Yeats's disillusionment with the Dublin middle-class audience who failed to appreciate the genius of John Synge and rioted at a premier performance of Synge's *The Playboy of the Western World* in 1907. Yeats drafted the first version in 1913. During the time of the poem's composition, Sir Hugh Lane, the nephew of Lady Gregory, was under severe public criticism for his campaign to give his collection of French impressionist paintings to Dublin if the city would build a proper gallery to host them. Accordingly, in the poem the speaker turns from this real, unappreciative audience—whom Yeats often called "the mob"—to an ideal audience represented by the fisherman, a symbol of native Irish culture. The poem ends with, in Roy Foster's words, "one of WBY's most magnificently assertive signatures" (*Life* 2 13): "Before I am old / I shall have written him one / Poem maybe as cold / And passionate as the dawn" (*CW1* 149).

When read with attention to its syntax, "The Fisherman" becomes more than a straightforward repudiation of the mass audience. The poem has two stanzas: in the first stanza, the speaker tells us that he first conceived of the fisherman twelve months ago; in the second, he remembers that original moment in one long sentence. Within that single sentence, tense shifts quickly, from present to past, from past to present, and then back to past and to future perfect. These tense shifts complicate and extend Yeats's sentence, creating a temporal drama in which the speaker looks back on his past self in a struggle to revive the original vision of the fisherman. In "The Fisherman," Yeats's syntax is not just a sign of an assertive self whose strong feelings distort his language; rather, it enacts a mind thinking, as the speaker tries to recapture his vision of an ideal audience but cannot fully believe in the possibility of realizing it.

A. Walton Litz argues that in the second stanza, the fisherman is transformed into "a vision of a possible future."[4] But Litz's characterization of the poem is more applicable to a version of the poem Yeats wrote the previous year. In May 1913 Yeats wrote "subject for a poem" into his notebook:

> Who is this by the edge of the stream
> That walking in a good homespun coat

And carries fishing in his hand
We singers have nothing of our own
All our hopes, our loves, our dreams
Are for the young for those whom
We sing in [?to] life. But is one
That I can see always though he is not yet born
He walks by the edge of the stream
In a good homespun coat
And carries a fishing rod in his hand.[5]

"Though he is not yet born" implies that although the fisherman is not born at present, he will be eventually. Yeats sounded this hopeful note more forcefully in the same month in a speech after a special Abbey performance: "I have no doubt that all we here in Ireland to-day are living more or less in the eyes of an unborn public, that we are more or less playing our part before an audience, not like this small audience, but a great audience of the unborn."[6] He went on to say: "The present generation was the one in which they saw Irishmen learning to love the arts for their own sake. It would be remembered as the generation in which the Irish people became a modern people."[7] In both the 1913 passage and the speech, the birth of an ideal audience who is appreciative of art seems to be possible. As suggested by "I can see always though he is not yet born," the audience does not exist yet but is always available to the imagination as a future vision to be realized. Imaginative time is continuous with real, historical time.

The 1914 version is not as idealistic, and the difference is apparent in the handling of syntax in the poem's second stanza. But first, I would like to analyze the opening stanza to demonstrate how shifts in syntax and thinking occur across the stanza break. The syntax of the first stanza is not as complex as that of the second, but a sense of disillusionment with the real Dublin audience is already present. The opening line immediately qualifies the optimism of the earlier version:

Although I can see him still,
The freckled man who goes
To a grey place on a hill
In grey Connemara clothes
At dawn to cast his flies,
It's long since I began
To call up to the eyes
This wise and simple man.
All day I'd looked in the face
What I had hoped 'twould be
To write for my own race
And the reality; (*CW1* 148)

"I can see always" is replaced by "Although I can see him still," which suggests that the fisherman he started imagining a year earlier might not be as vivid as he used to be. Rather than the idealized world of the continuous present in the draft, "The Fisherman" inhabits what the speaker calls "the reality." It is crowded with "[t]he living men that I hate"—those who scorn Yeats's and the Abbey's effort to create avant-garde art and to bring Lane's collection of paintings to Ireland. Through his involvement with the Abbey Theatre, Yeats wanted to create "an Irish literature which, though made by many minds, would seem the work of a single mind."[8] As Marjorie Howes argues, "between about 1899 and 1910, Yeats's Irish theatre represented, in part, an effort to forge and simultaneously theorize about the nation as a collectivity."[9] For him, the theater was "a potential means of mobilizing and 'nationalizing' the masses, something he recognized any successful nationalism in the age of mass politics must do."[10]

The first stanza uses paratactic syntax to emphasize the increasing pressure of a mass audience that resists being unified into what Howes calls a national "collectivity." "The dead man that I loved" refers to John Synge, but his presence is quickly drowned by a list of philistine audiences:

The living men that I hate,
The dead man that I loved,
The craven man in his seat,
The insolent unreproved,
And no knave brought to book
Who has won a drunken cheer,
The witty man and his joke
Aimed at the commonest ear,
The clever man who cries
The catch-cries of the clown,
The beating down of the wise
And great Art beaten down. (*CW1* 148)

Instead of describing the audience as a group, Yeats lists them in a paratactic sentence as discrete singulars: "the craven man," "the insolent," "no knave," "the witty man," "the clever man." There is no unity among these figures. In the face of this reality, art is powerless, and its defeat is rendered with an air of finality in a chiasmus: "The beating down of the wise / And great Art beaten down."

So far, Yeats's sentence is long but simple—a list of nouns that needs no parsing. Accordingly, the speaker's attitude toward the audience can be read as an unqualified snub. But the syntax twists and turns in the second stanza, when the speaker tries to push aside this repugnant reality by remembering how he originally conceived of the fisherman. Here, the speaker looks back to the past and reenacts the moment of his imaginative conception as if it is happening in the present moment of narration:

> Maybe a twelvemonth since
> Suddenly I began,
> In scorn of this audience,
> Imagining a man,
> And his sun-freckled face,
> And grey Connemara cloth,
> Climbing up to a place
> Where stone is dark under froth,
> And the down-turn of his wrist
> When the flies drop in the stream; (*CW1* 149)

Although the second stanza repeats many images from the first stanza, the shift from "It's long since" to "*Maybe* a twelvemonth since" immediately signals a change: in the second stanza, the speaker is trying harder to remember the fisherman, specifying the time that has passed, and bringing the past vision back into the present.

This imaginative effort is felt in Yeats's increasingly complex sentence structure. As the speaker remembers, the memory of the fisherman grows more intense; accordingly, the main clause is quickly left behind, and the subordinate clause dominates the rest of the stanza. The subordinate status of "since" is almost unnoticeable, because its main clause is abbreviated and grammatically incomplete ("Maybe a twelvemonth since" instead of "It has been a twelvemonth"). In other words, although the vision is remembered, it feels vivid as if it is happening in the present moment. The dactylic opening of the next line, "Suddenly," reinforces the intensity of the vision. The same word opens two of Yeats's famous visionary poems: "The Cold Heaven" ("Suddenly I saw the cold and rook-delighting heaven" [CW1 124]) and "Leda and the Swan" ("A sudden blow" [CW1 218]). In both poems, the sudden intensity of a visionary moment coincides with the beginning of a poem. Similarly, "Suddenly" in "The Fisherman" announces that this second stanza is not a mere continuation of the first stanza, but a new beginning. The pastness of the "since" clause is further diminished by the fact that the slant rhyme of "since" and "audience" is drowned by the triple *a* rhyme of "I beg**a**n [. . .] / Im**a**gining a m**a**n," which emphasizes the present intensity of the reenacted vision. As Helen Vendler points out, there is a metrical shift, too, from the "simple iambic predominance" of the first stanza ("It's l**o**ng since **I** beg**a**n / To c**a**ll up t**o** the **eyes** / This w**i**se and s**i**mple m**a**n") to the more "rhythmically alive" second stanza in the description of the fisherman,[11] with a trochee ("Climbing") and spondees ("down-turn," "flies drop").

The poem's focus on reviving the original moment of the fisherman's birth can also be seen in Yeats's revisions. He made two important changes. First, in the draft of "The Fisherman" in the Cornell manuscript edition of *The Wild Swans at Coole*, the second stanza begins: "In scorn of this audience / Suddenly I began."[12] The original opening of the second stanza puts more emphasis on the causal progression from the first stanza to the next: his rejection of the mass audience led him to imagine the fisherman. In the final version, Yeats obscures this transition by starting the stanza with "Maybe a twelve month since." This change makes the second stanza not just a continuation of the first stanza, but a fresh start on what has been said before, this time with more imaginative intensity. Second, in the draft version "Imagining a man" reads "Imagining *this* man."[13] The change from the demonstrative to the indefinite article suggests that the speaker is recalling his vision as if he is imagining the fisherman for the first time.

Reflecting this growing intensity, Yeats's sentence becomes longer and longer until it frees itself from the subordinate status of "since" as well as its pastness. After a series of tenseless present participles and noun phrases, the narrative past completely disappears:

Imagining a man,
And his sun-freckled face
And grey Connemara cloth,
Climbing up to a place
Where stone is dark under froth,
And the down-turn of his wrist
When the flies drop in the stream; (*CW1* 149)

Matthew Campbell comments on this passage: "There is a pointed simplicity and no little prosodic artfulness in the mimicry of the simple skills of the fisherman."[14] While the meter is simple, however, the syntax is not. By the time we get to the last line of this passage, the grammatical kernel of this clause, "I began," is so far behind that the fisherman seems to be freed from the past tense that opened the stanza. As Joseph Adams has argued, Yeats often subverts "the normal hierarchical structure of language."[15] In this passage, Yeats unmoors the sentence from "I began" by piling up phrase after phrase until the sentence drifts into the present tense.

Here Yeats is loosening up his syntax to recapture the intense experience of seeing the fisherman for the first time. Compare the spontaneous syntax of the above passage with the neat syntax of the first stanza, in which prepositions spatially orient the reader and make it clear where the fisherman is:

Although I can see him still,

The freckled man who goes
To a grey place on a hill
In grey Connemara clothes
At dawn to cast his flies, (*CW1* 148)

The second stanza repeats many of these images but in a more fragmentary sentence, as if the speaker is trying to grasp his vision for the first time, perceiving body parts first ("his sun-freckled face," "cloth," "the down-turn of his wrist") before grasping the whole picture. This initial fragmentariness testifies to the intensity of the vision. Similarly, the opening lines of "Leda and the Swan" suggest the rawness of the vision in fragmentary syntax:

A sudden blow: the great wings beating still
Above the staggering girl, her thighs caressed
By the dark webs, her nape caught in his bill,
He holds her helpless breast upon his breast. (*CW1* 218)

The perception of the scene is taking place at the present moment of speaking: the speaker lists a swarm of local perceptions ("wings," "thighs," "dark webs," "nape," "bill") before organizing them into the whole scene in a complete clause: "He holds her helpless breast upon his breast."

But this idealistic recuperation of the original intensity is subject to the speaker's awareness that he lives in a fallen present. While the vision of the fisherman in the 1913 version stays in the simple present of "always," it starts to diminish toward the end of the final version. The speaker admits that the fisherman is "[a] man who does not exist, / A man who is but a dream" (*CW1* 149). In the 1913 draft, the word "dream" meant the hope for a new audience: "All our hopes, our loves, our dreams / Are for the young." In the final poem, "dream" means "fictional." "A man who does not exist" also recalls "though he is not yet born" in the 1913 draft. The difference is that here the fisherman exists only in the speaker's imagination, but not in real, historical time.

This gap between imaginative time and real time becomes even starker when Yeats's sentence becomes as difficult as the stanza quoted at the beginning of this essay. Here, after a long detour into the present tense, the poem suddenly returns to the past tense:

A man who does not exist,
A man who is but a dream;
And cried, "Before I am old
I shall have written him one
Poem maybe as cold
And passionate as the dawn." (*CW1* 149)

Up to this point, the sentence has moved away from the narrative past and has been hovering in the present tense. Now it is suddenly pulled back to the narrative past as if the spell has been broken. This abrupt shift is created by the oddity of "and cried." The verb "cried" takes "I" as the grammatical subject, but this subject last appeared eleven lines earlier in "I began." This distance makes us pause and wonder who is doing the crying. This jarring shift is also metrical. The poem is written in the fast-moving tempo of iambic trimeter. But this sudden return to the narrative past coincides with the first internal punctuation in the poem, the comma that follows "cried," which arrests this metrical momentum. In Yeats's terms, this abrupt alteration of rhythm may be read as the breaking of a trance, as he suggests in "The Symbolism of Poetry":

> The purpose of rhythm [. . .] is to prolong the moment of contemplation, the moment when we are both asleep and awake, which is the one moment of creation, by hushing us with an alluring monotony, while it holds us waking by variety, to keep us in that state of perhaps real trance, in which the mind liberated from the pressure of the will is unfolded in symbols. (*E&I* 159)

The "alluring monotony" of the poem's trimeter creates a dreamscape in which the past vision of the fisherman is brought back into the present with its original intensity. This rhythm-induced trance is interrupted by the jolting syntactic punctuation of "and cried," waking the speaker up to reality.

It is true that if we accept Yeats's own account of his syntax, perhaps we are meant to take this syntactic distortion as a manifestation of his powerful feeling that cannot be expressed in ordinary syntax. The strong pause at "cried" could be there to emphasize a defiant note against the imaginative diminution happening in the previous two lines. The speaker has admitted that the fisherman is imaginary, but by crying out his resolution to write for the fisherman, he tries to maintain his hope for realizing an ideal audience in the future. The final lines are made particularly assertive by the future perfect tense. While the simple future "will write" suggests the speaker's wish to write such a poem, "shall have written" sounds more like a prophecy and takes the completion of the poem for granted.

Moreover, "Before I am old" is another defiant move that is rather uncharacteristic of Yeats. In his early poetry, Yeats often casts his speakers as prematurely old. The ending of "The Song of Wandering Aengus" is a good example, also because its language anticipates the closing lines of "The Fisherman": "Though I am old with wandering / Through hollow lands and hilly lands, / I will find out where she has gone, / And kiss her lips and take her hands" (*CW1* 56). The speaker of "The Fisherman" does not claim that he is already old, despite the fact that in the earlier version the speaker already groups himself with the old: "We singers have nothing of our own / All our hopes, our loves, our dreams / Are for the young." In the final version Yeats's speaker presents himself as not yet old, perhaps to reserve for himself the imaginative power to compose a poem before he yields to the young. To cite Foster again, this is indeed an "assertive" gesture.

But Yeats's confident note is qualified by the very forcedness of syntax and the abrupt shift from present to past tense. These features make it difficult to read the sentence with the ease that the coordinating conjunction "*and* cried" promises. This forced transition exposes the difficulty of reconciling imaginative time with real time, of locating the imaginary fisherman in the future. Even when the speaker seems to have broken away from the reality of mass audience into his imaginative vision, he must come back to the unfavorable time to which he belongs. "Cried" also recalls "the catch cries of the clown" in the first stanza, thus bringing the clamor of the mass audience back into a lyric space seemingly insulated from this "reality." Even in the poem's final lines, we hear an echo of uncertainty in "*maybe* as cold / And passionate as the dawn."

In "The Fisherman," the speaker looks back to the previous year, escaping from the mass audience and retrieving his vision of an ideal audience. As the sentence gets longer and longer, however, the speaker's thought process becomes more and more complex. Discussing Yeats's habit of extending a sentence with semicolons where a simple period would do, Michael Wood argues that Yeats "is trying to stave off an ending, even of sentences [. . .] as if every thought is tracked by another thought, a new qualification or additional sense or instance."[16] "The Fisherman" does not enact such qualification overtly, but the complex extension of Yeats's final sentence calls the dream of a timeless vision into question.

Once we are immersed in Yeats's "passionate syntax" and read it in time, we start to notice a less-than-confident tone. Attention to the poem's syntax reveals a speaker who is trying to envision an ideal audience for his art but feels uncertain about the possibility of realizing that audience. We share the speaker's uncertainty as we read on word by word, looking for syntactic coherence. In other words, syntax enacts a lived time in which the speaker—just like us—thinks, feels, and doubts, and we participate in that process. Read this way, the poet's passionate syntax is no longer a site of struggle where we must submit to his distorted sentence structure on his own terms and be often confused by it. Rather, it becomes an affective common ground where poet and reader meet.

Notes

1 John Holloway argues that Yeats's syntax is "always in the direction of speech in the sense of the poet's own most personal voice and presence: of an engagement of his own subjectivity and energy as the continuing focus of the poems and everything in them"; "Style and World in *The Tower*," in *An Honoured Guest: New Essays on W. B. Yeats*, ed. Denis Donoghue and J. R. Mulryne (New York: St. Martin's Press, 1966), 91. Bernard O'Donoghue agrees, identifying in Yeats's poetry "the force of feeling" that expresses itself through the distortion of syntax; "Dispassionate Syntax: Irish Poetry at the End of Yeats's Century," *Barcelona English Language and Literature Studies* 11 (2000): 171.

2 Joseph Valente, "Formal (Re)Introductions: New Criticism of Yeats," *Éire-Ireland* 47, nos. 3–4 (Fall/Winter 2012): 269. Valente discusses renewed interest in formalism in Yeats studies as he considers three books: Nicholas Grene, *Yeats's Poetic Codes* (Oxford: Oxford University Press, 2008); Helen Vendler, *Our Secret Discipline* (Cambridge, MA: Harvard University Press, 2007); and Michael Wood, *Yeats and Violence* (Oxford: Oxford University Press, 2010).

3 Derek Attridge, *Moving Words: Forms of English Poetry* (Oxford: Oxford University Press, 2013), 29. In recent years, there has been a growing interest in reexamining the process of reading from scholars of different dispensations. These scholars include Attridge and Rita Felski, who has emphasized the reader's affective relationship to texts, exploring how we are constantly "intertwined and entangled with texts." See Felski, *The Limits of Critique* (Chicago: University of Chicago Press, 2015), 84.

4 A. Walton Litz, "Yeats at Fifty," *Yeats: An Annual of Critical and Textual Studies* 12 (1994): 138.

5 W. B. Yeats, *The Wild Swans at Coole: Manuscript Materials*, ed. Stephen Parrish (Ithaca: Cornell University Press, 1994), 431.

6 "Municipal Art Gallery," *Irish Times*, May 10, 1913, 7.

7 *Irish Times*, May 10, 1913, 7–8.

8 W. B. Yeats, *The Autobiography of William Butler Yeats* (New York: Macmillan, 1965), 170.

9 Marjorie Howes, *Yeats's Nations: Gender, Class, and Irishness* (New York: Cambridge University Press, 1996), 67.

10 Howes, *Yeats's Nations*, 67.

11 Vendler, *Our Secret Discipline*, 190, 191.

12 Yeats, *The Wild Swans at Coole*, 141.

13 Yeats, *The Wild Swans at Coole*, 141, my emphasis.

14 Matthew Campbell, *Irish Poetry under the Union, 1801–1924* (New York: Cambridge University Press, 2013), 194.

15 Joseph Adams, *Yeats and the Masks of Syntax* (New York: Columbia University Press, 1984), 57. Adams's book is the most extensive study of Yeats's syntax to date. In it, Adams locates many places in Yeats's poetry where syntactic ambiguities are "more or less irresolvable" (4), revealing not a unified consciousness but a dispersed subjectivity. While Adams's approach is spatial, in that he tabulates local syntactical ambiguities in Yeats's work, I read Yeats's syntax as a temporal process, with an eye to the way an individual sentence unfolds as we read a poem.

16 Wood, *Yeats and Violence*, 121.

The Falconer is Dead: Reassessing Representations of Eternal Recurrence

Matthew Fogarty

In a letter addressed to Lady Gregory on December 26, 1902, William Butler Yeats first acknowledged the onset of what would become a lifelong fascination with Friedrich Nietzsche's philosophy: "Dear Friend," he confesses:

> I have written to you little and badly of late I am afraid for the truth is you have a rival in Nietzsche, the strong enchanter. I have read him so much that I have made my eyes bad again. They were getting well it seemed. Nietzsche completes Blake & has the same roots—I have not read anything with so much excitement, since I got to love Morris's stories which have the same curious astringent joy (*CL3* 284)

Less than three months later, Yeats expressed comparable sentiments to the New York lawyer, John Quinn, who had recently gifted him all of the available English translations of Nietzsche's books:

> I do not know how I can thank you too much for the three volumes on Nietzsche. I had never read him before, but find that I had come to the same conclusions on several cardinal matters. He is exaggerated and violent but has helped me very greatly to build up in my mind an imagination of the heroic life. His books have come to me at exactly the right moment, for I have planned out a series of plays which are all intended to be an expression of that life which seem[s] to me the kind of proud hard gift giving joyousness (*CL3* 313)[1]

The magnitude of Nietzsche's influence on Yeats has been well documented. However, those who have examined the specific nature and extent of this influence often note that Nietzsche's writing afforded Yeats a certain validation for values and ideas to which he already subscribed. As Otto Bohlmann succinctly puts it, Nietzsche provided "substantiation and a stable base for ideas Yeats might have felt unsure of."[2] This is not to denigrate in any way the scope of Nietzsche's importance to Yeats. Indeed, Conor Cruise O'Brien has even gone so far as to suggest that Yeats "might never have developed into a great poet without Nietzschean permissions."[3] But the complexity surrounding the matter of Yeats and Nietzsche's intertextual relationship serves as a timely reminder of the fraught theoretical terrain that invariably surrounds the question of authorial influence.

With this complexity in mind, this essay revisits the function that eternal recurrence performs in Yeats's middle-period occultism and re-evaluates its compatibility with the Nietzschean mode of eternal recurrence with which it has traditionally been aligned. It should be noted that there are representations of eternal recurrence in Yeats's later works that endorse the life-affirming potential that is in many ways the quintessential hallmark of Nietzsche's philosophy. In "A Dialogue of Self and Soul," for example, the speaker strikes a defiant and affirmative note: "I am content to live it all again / And yet again if it be life to pitch / Into the frogspawn of a blind man's ditch" (*VP* 479: 57–59). Likewise, in "Lapis Lazuli," there is a certain tragic joy to be discerned from the speaker's contention that "All things fall and are built again / And those that build them again are gay" (*VP* 566: 35–36). However, the cyclical historical model that Yeats presents in *A Vision* relies upon a historiological construct that is far more deterministic than the sentiments expressed in these later works. Over the past fifty years, those who have explored how this historical model manifests in Yeats's literary work have repeatedly turned to "The Second Coming."[4] Indeed, John Harrison has rightly pointed out that Yeats's "cyclical view of history" is not strictly compatible with Nietzsche's life-affirming antecedent.[5] However, I would argue that Harrison's distinction does not go far enough. Focusing on *A Vision* and "The Second Coming," this essay demonstrates that Yeats's historical metanarrative and the occult principles that bolster it are fundamentally incompatible with Nietzsche's philosophical values.

The theory of eternal recurrence is arguably the most elusive of the many elusive ideas that feature in Nietzsche's philosophy. In its most traditional form, the theory proposes that, "whatever in fact happens, has happened infinitely many times and will re-happen an infinity of times, *exactly* in the same way in which it happens now."[6] Its origins can be traced to pre-Socratic Greek philosophy, Buddhism, and Middle Eastern pagan religions.[7] As a non-theistic cosmological hypothesis, it requires neither a beginning nor an end; or, to put it in Aristotelian terms, a hypothesis which requires neither a prime mover nor a final *telos*. With respect to Nietzsche's philosophy, there are passages in the *Nachlass*—the posthumously published notes he compiled between 1883 and 1888—that contemplate this theory's potential to function as a viable cosmological hypothesis. But these reflections are tempered by the persistent sense that Nietzsche identified a hitherto unknown and incredibly powerful axiological potential in all of this.[8] Indeed, Alexander Nehamas has observed that one must at least attempt to demonstrate that such a hypothesis might be true if it is to be regarded as a genuine philosophical proposition, and Nietzsche never does so in his published work. Turning to *Thus Spake*

Zarathustra (1883–1885), Nehamas further notes that Nietzsche's prophetic title character never actually suggests that this theory might function as a viable cosmological hypothesis.[9] In the passage where eternal recurrence is most explicitly discussed, it is, in fact, the surrounding animals who regurgitate what they understand Zarathustra to have taught:

> Everything goes, everything comes back; eternally rolls the wheel of being. Everything dies, everything blossoms again; eternally runs the year of being. Everything breaks, everything is joined anew; eternally the same house of being is built. Everything parts, everything greets every other thing again; eternally the ring of being remains faithful to itself.[10]

Considered in the broader context of Nietzsche's philosophy, these animals appear the embodiment of the "Nietzschean Herd," both in appearance and in their pliant acceptance of a cosmological hypothesis that Zarathustra promptly dismisses as "a hurdy gurdy song."[11]

The only other passage in Nietzsche's published work that discusses the theory of eternal recurrence in any detail is imbued with comparable ambiguity. In this instance, Ivan Soll observes that "the entire question of its veracity is neatly side-stepped by presenting it not as a truth but as a thought experiment."[12] Published in *The Gay Science* (1882), this passage begins with an all-important question:

> What if some day or night a demon were to [. . .] say to you: "This life as you now live it and have lived it you will have to live once again and innumerable times again; and [. . .] all in the same succession and sequence." Would you not throw yourself down and gnash your teeth and curse the demon who spoke thus?[13]

The ambiguity generated by this non-committal prompt is compounded by the question that immediately succeeds it: "Or have you once experienced a tremendous moment when you would have answered him: 'You are a god and never have I heard anything more divine.'"[14] Although a statement then follows, it incorporates yet another question: "If this thought gained power over you, as you are it would transform and possibly crush you; the question in each and every thing, 'Do you desire this again and innumerable times again?' would lie on your actions as the greatest weight!"[15] Indeed, it concludes by posing one final question to the reader: "Or how well disposed would you have to become to yourself and to life *to long for nothing more fervently* than this ultimate eternal confirmation and seal?"[16] Much like the prophetic Zarathustra, then, Nietzsche's demon narrator never proposes that the theory of eternal recurrence might operate as a viable cosmological hypothesis. For these reasons, Nietzschean scholars in the late twentieth and early twenty-first centuries almost univocally propose that Nietzsche reformulates the cosmological iteration of eternal recurrence to function as an axiological imperative: If you had to live the same life over and over again, would you be happy to make the same choices, or to adhere to the same value systems that underpin these choices?

This understanding of Nietzschean eternal recurrence can be traced to concerted post-war efforts to reclaim his philosophy from the taint of his posthumous association with Nazism.[17] It was first advanced by Georges Bataille in *Sur Nietzsche* (1945):

> I think the idea of eternal return should be reversed. It's not a promise of infinite and lacerating repetitions: It's what makes moments caught up in the immanence of return suddenly appear as ends. In every system, don't forget, these moments are viewed and given as means: Every moral system proclaims that "each moment of life ought to be *motivated*." Return *unmotivates* the moment and frees life of ends—thus first of all destroys it.[18]

The emphasis Bataille places on these ethical dimensions laid much of the intellectual groundwork for Gilles Deleuze's 1962 contention that Nietzsche's eternal recurrence establishes an ethical principle as rigorous as Immanuel Kant's categorical imperative.[19] Deleuze argues that, "as an ethical thought, the eternal return is the new formulation of the practical synthesis: *whatever you will, will it in such a way that you also will its eternal return*."[20] However, this reading of Nietzschean eternal recurrence has largely been ignored by those who have written about the potential correlations between this aspect of his philosophy and Yeats's occult speculation. For example, David Thatcher proposes that Yeats's interest in eternal recurrence was magnified by "Nietzsche's reformulation of it and from the attitude he adopted."[21] Likewise, Erich Heller argues that Yeats's *A Vision* "owes something to Nietzsche's vision of [. . .] Eternal Recurrence."[22] Frances Nesbitt Oppel suggests that, as Yeats "charts his own system" in *A Vision*, he tries "to follow Nietzsche into the paradox of Eternal Return, which demolishes sequential or linear time altogether."[23] Patrick Bridgewater claims that it was "Eternal Recurrence, as annunciated in *Thus Spake Zarathustra*, that caught and held Yeats's attention."[24] For his part, Otto Bohlmann turns to *The Gay Science* to provide evidence of the supposed affinity between Nietzsche's and Yeats's engagement with the theory of eternal recurrence. He claims that Nietzsche "speaks of a demon who whispers the prophecy that your life as you lived it 'will have to return to you, all in the same succession and sequence [. . .] The eternal hourglass of existence is turned upside down again and again, and you with it, speck of dust!'"[25] Although Nietzsche does use the term "prophecy" once when referring to theory of eternal recurrence in the *Nachlass*,[26] it appears somewhat dubious to reformulate this passage's opening question as a statement and designate it a "prophecy." In doing so, Bohlmann jettisons the critical ambiguity generated by the demon narrator's initial utterance. It is, perhaps, understandable that Thatcher and Bridgewater do not consider the "thought experiment" argument. Both of their studies were published before Soll's 1973 re-evaluation of Nietzschean recurrence. It is more difficult to account for Bohlmann's and Heller's reluctance to acknowledge these developments in Nietzschean studies, as their respective works were published in 1982 and 1990. There is no question that Yeats identified a certain philosophical justification for his occult speculation within the depths of Nietzsche's philosophy. It is deeply problematic, however, to insinuate that Yeats's justification is well founded in Nietzsche's philosophy.

In the decades prior to 1969, when George Mills Harper and Katherine Raine began exploring Yeats's extant occult papers, it was generally assumed that these mystical interests could be separated from his literary works.[27] This longstanding critical consensus now appears rather extraordinary, especially in light of the fact that Yeats openly acknowledged the abiding relevance of these occult interests in his 1921 preface to *Michael Robartes* and *the Dancer*:

> Goethe has said that the poet needs all philosophy, but that he must keep it out of his work. After the first few poems I came into possession of Michael Robartes' exposition of the *Speculum Angelorum et Hominum* of Giraldus, and in the excitement of arranging and editing could no more keep out philosophy than could Goethe himself at certain periods of his life. (*VP* 853)

Yeats is referring to the "philosophy" that was subsequently published in the 1925 edition of *A Vision*, in which he claimed to have gleaned these insights from a mysterious "Arabian traveller."[28] In the heavily revised 1937 edition, Yeats provides an alternative account of this philosophy's origins:

> On the afternoon of October 24th 1917, four days after my marriage, my wife surprised me by attempting automatic writing. What came in disjointed sentences, in almost illegible writing, was so exciting, sometimes so profound, that I persuaded her to give an hour or two day after day to the unknown writer, and after some half-dozen such hours offered to spend what remained of my life explaining and piecing together those sentences.[29]

Yeats maintained that these ethereal entities chose to communicate using the terminology and themes that featured in his earlier occult exposition, *Per Amica Silentia Lunae* (1917), and that this accounts for the similarity of these two texts. Regardless of whether or not one finds this proposition credible, the system that appears in *A Vision* represents the culmination of Yeats's lifelong interest in all things phantasmagorical.

These occult interests were initially sparked by his relatives and their servants at the Pollexfen family home at Merville in County Sligo, who were unified by their infatuation with the paranormal, despite their disparate social backgrounds (*Life1* 20–21). By the time he reached his early twenties, Yeats's interest in the supernatural had broadened to encompass strands of Eastern mysticism, which he first encountered in A. P. Sinnet's *The Occult World* (1881) and *Esoteric Buddhism* (1883).[30] Shortly after receiving a copy of the latter text in late 1884 from his aunt, Isabella Pollexfen Varley, Yeats discovered the Dublin Hermetic Society. Popular among many important figures in the Irish intelligentsia, such as AE (George Russell), Eglinton, Charles Johnston, Charles Weekes, and Claude Falls Wright, as well as scholars of Eastern philosophy such as Mir Alaud Ali, Professor of Persian, Arabic, and Hindustani at Trinity College Dublin, the Society provided a space for the exchange of ideas derived from Eastern schools of thought (*Life 1* 46-47). In April 1886, the Dublin Hermetic Society became the Dublin Theosophical Society, that is, an official branch of the Theosophy movement co-founded by Helena Blavatsky in 1875. After moving back to London in 1887, Yeats became a member of Blavatsky's London Lodge, also known as the "Blavatsky Lodge," before joining the Hermetic Order of the Golden Dawn in 1890.[31] Where the quasi-religious Theosophy movement drew inspiration from a heady mixture of Neoplatonism, Buddhism, and Hinduism, the Hermetic Order of the Golden Dawn was a secret society dedicated to the study and performance of magic and occult practices. Yeats also discovered various modes of spiritualism while living in London, such as the automatic writing that would later give rise to *A Vision*.[32] To add to this already potent and eclectic range of occult influences, one might also point to Yeats's familiarity with Rosicrucianism, Cabbalism, Gnosticism, alchemy, astrology, and the Tarot, to say nothing of his interest in the Western mysticism of Emanuel Swedenborg, Jakob Böhme, and William Blake.[33]

Between 1925 and 1937, while Yeats immersed himself in a range of Eastern beliefs and practices, he also familiarized himself with the work of Giambattista Vico, Arthur Schopenhauer, and Oswald Spengler.[34] Indeed, Yeats acknowledges the many similarities between his and Spengler's historical metanarratives in the preface to the 1937 edition of *A Vision*. He does, nonetheless, contend that his paranormal communicators shared this "symbolical map of history" with him before the 1918 publication of Spengler's *The Decline of the West*.[35] The section titled "Dove and Swan," in which Yeats sets out this historical metanarrative, was one of only two sections that were republished more or less untouched in the second edition. This is not really surprising, however, as Yeats would have found little in these Eastern schools of thought, or in the works of

Vico, Schopenhauer, and Spengler, to have prompted a reconsideration of this historical determinism.

In addition to appearing in *Michael Robartes and the Dancer*,[36] the collection in which Yeats underscored the significance of the philosophy that bolsters this historical model, the esoteric discourse of *A Vision* makes its presence felt from the outset of "The Second Coming": "Turning and turning in the widening gyre / The falcon cannot hear the falconer; / Things fall apart; the centre cannot hold" (*VP* 401: 1–3). In the context of *A Vision*, Yeats uses the term "gyre" to denote the two interpenetrating cones that form the nucleus of his elaborate amalgamation of various strands in Western mysticism. For example, he acknowledges the correlations between his gyres and Swedenborg's contention that "all physical reality, the universe as a whole, every solar system, every atom, is a double cone."[37] Yeats draws additional inspiration from Blake's *The Marriage of Heaven and Hell* (1790), which was principally conceived as a riposte to Swedenborg's *Heaven and Hell* (1758). Blake challenged Swedenborg's steadfast adherence to the primacy of orthodox moral structures, and indeed the mutual exclusivity of perceived opposites. Instead, Blake proposes that conflictual forces are "necessary to human existence."[38] This Blakean influence makes itself most keenly felt as Yeats assigns the qualities of "Concord" and "Discord" to each of his gyres.

Even at this most basic level, the principles that underpin Yeats's design are incompatible with Nietzsche's philosophical values. Writing on the potential value of "mystical knowledge," Nietzsche plainly stipulates that such "explanations are thought to be deep; the truth is they are not even shallow."[39] There may be certain parallels between Nietzsche's Apollonian and Dionysian energies and the Blakean contraries that Yeats associates with his concordant and discordant gyres.[40] As Charles I. Armstrong has noted, these parallels are likely attributable to Yeats's and Nietzsche's familiarity with the pre-Socratic philosophies of Heraclitus and Empedocles, both of whom placed great emphasis on the metaphysical significance of contraries.[41] However, Nietzsche would have objected most strenuously to Yeats's somewhat Hegelian attempt to systematize these conflictual energies into what he called a "logical form."[42] The structural arrangement of this logical symbiosis is also at odds with Nietzsche's philosophy insofar as it designates the concordant gyre as "primary" and its discordant opposite as "antithetical." As Yeats puts it:

> the subjective cone is called that of the antithetical tincture because it is achieved and defended by continual conflict with its opposite; the objective cone is called that of the primary tincture because whereas subjectivity [. . .] tends to separate man from man, objectivity brings us back to the mass where we begin.[43]

This idea that an individual might begin their journey on the "primary" side of Yeats's schema and eventually return there having traversed the antithetical terrain of the opposing gyre implies that the subject's natural position is akin to that which Nietzsche repeatedly renounces as herd mentality. In spite of these fundamental incongruities, it has long been believed that Yeats's occult speculation in *A Vision* is compatible with Nietzschean eternal recurrence. For instance, Bridgewater has proposed that Yeats was attracted by "the many parallels between Nietzsche's work and the occult literature with which he was already familiar."[44] Bohlmann stretches the point further by claiming that "many of the premises" which underpin this "intricate system [. . .] clearly find much precedent in Nietzsche, who lends immediacy to ancient notions."[45] Notwithstanding Harrison's rejection of the perceived affiliations between Yeats's and Nietzsche's eternal recurrence, these misapprehensions concerning the similarities between Yeats's occultism and Nietzsche's philosophy have stood unchallenged for over thirty-five years.

Although Bridgewater and Bohlmann do acknowledge that Yeats's system is more elaborate than the cosmological version of eternal recurrence which they attribute to Nietzsche, they do not consider how these elaborations render this system at odds with Nietzsche's philosophical principles. This is especially true of Yeats's reliance on Böhmean mysticism. Yeats's deployment of the term "tincture" alerts us to the influence of Böhme, for whom it designates a miraculous, life-giving energy that facilitates all growth and transformation.[46] It is ultimately this miraculous energy that transforms Swedenborg's "double cone" into a spiralling double vortex of perpetual motion that facilitates growth and transformation within the contrasting parameters set by Blake's intimately related contraries. With regard to "The Second Coming," it is Böhme's tincture that keeps the Yeatsian gyres "turning and turning" (*VP* 401: 1). However, Nietzsche was characteristically firm in his insistence that "the believer in magic and miracles reflects on how to *impose a law on nature*–: and, in brief, the religious cult is the outcome of this reflection."[47] Indeed, he was equally forthright in his dismissal of astrological practices and the foolish pride of those who believe "the starry firmament revolves around the fate of man."[48] And yet, Yeats further complicates this amalgamation of Western mysticism by setting "a row of numbers upon the sides," denoting "a classification [. . .] of every possible movement of thought and life, [which] correspond to the phases of the moon."[49] Yeats called this metaphysical construct the "Great Wheel" and proposed that every individual is preordained to pass through these twenty-eight stages of incarnation. As Ellmann explains:

> the soul may be said to pass through all the phases within a single lifetime, beginning with the completely unindividualized or objective state of infancy

> (phase 1), rising to the full individuality or subjectivity of maturity (phase 15), and sinking back at last into childhood and mere oblivion (phase 28), where it dies and then after a period begins the round once more.[50]

This suggests that each individual is effectively manoeuvred through these twenty-eight phases of incarnation, ensuring that all their lived experiences correspond to a process that sees them pass from the primary, objective state, through the antithetical, subjective state, and ultimately returned to the primary, objective state, where the cycle begins anew.

Critics who separate "The Second Coming" from the philosophical backdrop set out in *A Vision* have tended to interpret the poem as a relatively straightforward meditation upon the oscillating socio-political climate of interwar Europe. Certainly, the poem "responds to and participates in the pan-European militarization of politics that put an end to nineteenth-century liberalism," as Seamus Deane suggests.[51] This reading is borne out by the topical allusions that feature in the early drafts. As Helen Vendler has observed, these include references to the French and Russian revolutions, and possibly the militant unrest in early twentieth-century Ireland.[52] However, the specificity of Yeats's "response," and the precise nature of this "participation," comes far more sharply into focus when the poem is set against this philosophical backdrop. The significance of this backdrop is underscored by the disparate interpretations of the poem's "falcon" metaphor advanced by Ellmann and Denis Donoghue. The former argues that Yeats "was careful not to require knowledge of his prose [and] made it possible to suppose that the gyre is merely the falcon's flight."[53] Donoghue cautions against discounting the importance of *A Vision*, however, noting that such readings tend to pay disproportionate attention to the poem's socio-political context and reductively translate "the falconry into specifically political terms."[54] The key difference is that Ellmann perceives the "falcon's flight" as being emblematic of Yeats's gyres; whereas Donoghue rightly points out that these gyres are signified by the act of "falconry." This distinction is not insignificant, nor is it a simple matter of semantics. These contrasting interpretations point toward the time-honored philosophical question of free will versus determinism. By Ellmann's estimation, the falcon remains in control of its own destiny as the gyre is generated by the falcon's flight. But when the act of falconry is associated with the image of the gyre, as Donoghue suggests, it operates as a powerful metaphor of humankind's unawareness of the ordinance this casual configuration exerts. Hence, "the falcon cannot hear the falconer" (*VP* 401:2). Falcons are renowned for their flight speed and capacity to rapidly shift direction. And yet, these majestic birds are routinely trained to hunt upon command. From the vantage point of *A Vision*, the relationship that binds the unknowing human subject to the ordinance of the Great Wheel shares a great deal with the affiliation that binds the falcon to its falconer.

Donoghue's clarification becomes all the more significant when the implications of Yeats's philosophical conjecture are considered, not only at the microcosmic level that relates to every individual's lived experience, but also at the macrocosmic level that applies this cyclical process to the collective history and cumulative fate of all humankind. This is the "symbolical map of history" that Yeats republished largely without revision in the 1937 edition of *A Vision*.[55] He calls this macrocosmic version of the Great Wheel the "Historical Cones." This construct implies that all of humankind's known history is nothing more than a carefully choreographed and repetitive oscillation between these primary and antithetical gyres. Like some prodigious square dance, doomed to eternally repeat itself, these macrocosmic cycles, or "Great Years," are directed by the same amalgamation of mystical and astrological principles that comprise the Great Wheel. As Matthew Gibson explains, the term "Great Year" was used by both Neoplatonists and Stoics to describe a "continuum in history, computed to be either 36,000 or around 26,000 years long, [. . .] involving the alignment and return of the planets to the same point."[56] Whatever about the overall length of this astrological cycle, Yeats notes that the two thousand years of Christianity is "an entire wheel," much "like the two thousand years [. . .] that went before it."[57] The apocalyptic imagery described in "The Second Coming" bears witness to the decline of the two-thousand-year Christian cycle. In fact, the "twenty centuries of stony sleep" (19–22) described by the poem's speaker corresponds with Yeats's contention that the "Christian era, like the two thousand years [. . .] that went before it, is an entire wheel."[58] If one follows Ellmann's lead, assuming that the falcon's flight is emblematic of the turning gyre, it seems reasonable to conclude that the contemporaneous collapse of European order is manifested in the falcon's apparent incapacity to heed the falconer's directives. When set against the historical metanarrative constructed in *A Vision*, however, this collapse appears entirely analogous with the necessary chaos that is ushered in with the dawning of the antithetical era. From this perspective, chaos does not reign supreme in "The Second Coming" because "the falcon cannot hear the falconer" (*VP* 401:2). This phrase instead refers to humankind's obliviousness to the fact that this chaos has been predestined to occur as the concord initiated by the primary gyre gives way to its antithetical opposite. As the speaker succinctly puts it, "things fall apart; the centre cannot hold" (*VP* 401:3).

While acknowledging that "Yeats himself liked to talk as if it made everything predestined," Ellmann argues against a fatalistic reading of Yeats's design and insists that one may still "choose between several alternatives."[59] In theory, this might be true of the microcosmic existential level that Yeats associates with his Great Wheel. However, this non-fatalist reading simply cannot function at the macrocosmic historical level that Yeats associates with the Great Years. Should one possess the capacity to make meaningful life choices, as Ellmann proposes, these choices would invariably, by their very definition, possess the capacity to alter the uniformity that Yeats ascribes to the recurring historical cycles that comprise the Great Year. If, for example, a substantial mass of subjects freely chose to adhere to "primary" principles during an "antithetical" age, could it still be characterized by the values Yeats associates with the antithetical gyre? Indeed, it was the matter of the system's fatalism that elicited the strongest criticism from Yeats's friend, George Russell (AE):

> I feel to follow in the wake of Mr. Yeats's mind is to surrender oneself to the idea of Fate and to part from the idea of Free Will. I know how much our life is fated once life animates the original cell, the fountain from which the body is jetted; how much bodily conditions affect or even determine our thought, but I still believe in Free Will and that, to use the language of the astrologers, it is always possible for a man to rise above his stars. Now Mr. Yeats would have me believe that a great wheel turns ceaselessly, and that I and all others drop into inevitable groove after groove. It matters not my virtue to-day, my talent which I burnish, the wheel will move me to another groove where I am predestined to look on life as that new spiritual circumstance determines, and my will is only free to accept or rebel, but not to alter what is fated.[60]

We would do well to take Russell's misgivings under advisement; he was certainly no stranger to the occult circles in which Yeats moved.[61] More than this, however, the determinism that he identifies at the nucleus of Yeats's metaphysical configuration appears to permeate the form and meaning of "The Second Coming."

For all its descriptions of the impending terror that will arise in conjunction with the dawning of the antithetical age, there is little variation from the decasyllabic metre established in the poem's opening lines. In fact, where there is a slight deviation in the first stanza from the iambic pentameter that features predominantly throughout, this deviation is specifically contrived to establish a certain parallelism between the poem's form and content. The initial foot in the poem's opening line, "Turning," is a trochaic inversion of the dominant pattern in the lines that follow. As a consequence, the textual form works in tandem with the "Turning" it describes (*VP* 401:1). This structured uniformity persists even while the speaker insists that "things fall apart; the centre cannot hold" (*VP* 401:3). In this instance, the semicolon fuses two separate, yet closely related clauses using a strict iambic pentameter that flouts the line's expressed meaning. This forges an alliance that is, within the context of the poem, as symmetrical as it is disruptive because this dissolution of order and descent into chaos is not in itself chaotic. The poem's formal structure never relinquishes its power over the content; it coaxes stealthily and from a distance, much as the causal configuration represented by Yeats's falconry looms ever constrictively and yet beyond the comprehension of his falcon. This decasyllabic pattern is sustained throughout the five lines that complete the first stanza, where the speaker's cool and detached register further infuses these apocalyptic descriptions with a certain sense of inevitability: "Mere anarchy is loosed upon the world, / The blood-dimmed tide is loosed, and everywhere / The ceremony of innocence is drowned; / The best lack all conviction, while the worst / Are full of passionate intensity" (*VP* 401:4–8). It is also telling that the spondaic feet at the beginning of line four stresses that it is "*mere* anarchy" that "is loosed upon the world." Indeed, this anarchy is "mere" precisely because this dissolution of order is an entirely natural and preordained by-product of Yeats's antithetical age. In addition to the quartet of slant rhymes that lend the first four lines of this octave a loose sense of stability, "gyre," "falconer," "world," and "hold" (*VP* 401:1–4), Vendler notes that this first stanza is "constructed in a series of half-lines, separated by medial breaks, in which the 'left' half represents the dissolution of form, and the 'right' half represents the threatened world order":

Chaos	**Order**
Turning and turning	in the widening gyre
The falcon cannot hear	the falconer
Things fall apart	the centre cannot hold
Mere anarchy is loosed	upon the world
The blood-dimmed tide is loosed	and everywhere
The ceremony of innocence is drowned	
	The best
lack all conviction, while	
The worst are full of passionate intensity.[62]	

Even the violent, oceanic imagery that Yeats uses in this stanza implies the presence of some underlying gravitational force; a force strong enough to orchestrate and conduct this ostensibly spontaneous implosion.

As Deane proposes, it is possible to determine "what the falcon, the tide, the ceremony, the best, [and] the worst" refer to from the surrounding poems in *Michael Robartes and the Dancer*.[63] Nevertheless, the meanings ascribed to these poetic components take on greater significance if one is familiar with the version of eternal recurrence that Yeats outlines in *A Vision*. The second and final stanza of the "The Second Coming" also exploits the radical sense of oscillation that characterizes this mode of historical determinism. Drawing on the intertextuality set up by the poem's title, which evokes the day of judgement traditionally associated with the return of Jesus Christ, this stanza imbues the "rocking cradle" and the town of "Bethlehem" with all the ungodly menace that Yeats ascribes to his antithetical age. This is not "the glorious Second

Coming of Christ," as Vendler succinctly puts it, "but a reprise, in grotesque form, of a new energy at Bethlehem."[64] Deane has rightly observed that this poem engages with the contrasting themes of "ending" and "beginning" in a way that problematizes the distinction between the two.[65] But the origin of this difficulty is twofold. On the one hand, it arises because the poem's speaker refuses to draw a value-based distinction between the contrasting principles that will reign supreme in the disparate historical cycles that clash in Yeats's text. On the other hand, it remains elusive because, for Yeats, these cycles are just equivalent constituents of an all-encompassing whole. Much like the first stanza, the poem's second stanza adheres to a certain formal consistency; in fact, its fourteen decasyllabic lines comprise a variation on the traditional sonnet, composed in a predominantly blank verse, that parallels the carefully controlled chaos of the first stanza. In this way, the formal synchronicity that underpins the apocalyptic imagery conjured up in this second stanza further mirrors the underlying causal force that orchestrates the fate of humankind in accordance with Yeats's historical metanarrative.

It is certainly true that Yeats's "shape with lion body and the head of a man, / A gaze blank and pitiless as the sun" (*VP* 401:14–15) is reminiscent of Nietzsche's "blond beast." As Patrick Bixby explains, this creaturely signifier is "associated with everything from the dauntless heroes of ancient Greek culture to the predatory instincts of the lion" across the breadth of Nietzsche's writing.[66] However, the determinist iteration of eternal recurrence that underpins the historical metanarrative that Yeats communicates in *A Vision*, and makes its present felt at the levels of form and content in "The Second Coming," does not align with the axiological reformulation of eternal recurrence that modern and contemporary scholars associate with Nietzsche. Notwithstanding the ostensible similarities between Nietzsche's Apollonian and Dionysian energies and the Blakean contraries that feature in Yeats's cyclical design, it is difficult to substantiate Bridgewater's and Bohlmann's contention that there are many parallels between Nietzsche's philosophy and Yeats's middle-period occultism. If indeed there are correlations between Nietzsche's philosophy and Yeats's occult speculation in *A Vision*, they are akin to those described by Harold Bloom as "misprision," insofar as Yeats misreads Nietzsche "to clear and imaginative space" for himself.[67]

In addition to the incompatibilities previously noted, it is difficult to reconcile this occult speculation with one of Nietzsche's most basic and immediately recognisable philosophical principles, "God is dead." This proclamation of God's death does not only reject *all* monotheistic claims to absolute authority; it rejects all claims to absolute authority, whether they are made in the name of religion, science, morality, politics, or quasi-religious occult speculation. In his 1873 essay, "David Strauss, the Confessor and

Writer," Nietzsche admonished those who wished to inscribe a "new faith" by "constructing the broad universal highway of the future"; in fact, he equated such efforts equated to those of a "trundling hippopotamus" whose "growling and barking had changed into the proud accents of the founder of a religion."[68] Just one year later, in an essay entitled "On the Uses and Disadvantages of History for Life," Nietzsche warns that the individual who learns:

> to bend his back and bow his head before the "power of history" at last nods "Yes" like a Chinese mechanical doll to every power, whether it be government or public opinion or a numerical majority, and moves his limbs to the precise rhythm at which any "power" whatever pulls the strings.[69]

By the time Nietzsche published *Human All Too Human* in 1878, he had already rejected the ascetic determinism espoused by his one-time mentor, Arthur Schopenhauer, and concluded that one "must remove the motley leopard-skin" of Schopenhauerian metaphysics "if one is to discover the real moralist genius behind it."[70] All of these remarks appeared in Nietzsche's writing before he proclaims God's death for the first time in *The Gay Science* (1882), in which he further cautions that "there may still for millennia be caves in which they show [God's] shadow. – And we – we must still defeat his shadow as well."[71] It is not simply that eternal recurrence holds a different significance for Yeats and Nietzsche, as Harrison observes in his analysis of "The Second Coming." The version of eternal recurrence that makes its presence felt in this poem stands in diametrical opposition to the life-affirming potential that Nietzsche wishes to unlock with all these denunciations of claims to absolute authority. Indeed, for Nietzsche, even the shadow of God-like omnipotence that manifests in the form of Yeats's falconer is dead.

NOTES

1 It may be the case that Yeats did not read Nietzsche's work in a focused and intense fashion prior to 1902. But he almost certainly encountered the German's ideas no later than April 1896, when his short story, "Rosa Alchemica," appeared in the April issue of *The Savoy* magazine alongside the first of Havelock Ellis's trilogy of essays on Nietzsche's life and work. See "Rosa Alchemica: A Story by W. B. Yeats," in *The Savoy*, No. 2, ed. Arthur Symons (London: Leonard Smithers, 1896), 56-70. In fact, two of Yeats's essays on "William Blake and his Illustrations to the Divine Comedy" appeared in the magazine's July and August issues, alongside Ellis's subsequent essays on Nietzsche. See "William Blake and his Illustrations to the Divine Comedy: His Opinions Upon Art (The First of Three Articles by W. B. Yeats)," in *The Savoy*, No. 3, ed. Arthur Symons (London: Leonard Smithers, 1896), 41-57, and "William Blake and his Illustrations to the Divine Comedy: His Opinions Upon Dante (The Second of Three Articles by W. B. Yeats)," in *The Savoy*, No. 4, ed. Arthur Symons

(London: Leonard Smithers, 1896), 25-41. URL: http://onlinebooks.library.upenn.edu/webbin/serial?id=savoy1896

2 Otto Bohlmann, *Yeats and Nietzsche: An Exploration of the Major Nietzschean Echoes in the Writings of William Butler Yeats* (Totowa, NJ: Barnes and Noble, 1982), 7.

3 Conor Cruise O'Brien, *The Suspecting Glance: The T. S. Eliot Memorial Lectures delivered at Eliot College in the University of Kent, at Canterbury, November, 1969* (London: Faber and Faber, 1972), 63.

4 See, for example, Richard Ellmann, *Yeats: The Man and the Masks* (London: Faber and Faber, 1961), 223–43, Denis Donoghue, *Yeats* (London: Fontana, 1971), 90–94, Seamus Deane, *Strange Country: Modernity and Nationhood in Irish Writing since 1790* (Oxford: Clarendon Press, 1998), 172–81, Peter Hühn, *The Narratological Analysis of Lyric Poetry: Studies in English Poetry from the 16th to the 20th Century*, trans. Alastair Matthews (Berlin: Walter de Gruyter, 2005), 177–86, and Patrick Bixby, "Frightful Doctrines: Nietzsche, Ireland, and the Great War." *Modernist Cultures* 13, no. 3 (2018): 334–38.

5 John R. Harrison, "What rough beast? Yeats, Nietzsche, and Historical Rhetoric in the 'The Second Coming,'" *Papers on Language and Literature* 31, no. 4 (Fall 1995): 373.

6 Arthur Danto, "The Eternal Recurrence," in *Nietzsche: A Collection of Critical Essays*, ed. Robert C. Solomon (New York: Anchor Books, 1973), 316.

7 Martin S. Bermann, "The Conflict between Enlightenment and Romantic Philosophies as Reflected in the History of Psychoanalysis," in *The Origins and Organization of Unconscious Conflict: The Selected Writings of Martin S. Bergmann* (Abingdon and New York: Routledge, 2017), 101.

8 Friedrich Nietzsche, *The Will to Power*, trans. Walter Kaufmann and R. J. Hollingdale (New York: Vintage Books, 1968), 544–50.

9 Alexander Nehamas, *Nietzsche: Life as Literature* (Cambridge, MA: Harvard University Press, 1985), 143–46.

10 Friedrich Nietzsche, "Thus Spoke Zarathustra," in *The Portable Nietzsche*, ed. and trans. Walter Kaufmann (New York: Penguin Books, 1976), 329.

11 Nietzsche, "Thus Spoke Zarathustra," 330.

12 Ivan Soll, "Reflections on Recurrence: A Re-examination of Nietzsche's Doctrine, *die Ewige Wiederkehr des Gleichen*," in *Nietzsche: A Collection of Critical Essays*, ed. Robert C. Solomon (New York: Anchor Books, 1973), 323.

13 Friedrich Nietzsche, *The Gay Science: With a Prelude in German Rhymes and an Appendix of Songs*, ed. Bernard Williams, trans. Josefine Nauckhoff and Adrian Del Caro (Cambridge: Cambridge University Press, 2003), 194.

14 Nietzsche, *The Gay Science*, 194.

15 Nietzsche, *The Gay Science*, 194.

16 Nietzsche, *The Gay Science*, 194–95. Emphasis in original.

17 This literal reading of eternal recurrence was among the many misinterpretations of Nietzsche's philosophy that proved amenable to Nazi philosophers, such as Alfred Baeumler, who used it to legitimize the Party's dogmatic principles in *Nietzsche, der Philosoph und Politiker* (1931). See Max Whyte, "The Uses and Abuses of Nietzsche in the Third Reich: Alfred Bauumler's 'Heroic Realism,'" *Journal of Contemporary History* 43, no. 2 (2008): 180.

18 Georges Bataille, *On Nietzsche*, trans. Bruce Boone (London and New York: Continuum, 2004), xxix. Emphasis in original.

19 Kant's categorical imperative is a refinement of the golden rule, which suggests you should treat others as you would like to be treated. Kant proposes that one should act only as one would like every other rational subject to act in order to establish a more objective ethical principle.

20 Gilles Deleuze, *Nietzsche and Philosophy*, trans. Hugh Tomlinson (New York: Columbia University Press, 1983), 68. Emphasis in original.
21 David S. Thatcher, *Nietzsche in England, 1890–1914: The Growth of a Reputation* (Toronto: Toronto University Press1970), 171.
22 Erich Heller, *The Importance of Nietzsche: Ten Essays* (Chicago: Chicago University Press, 1990), 133.
23 Frances Nesbitt Oppel, *Mask and Tragedy: Yeats and Nietzsche, 1902–10* (Charlottesville: University Press of Virginia, 1987), 61.
24 Patrick Bridgewater, *Nietzsche in Anglosaxony: A Study of Nietzsche's Impact on English and American Literature* (Leicester: Leicester University Press, 1972), 73.
25 Bohlmann, *Yeats and Nietzsche*, 157.
26 Kaufmann notes that Nietzsche uses the phrase "A Book of Prophecy" in this section of the manuscript in reference to a plan for a book, *The Eternal Recurrence*. See Nietzsche, *The Will to Power*, 544.
27 For an overview of the scale and importance of these papers, see George Mills Harper, "Yeats's Occult Papers," in *Yeats and the Occult*, ed. George Mills Harper (London: Macmillan Press, 1976), 1–11.
28 W. B. Yeats, *A Vision*, 2nd edn. (London: Macmillan Press, 1981), 19.
29 Yeats, *A Vision*, 2nd edn., 8.
30 Terence Brown, *The Life of W. B. Yeats: A Critical Biography* (Oxford: Blackwell Publishers, 2001), 33.
31 For a detailed exposition of Yeats's involvement with the Theosophical Society and the Hermetic Order of the Golden Dawn, see Ken Monteith, *Yeats and Theosophy* (New York: Routledge, 2008), and George Mills Harper, *Yeats's Golden Dawn* (London: Macmillan Press, 1974).
32 Margaret Mills Harper has written extensively on the automatic writing exercises that gave rise to *A Vision* and the pivotal role performed by George Yeats in this collaborative production. See, for example, Harper, *Wisdom of Two: The Spiritual and Literary Collaboration of George and W. B. Yeats* (Oxford: Oxford University Press, 2006).
33 Timothy Materer, "Occultism," in *W. B. Yeats in Context*, eds. David Holdeman and Ben Levitas (Cambridge: Cambridge University Press, 2010), 237–46.
34 Margaret Mills Harper and Catherine E. Paul, "Editors' Introduction," in *AVB* xxiii–li.
35 Yeats, *A Vision*, 2nd edn., 11.
36 The poem was written in 1919 and originally published in *The Dial* in November 1920. See W. B. Yeats, "Ten Poems," *The Dial* LXIX, no. 5 (1920): 455-66.
37 Yeats, *A Vision*, 2nd edn., 69.
38 William Blake, *The Marriage of Heaven and Hell* (London: Oxford University Press, 1975), xvi.
39 Nietzsche, *The Gay Science*, 121.
40 In *The Birth of Tragedy*, first published in 1872, Nietzsche uses the terms "Apollonian" and "Dionysian" to describe two opposing artistic energies. He associates the Apollonian with the kind of measured restraint exemplified by the practice of sculpting; the Dionysian with the intoxication of music and its capacity to facilitate the erosion of all subjectivity. See Nietzsche, "The Birth of Tragedy," in *Basic Writings of Nietzsche*, ed. and trans. Walter Kaufmann (New York: Random House, 2000), 33–38. This was Nietzsche's first book, written when he was just twenty eight years old and still very much under Schopenhauer's pessimistic spell. He rejected much of what appeared in this book in his preface to the 1886 edition, entitled "An Attempt at Self-Criticism". See "The Birth of Tragedy," 16–27.

41 Charles I. Armstrong, "Ancient Frames: Classical Philosophy in Yeats's *A Vision*," in *W. B. Yeats's A Vision: Explications and Contexts*, eds. Neil Mann, Matthew Gibson, and Claire V. Nally (Clemson: Clemson University Digital Press, 2012), 96.
42 Yeats, *A Vision*, 2nd edn., 72.
43 Yeats, *A Vision*, 2nd edn., 71–72. Emphasis in original.
44 Bridgewater, *Nietzsche in Anglosaxony*, 69.
45 Bohlmann, *Yeats and Nietzsche*, 173.
46 For a detailed description of the function performed by the tincture in Boehmean mysticism, see Andrew Weeks, *Boehme: An Intellectual Biography of the Seventeenth-Century Philosopher and Mystic* (Albany, NY: State University of New York Press, 1991), 122–24.
47 Friedrich Nietzsche, *Human, All Too Human: A Book for Free Spirits*, trans. R. J. Hoilngdale (Cambridge: Cambridge University Press, 1986), 64. Emphasis in original.
48 Nietzsche, *Human, All Too Human*, 14.
49 Yeats, *A Vision*, 2nd edn., 78.
50 Ellmann, *Yeats*, 226–27.
51 Deane, *Strange Country*, 172.
52 Helen Vendler, *Our Secret Discipline: Yeats and Lyric Form* (Oxford: Oxford University Press, 2007), 171.
53 Vendler, *Our Secret Discipline*, 237.
54 Donoghue, *Yeats*, 91.
55 Yeats, *A Vision*, 2nd edn., 11.
56 Matthew Gibson, "Yeats, the Great Year, and Pierre Duhem," in *Yeats, Philosophy, and the Occult*, eds. Matthew Gibson and Neil Mann (Clemson: Clemson University Digital Press, 2016), 179.
57 Yeats, *A Vision*, 2nd edn., 267.
58 Yeats, *A Vision*, 2nd edn., 267.
59 Ellmann, *Yeats*, 230.
60 George Russell, "A Vision," *The Irish Statesman*, February 13, 1926, 714.
61 Like Yeats, Russell was a member of the Theosophical Society. In fact, both Yeats and Russell were founding members of the Dublin Lodge of the Irish Theosophical Society, established in 1886. Russell derived the pseudonym, "AE," short for "Aeon," from the name of the first created being according to Gnostic mythology. Russell did not join The Hermetic Order of the Golden Dawn, however, as he held misgivings regarding the practice of ritualistic magic.
62 Vendler, *Our Secret Discipline*, 172–73.
63 Deane, Strange Country, 173.
64 Vendler, *Our Secret Discipline*, 172.
65 Deane, Strange Country, 173.
66 Bixby, "Frightful Doctrines," 324.
67 Harold Bloom, *The Anxiety of Influence: A Theory of Poetry* (New York: Oxford University Press, 1973), 5.
68 Friedrich Nietzsche, "David Strauss, the Confessor and the Writer," in *Untimely Meditations*, trans. R. J. Hollingdale (Cambridge: Cambridge University Press, 1983), 14.
69 Friedrich Nietzsche, "On the Uses and Disadvantages of History for Life," in *Untimely Meditations*, trans. R. J. Hollingdale (Cambridge: Cambridge University Press, 1983), 105.
70 Nietzsche, *Human, All Too Human*, 222.
71 Nietzsche, *The Gay Science*, 109.

Rapallo Notebooks A and B

Neil Mann

The Rapallo Notebooks

This is the first of a series of essays in *IYS* covering the five notebooks that W. B. Yeats kept between 1928 and 1931, referred to as "Rapallo Notebooks," which are now held by the National Library of Ireland as MSS 13,578–13,582. As well as the Italian town of Rapallo, the notebooks bear traces from other places, including Dublin, Coole, and London, as Yeats tended to use bound notebooks as a portable means of keeping his work together when traveling, preferring loose-leaf notebooks when at home. However, the name is apt, as W. B. and George Yeats returned to Rapallo for three successive winters for Yeats's health,[1] and it is also likely that the notebooks were purchased in Italy.[2] They were not the only notebooks used when the Yeatses were in Rapallo, and others overlap with them, including, for instance, the diary that Yeats kept in 1930, but these five have a uniformity of dimensions and paper,[3] and were early on treated as a group, now labeled A, B, C, D, and E.[4] Notebooks A, B, and E are identical, with a yellow cover decorated with vertical lines made of lozenge shapes, while C and D have a cover design in olive green, blue, and white, with small flowers.

A detailed overview of the five notebooks, "Yeats's Rapallo Notebooks," appears in the forthcoming *Yeats Annual* issue dedicated to manuscript materials.[5] As that essay indicates, it is in fact likely that Rapallo Notebooks A, B, and E were all started in 1928, with B being the first, while E had all the early material removed.[6] Because of particular overlap of time and material between Rapallo Notebooks A and B, they are presented together in this issue, though treated separately for the sake of clarity. And, although Rapallo Notebook B precedes Rapallo Notebook A in terms of starting date and, to a large extent, of use, they are examined in the order of their labeling. Subsequent essays by Wayne Chapman, Margaret Mills Harper, and Warwick Gould will deal with the other notebooks singly.

If there is a common thread to the notebooks, it is in the drafts and notes where Yeats was struggling with a new exposition of the system of *A Vision*. After publication of the first version of *A Vision* in 1925,[7] he had immediately started to revise his thinking about important elements, to read more widely in philosophical literature, and to rewrite sections of the book. By 1928 he was seriously drafting for a new edition, and all five Rapallo notebooks contain *Vision* material—though Rapallo Notebook D has relatively little, while Rapallo

Notebook B is almost exclusively dedicated to such drafts. Some of the material is completely new, but much could be termed "intermediate" between the formulations of *A Vision A* and those of *A Vision B*. For students of *A Vision*, therefore, they often reveal how the thought itself was developing, so that what is expressed concisely and sometimes too laconically in *A Vision B* (1937) may be explained a little more fully or tentatively here, or even in completely different ways. In fact, relatively little of the material contained in the notebooks' drafts appears in the 1937 edition without significant transformation, with the exception of material for *A Packet for Ezra Pound* and some of what became "The Great Year of the Ancients."

The notebooks also bear witness to the poetic creativity of the late 1920s, including poems that would appear in the Cuala Press's *Words for Music Perhaps* (1932) and Macmillan's edition of *The Winding Stair and Other Poems* (1933), drafts for *The Words upon the Window-pane* (first staged in 1930) and *The Resurrection* (the revised version of 1931). There are also minor emendations for *The Player Queen*, material associated with *The Cat and the Moon*, drafts for essays, prefaces, letters to the press, and unpublished material, both poetry and prose, including ideas for poems that were probably never written. Mixed in with these are diary entries and analyses of friends, reading lists, notes from Yeats's reading and researches, a week's appointments, calculations, and a record of payments.

Because of their binding, the notebooks preserve a fuller record of the genesis of poetry and drama than Yeats's preferred format of loose leaf, though all of the notebooks show signs of pages having been torn out or removed with a blade. Above all, it is the heterogeneity and the miscellaneous quality of the material in the notebooks that makes them a singular and very immediate record of Yeats's mind and concerns at a crucial stage of his career. The poet may not be "the bundle of accident and incoherence that sits down to breakfast," but rather someone who "has been reborn as an idea, something intended, complete" (*E&I* 509, *CW5* 204), yet both poet and bundle of accident are present in the notebooks' ferment of the esoteric, the poetic, and the day-to-day. Indeed, just as some alchemists claimed that the raw material for the Philosophers' Stone was to be found on the common dungheap,[8] Yeats acknowledged that the poet's "masterful images" began in "A mound of refuse or the sweepings of a street" (*VP* 630, *CW1* 355), and, though it would be unnecessarily disparaging to describe the notebooks as such sweepings, they do show the jostle of disparate elements.

This disparateness is lost when drafts are removed from their context. Most of the poetry and drama is now readily available in facsimile in the Cornell manuscripts series, but in extracted form, presented page by page and often reordered, as Yeats tended to use the right-hand side of a spread first, with the left-hand side for later revisions.[9] The Cornell series's presentation, of course, serves well the purpose of showing how the works evolve and brings together drafts from a variety of places, but it risks creating a false sense of teleology or smoothing over the cross-fertilization of other interests.[10] These notebooks may contain multiple drafts of a single poem, just one, or even just a few lines adumbrating something filled out elsewhere, but this version is placed not with any preceding states nor with later typescripts and more final versions, but rather with the mix of other writings and concerns.[11] The tables presented in the Appendix make it possible to map how this material appears in the notebooks, at least partially, and they also indicate some other places that offer relevant transcriptions.[12]

Because almost none of the material in Rapallo Notebooks A and B has been transcribed or reproduced before, I have erred on the side of fullness when presenting transcriptions in the following essay. This has made the article significantly longer than originally projected, but I trust that there is enough of interest to students of Yeats to justify the length and the detailed—though far from exhaustive—treatment of the material.

NOTE ON TRANSCRIPTION PRINCIPLES, CONVENTIONS, AND SYMBOLS

The transcriptions in this examination seek to illustrate the wealth of material contained in the notebooks, most of it not published before.

In general, readability is paramount. Cancelled text is not included in the transcription, unless a cancelled word makes the syntax more comprehensible. Where the line striking content through does not reach a word that is evidently no longer intended, that word is omitted as if it had been struck through. However, in examples where the process of composition is a point of consideration, the cancellations are, of course, included, to show how Yeats rethought and refined his expression. In cases of multiple levels of cancellation, I have tried to indicate these as far as possible with standard typography, with single strikethrough, double strikethrough, and lines drawn in.

Similarly, in text for reading, insertions are usually included silently, but when the process of writing is important, they are indicated by placing the text in <pointed brackets>, omitting any caret mark or lines. Material inserted from the opposite verso is placed in {curly brackets}.

Punctuation is only added in [brackets] when the reader might otherwise stumble over the construction, so the text is usually left with Yeats's very light and slightly wayward punctuation. Uncertain readings show the word(s) [?queried in brackets]. Supplied words and clarifications are in [*italics in brackets*], as is the occasional [*sic*] where the reader might suspect a misprint, although most misspellings and repetitions are given as they appear without comment. As Yeats occasionally uses his own ellipses, my ellipses signifying omitted text are also placed in brackets, with three [. . .] or four points [. . . .] according to standard convention of whether or not at least one period is omitted. In transcriptions where cancelled text is being shown, repetitious material that is cancelled is sometimes omitted and shown as [. . . .].

Yeats's spelling was never conventionally strong and, while his handwriting is seldom easy, in these personal notebooks it is sometimes little more than gestural shorthand: paradoxically, therefore, words with clearer lettering appear with Yeats's (mis)spelling, while those with outlines that are understandable only in context appear more conventionally.

The illustrations of the pages from the notebooks are intended to give some instances of how the transcriptions relate to the real material, in particular the appearance of the pages, and to show readers some words that have remained impossible for me to transcribe with confidence.

The Sequence of Rapallo A and B

Both Rapallo A and B are dominated by material associated with *A Vision*, Rapallo A significantly, and Rapallo B almost exclusively. From internal dating, it appears that Rapallo B was started in March 1928, while it is likely that Rapallo Notebook A was started in July 1928. The two notebooks ran in parallel during the summer and early fall of 1928; Rapallo Notebook B was finished in October and Notebook A a month later in November 1928, only for a blank page to be used two years later to extend an entry from the 1930 diary.

The sequence and relationship of the notebooks can be illustrated by one section from the Rapallo Notebooks' immediate predecessor, and the versions that developed in the two notebooks themselves. Prior to the Yeatses' arrival in Rapallo, W. B. Yeats had been using a leather notebook, which he had probably brought along with him when his health problems led the couple to sail for the south in November 1927.[13] It contains drafts of poems that would go into *The Winding Stair* (1929), some of which appear to be in relatively fair form while others are still very much in progress.[14] At the end of these poems Yeats gives a date of "Dec 1927"; they are followed by notes relating to the system of *A Vision* and records of "Sleeps" in Cannes, where the Yeatses stayed from the end of November 1927 until the middle of February 1928. The last date in this book (though not the last entry) is "Sleap March Rapallo."[15]

One of the more extended notes in this volume is titled "suggested first paragraph of system," two pages after the date of "Dec 11" 1927. In this projected opening for the new edition of *A Vision*, Yeats starts with the *Daimon*. Realizing that he had not stated the subject of the paragraph clearly, Yeats indicated the insertion of an introductory sentence stating, "all that can <need> be said of the daimon in this place can [*be*] put into a few sentences."[16] This prefaces the following presentation:

> It is a self creating power none is like another, for what in a man personally is unique is from the daimon and this daimon seeks to unite itself now with one now with another daimon but can only do so through the human mind it has neither reflection nor memory. We represent it thus

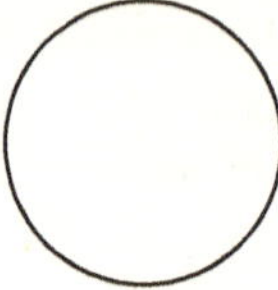

> because it does not perceive, as does the linear mind of man, object following object in a narrow stream, but all at once & because it perceives objects arranged about as it were in order of their kinship with itself, those most akin the nearest & not as they are in time & space.[17]

The treatment goes on to consider the relation between human and daimon in some depth, with many cancellations and second thoughts.

The next draft in Rapallo B, titled "First things" and dated March 1928 at the end, shows more confidence, though Yeats decided to insert yet another introductory paragraph in front of the text, indicating its insertion from the opposite verso.[18] The few sentences about the *Daimon* are introduced by the disclaimer, "I begin with the daimon & of the daimon I know little," a lack of knowledge that is brushed aside in characteristically Yeatsian style by piling up quotations from a an proto-Christian heretic, the Upanishads, and a Zen koan (see the section on Rapallo B below). He then recounts an argument with the instructor, in fact very recent as it was one of the last entries in the previous, leather-bound notebook, "Sleap March Rapallo." Yeats recounts that the instructor was "cross because I did not realize that the daimon was perfect" and had explained to him how *Daimons* could be both unique and perfect.[19] Yeats records in Rapallo B:

> I did not dare to ask why, if the daimon is perfect, ~~it was necessary to create man~~ <man comes into existence>; I did not want another scene & besides one cannot know everything. I accept his thought & say that nothing can be taken from or added to the daimon & being a symbolist & no philosopher I declare that this is its shape[20]

This comes at the bottom of a page and the following page was torn out, but Yeats appears to remove the explanation of why the *Daimon* is symbolized by the circle; further explanation is separated into the following section and consideration of how the *daimonic* mind connects to and differs from the human mind is briefer. This whole page was later completely cancelled.

In Rapallo A, the list of contents on the book's first verso notes that the section titled "First Things" has the "first page lacking."[21] Because of this, the notebook does not show how the opening section developed, but the text of its section II echoes Rapallo B:[22]

> I did not dare to ask why if each be perfect man should come into existence; I did not want another scene & besides one cannot know everything. I accept his thought & say <to introduce the chief person of my ~~play~~ drama> that nothing can be taken from or added to the Daimon & being a symbolist <dramatist> & ~~know~~ ~~no philosopher~~ <~~logician~~> <not a dialectician> declare that this is its shape[23]

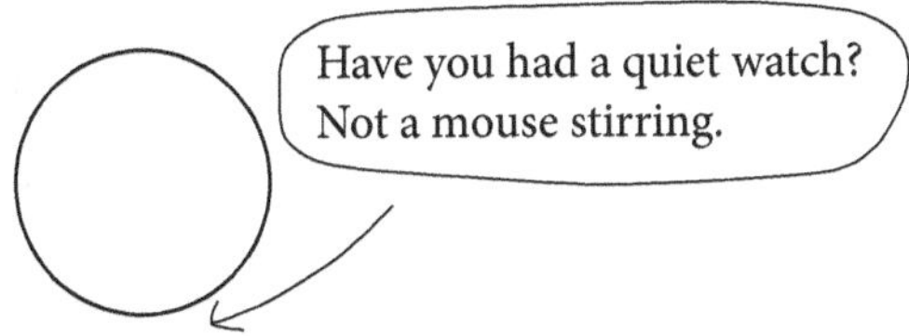

What were additions and corrections to the text of Rapallo B are incorporated into the text of Rapallo A, with slight changes, generally in the direction of more formal language, so that "why if the daimon is perfect man comes" is amended to "why if each be perfect man should come." Further elaborations are added, so that Yeats declares the *Daimon* "the chief person of my drama," and refines his thinking, deciding, for instance, not to disqualify himself as a philosopher but to admit that he is no dialectician. The miswriting of "know" for "no" may indicate that the text was being dictated directly from its source, whether Rapallo B or the associated typescript. He also adds a gnomic quotation from *Hamlet*, alluding to the presence of a spirit, which persists through a series of drafts.[24]

These three extracts show the relatively straightforward development of a single concept,[25] and also indicate the order of the Rapallo Notebooks, which is also indicated by the first bloc of material in Rapallo A being listed as "Great Year (final version),"[26] while the fourth bloc of material in Rapallo B is listed as "Great Year (early version)," with the text in Rapallo A adopting the later versions of Rapallo B's drafts, though there are relatively few points of direct contact between the two.[27] The "Great Year" section in Rapallo B follows a bloc dated "May 1928" (after a few intervening notes),[28] and takes up more than twenty-four leaves, so it is unlikely that "The Great Year" that opens Rapallo A was started before June of that year, and July seems more probable.

The following tabulation sets out the approximate periods during which the three notebooks examined above were in use.

Table 1. Approximate dates and places of use of Yeats's notebooks NLI 30,359, Rapallo A, and Rapallo B.

year	*month*	*main places*	Leather NB NLI 30,359	Rapallo A NLI 13,578	Rapallo B NLI 13,579
1927	Dec	Cannes			
1928	Jan				
	Feb				
	Mar	Rapallo			
	Apr	Rapallo / Dublin			
	May	Dublin			
	Jun	London			
	Jul	Dublin			
	Aug	Coole			
	Sep	Dublin			
	Oct				
	Nov	Rapallo			
	Dec	Rome / Rapallo			
1929					
1930					
	Nov	London / Dublin			

Rapallo Notebook A

Rapallo Notebook A is, therefore, probably the second of the Rapallo Notebooks Yeats started, and its main period of use was from before August 1928 until later that year, when Yeats put one of the notebook's two explicit dates at the end of a long draft of material related to the Great Year for *A Vision*, "Nov 1928."[29] The other date contained in the notebook actually comes from 1930 and relates to an isolated late item dated "Oct 20," continuing an entry from the 1930 diary. However, much of the other material in Rapallo A is clearly datable by external factors including letters and periodical publication.

The November date for the *Vision* material is squeezed vertically into a lower corner and evidently relates to revision and possible addition, as it is followed by material from before that date: drafts for articles on censorship published in September 1928;[30] early drafts for his essay on the Irish coinage (the final draft finished, according to a letter, by August 28, [1928], *CL InteLex* 5150); and a draft letter responding to Annie Horniman's carping criticism in the *Irish Statesman* on 6 October 1928 (Yeats's letter was published 13 October 1928, *CL InteLex* 5176).[31] The notebook also contains revisions to *The Player Queen* for upcoming performances at the Abbey in September 1928, as well as notes from reading Stephen MacKenna's translation of Plotinus and on the long ages of Indian tradition. It appears to have been treated as finished and put aside at the end of 1928, but it was taken up two years later to take advantage of the plentiful blank space at the end of the notebook to add to the diary of 1930,[32] which had been filled up; Yeats extended the diary entry dated "October 20" and also added a coda to a later undated entry. As the diary was finished in November 1930—its final entry is dated "Nov 18"—it is likely that the extension was actually added after that date.

CONTENTS: OVERVIEW

Over half of the notebook is taken up with revisions for *A Vision*, focused on two areas that changed significantly: the vastly expanded treatment of the "Great Year" and Yeats's continuing struggle with how best to start his presentation of the system.[33] The main treatment of the Great Year in *A Vision A* (1925) had been a lengthy exploration in Book II, section "X | The Great Year in Classical Antiquity," which is supplementary to the system as such, illustrating how Yeats's idea relates to its many precedents (*AVA* 149–58, *CW13* 121–28). The drafts in Rapallo A and B build on this material but contain further research on ancient cosmology, furnished by wider reading, although Yeats had yet to be introduced to some of the illustrations he would use, such as the work of Leo Frobenius that was Ezra Pound's enthusiastic recommendation.[34] Many pages of the drafts also relate the Great Year to more technical aspects of the system, but little of this material reached the published version. Like its slighter predecessor in *A Vision A*, therefore, much of "Book IV: The Great Year of the Ancients" as published in *A Vision B* (1937) is not particularly connected to the esoteric system. Rather, it is mainly concerned with drawing parallels between the long periods of *A Vision*'s historical cycles and various schemes of antiquity—whether the return of all the planets to the same positions or the precession of the equinoxes—as well as more modern anthropological research and discussion of writers such as Oswald Spengler and Henry Adams.

As alluded to in the earlier examination of the notebooks' order, Rapallo A's section on "First Things" redrafts the material of Rapallo B, intended for the new edition of *A Vision*. It opens with the *Daimon* before moving to the intersecting cones and the presentation of the gyres—drawing on Plotinus, Heraclitus, Proclus, and Cavalcanti—to explain the underlying foundations that Yeats felt he had avoided in *A Vision A*. Convinced of the *Principles*' more fundamental importance, Yeats also decides to explain the gyres in terms of the *Principles* rather than the *Faculties*, describing the movements of *Husk* and *Passionate Body* instead of *Will* and *Mask*, along with *Spirit* and *Celestial Body* instead of *Creative Mind* and *Body of Fate*. This treatment breaks off in a tortuous swirl of cancellation and correction as Yeats struggles to work in the opposition of Christ and St. John in the Christian year, already included in *A Vision A* (cf. *AVA* 164, *CW13* 133; *AVB* 212, *CW14* 156), and pages have evidently been removed.

Interjected between these two drafts comes the first of two essays relating to the Censorship Bill that was going through the Dáil, which had had its first reading the day after Yeats last spoke in the Senate in July 1928.[35] The two articles appeared in September 1928, and the drafts here probably date from late July or August (there are later, fuller typescripts).[36] They show Yeats's continued interest and activism in national politics, despite his physical infirmity and frustrations with the state of affairs. The notebook also contains a draft of a letter connected to the first article: Yeats mentions Wagner's inspiration by the Palatine Chapel in Palermo, which prompted a letter to the editor from Annie Horniman—and this subsequent rejoinder.[37] There are also pages drafting parts of the "Editorial" or introduction to *The Coinage of Saorstát Éireann*, giving an account of the process involved in deciding on the designs for the new Irish coins, another aspect of his engagement in the public life of the Free State.[38]

The only direct reference to any poetic or dramatic work comes in some revisions to *The Player Queen* so that "no dancer has to speak" (to George Yeats, August 17, 1928, *CL InteLex* 5145; *YGYL* 194). These changes appear to have been undertaken in preparation for the Abbey's production of the play in September 1928 alongside dance programs given by Ninette de Valois' company.[39]

Other pages of the notebook are taken up with stray notes on his reading, and there are many blank pages. The only real date in the notebook comes after Yeats apparently returned to revise and probably add to his drafts on the Great Year, and this is followed by three completely blank leaves, so Yeats had clearly left empty pages available for finishing off this section, possibly recognizing the need to start drafting something on censorship. There is a similar gap after the article on censorship and Aquinas,[40] probably showing Yeats again starting a new project while still expecting to add to the preceding material. As there are no obvious changes in handwriting or ink, it is impossible to say how many pages he originally left and subsequently used, but they do show the need to move from one area of interest to another, while knowing that there was still work to do. Indeed, the date of "Nov 1928" at the end of the notebook's first large bloc, "The Great Year," may well indicate that revising and adding to this section was the last sustained work in the notebook. However, as mentioned earlier, in the plentiful space towards the end of the book,[41] a single blank page was convenient when Yeats wanted to expand on one of the entries toward the end of the diary he kept during 1930, thus briefly bringing the notebook back into service.

Rapallo Notebooks A and B contain no poetry. Yeats had told Olivia Shakespear in October 1927 that he had undertaken to provide "sixteen or so pages of verse" for a New York publisher for £300, adding later that "These new poems interrupted my re-writing of 'A Vision'" (*CL InteLex* 5034; cf. *L* 730). Having contended with ill health over the winter and having fulfilled his poetic commitment when the typescript of the poems went off to the press on March 13, 1928,[42] Yeats appears to have restarted work on *A Vision* in Rapallo B with redoubled focus, and in July he was telling Lady Gregory that he had "snatched every moment to finish 'A Vision' & put off till tomorrow everything else" (July 30, [1928], *CLInteLex* 5137; cf. *L* 745).

Despite this focus, timeliness was obviously crucial for his contributions to the censorship debate, and other commitments such as the report on the currency had some urgency too, as did rehearsals for the Abbey's new season, so that these intruded into the notebook he began slightly later, Rapallo A, but only insofar as they were pressing. Rapallo A is thus largely confined to the prosaic, albeit essential aspects of Yeats's life in the 1920s, both the private esoterica of *A Vision* and public politics, represented here by censorship and coinage. The only aspects of the poet or dramatist glimpsed are those of the practical man of the theater adapting a play for particular upcoming circumstances and perhaps the lyrical prose of "Rapallo in Spring" that opens Rapallo B. However, the following year, when, "in the spring of 1929 life returned to me as an impression of the uncontrollable energy and daring of the great creators," as Yeats recalled in the introduction to the *Winding Stair and Other Poems* (1933, *VP* 831), renewed inspiration would fill subsequent notebooks with poetry.

In Greater Detail

[Cover][43]

This notebook has a large letter "D" on the cover, the relic of a previous labeling system that was certainly in operation in late 1930: at the end of the entry for October 20 in the 1930 diary, Yeats indicated where to locate the continuation: "see book D."[44] The only other notebook to have a letter written on the front cover is Rapallo E,[45] and indeed these two could well have been "neighboring" volumes in a different sequence of notebooks. It is very probable that Rapallo E was started before the current Notebooks C and D, and contained the *Vision* material that is indicated in the cancelled list written on the cover above the letter "E." Though the three lines have been scratched through to the point of illegibility, they appear to read "Principle [sic] symbols | hourglass &

diamond | To [illegible] Great Wheel." This content does not appear in Rapallo E as it now is, but a significant number of pages have been removed from the beginning of the notebook.[46] The relabeling of notebook "D" as "A" appears to have been done by the Yeatses, with "A" and "B" appearing on the first rectos of these notebooks, even though this ordering is out of chronological sequence.[47]

[1r–3r]

The rebinding of the notebook has added two leaves at the front of the notebook, but the first page proper bears a large letter "A" on the recto, while the verso gives a list in W. B. Yeats's hand of the book's "Contents":

> Great Year (final version) 20 pages
> Censorship & Thomas Acquinas
> First Things 12 pages (first page lacking)
> Player Queen (corrections) 6 pages
> Essay on Coinage 3 pages
> Censorship 10 pages
> letter in Reply to Miss H 1 page

This table of contents reflects fairly accurately the notebook's main material, and the list was evidently drawn up after the book was finished, probably in 1928 and before the addition of the 1930 diary entry. The pages were counted and it was possibly at this stage that Yeats numbered or renumbered the pages of each section, usually restarting at "1" for each new stretch and occasionally skipping numbering for pages with rejected material or moving out of sequence to reflect changes in order (in Rapallo B).[48]

The brief chain of notes below these contents shows, however, part of the provocative juxtaposition that comes in Yeats's bound volumes: he links with vertical lines "One absolute," "manifold one. Int Prin," "Each one among many. soul (individuals)," jottings that evidently relate to his notes on Plotinus on the facing page [2r]. Brief though they are, Yeats was looking for them in August 1928, writing to George from Coole:

> I am so sorry but I have found those notes you have been searching for in one of those Italian MSS books. They were not in the leather bound book I put you looking for. I am ashamed of myself. Next time you are in Dublin send me the fourth Plotinus volume for it is to that they refer. ([August 17, 1928], *CL InteLex* 5145; cf. *YGYL* 194)

This letter indicates that Yeats must certainly have started the notebook before he arrived at Coole on August 14, 1928, and if the volume of Plotinus was located in Dublin, Yeats had probably made the notes while there—he and George had arrived in April 1928 and he spent much of his time there.[49] The notes refer to MacKenna's *Plotinus: The Divine Mind, Being the Treatises of the Fifth Ennead*, noting the symbolism of "intellection symbolized by [circle] | sensation by line" and locating such connections as "p12 par[agraph] 3 | sphere," which gives an account of Parmenides, comparing his unity "to a huge sphere in that it holds and envelops all existence."[50] Such notes show Yeats writing only for himself and a full blank leaf left before the following item, [3r/3v], may indicate that he contemplated more notes on Plotinus or other reading.

[4r–26r] "Great Year (final version) 20 pages"

The leaf that follows [4r] starts a formal draft of "The Great Year" for *A Vision* and, after rejecting at least two openings, begins with what would be the second paragraph of "Book IV: The Great Year of the Ancients" in *A Vision B*—"To the time when Marius sat at home planning a sedition that began the Roman civil wars, popular imagination attributed many prodigies" (*AVB* 243, *CW14* 177)—but there is much correction, cancellation, and insertion. The general shape and text are relatively close to the published version for the first five pages (two sections), while also including ideas that were incorporated into the introduction for *The Resurrection* in *Wheels and Butterflies* (1934), such as the comment on the Great Year, that "To measure it according to Proclus we should know the life period of all living things gods, whales & gudgeons for when it ends all must end[,] when it begins all begin."[51]

Section III, however, starts on a provocative tack that was not included in *A Vision B*, and the implications, though characteristic of Yeats's thinking, are slightly confused and confusing, albeit clearer than the version outlined in Rapallo B:

> I delight in a symbolism that can thrust Christianity back into the crises where it arose & then display it not as an abstract ideal but united to its opposite, & thrust it forward in crissis after ~~criss~~ crisis, where the actors must change roles, & the defeated Tincture triumph in its turn. An ideal separated from its opposite is lyrical & its fantastic immobility ~~appals us~~ palls upon us but an ideal united to its opposite is tragic & stays always like the poetry of Dante. I am tired of Shellean Christianity—I prefer to any song in the air a Phoenix, that rises twelve times form a body twelve times consumed to ashes.[52]

The opposition of lyrical and tragic—the two forms most characteristic of Yeats's own poetry and drama—is slightly strange, as it seems to disparage his lyric mode, though there is evidently some of the bravura provocation that would later inform *On the Boiler*. Though this formulation went through drafts in Rapallo B and then A, this approach and tone were not used in *A Vision*. In general, the drafting here shows signs of hurry in the handwriting, which is often illegible or intelligible only from context, sentences that are ungrammatical as they change course with deletion and substitution, and thinking that is exploratory, even muddled. Yeats is possibly, as Jon Stallworthy suggests, "*thinking* on paper," projecting ideas provisionally in an act of discovery rather than statement.[53]

Yeats also shows uncertainty about how to relate various elements of *A Vision*'s scheme of historical gyres and the phases of the moon to the solar year, with tables presenting significantly different alignments of various cycles within the system, as his examination passes into more technical aspects of the symbolic year. Several schemes that place the phases and zodiac signs in correspondence with the 2,200-year months of the Great Year are all rejected, as Yeats abandons all but the simplest arrangement. The draft proceeds to an exposition of the *Principles* showing "the different phases of the wheel of month or year" in the geometrical arrangement of the cones,[54] before differentiating the historical Great Year from "the great wheel of incarnations."[55] The treatment then provides an explanation for the special arrangement of the diagram prefacing "Dove or Swan" which survives into the version published in 1937, discussing how "My instructors have adopted this arrangement of the cones & gyres . . . because it enables them in figure [*gap for number*] to stretch out in a line four periods which are in Spengler's sense 'contemporaneous,'" noting that the instructors "scrawled it once or twice on the margins of a manuscript, while writing something else & left me to discover its meaning. They seem to play with their abstractions as we do with words" (cf. *AVB* 256, *CW14* 187).[56]

The following section expands on the concept of the Phoenix mentioned earlier, comparable to the divine avatars of Hinduism:

> VIII.
>
> The Twelve beings who start the twelve months of my year are called incarnations of Buddha in the east but as we have [*no*] name for them I shall call them the twelve Phoenixs because a Phoenix rises from its predecessors ashes. Each must create itself, so fully that all the past is taken up into its nature, & upon completeness of this act not upon any reality beyond the mind depends the stability of civilization, & only through this act which leaves nothing beyond itself can the will of man be free. We approach a multiform Phoenix because antithetical revelation though its Master may show certain dominant types can never be the same for any two personalities. Its God is immanent, Shelleys Demigorgan rising from the earth as from the daimonic sphere to overturn quantative nature, transcendant law, his serpent struggling with an eagle.[57]

The next pages return to diagrammatic representations of the Great Year mapped to the zodiac, the possibility of spiritual release from the wheel of incarnation, and Plotinus's "Three Authentic Existants" (Yeats's very partial reading of MacKenna's translation of *The Enneads*):[58]

IX

The diagrams frequently make each of these months a half month, a bright or dark fortnight, that they may turn the 26 000 years we have thought of as the great year into the first half of a year of 52 000. When they do this they still enumerate the zodiac twice over. The *Spirit* of the year of 52 000 years moves twice through the zodiac

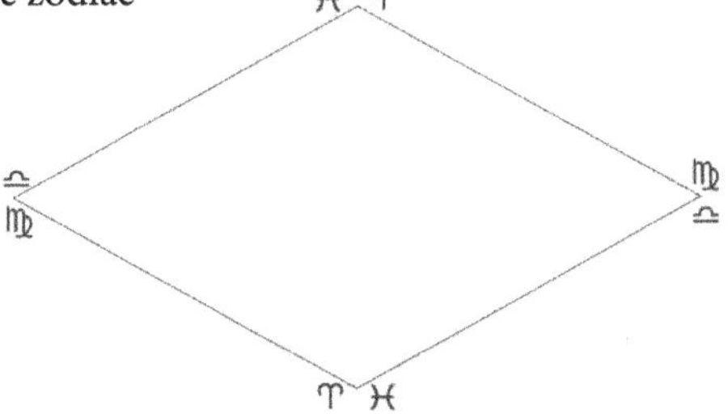

before it completes its circle.[59] The object is to get the second half of the greater, a new zodiac a new series of twelve cycles, which may contrast with the first as primary with antithetical but — being preceded by a kind of death p[*hase*] 22 — may[,] should the soul have earned its freedom, be a spiritual existence. If a spiritual existence they are no longer twelve [?then/?there], no longer gyres but spheres one within an other. The Three Authentic existants of Plotinus & from the first of these — called the thirteen cycle [—] the Antithetical Tincture is reflected, from the second the Primary[,] while in the third is the union of the first two. It is from this 3 fold world that the greater spirits descend. It will be present[*ly*] seen that ~~they are~~ being related to those in the first twelve cycles as the principles are to the faculties and come without intermediary not being means to an end.[60]

This treatment, which continues onto the next page, shows Yeats still thinking in terms of the stages beyond incarnation as three "cycles" or spheres (cf. *AVA* 176, 236; *CW13* 143, 194), a formulation that was in the process of being assimilated into a single *Thirteenth Cone* or *Sphere*. He writes of the Great Year as containing all the lesser cycles within it (see Figure 1), stating that:

> Sometimes my instructors have compared the great year to a whole number, & the months or days of the other wheels, where all wheels finish at the same moment to integers that multiply into the whole number, as 1, 2 & 3 multiply into 6, to a work of art where every thing is a part of everything, flows back as it were into the whole, & the days & months of those wheels where the wheels do not coincide to numbers, where the integers do not multiply into the whole number but pass as it were beyond [?indefinitely], & to all kinds of practical & scientific work that is a means to something else, information as distinguished from knowledge. Indeed their whole morality, when they speak of the soul liberating itself, they mean that ~~it can at last enter~~ the sphere, escapes from the gyre into the sphere because it has so lived that the clocks chime midnight at the same instant.[61]

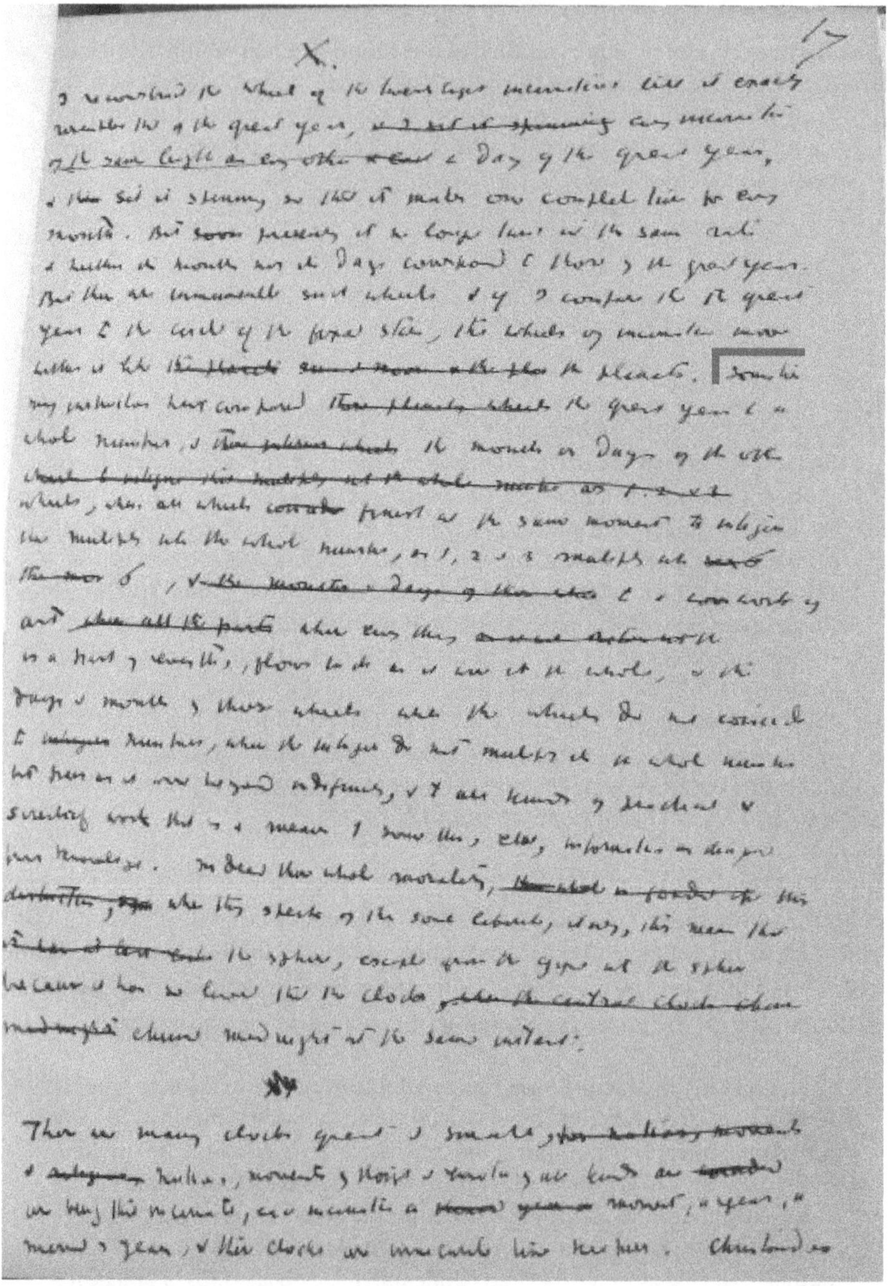

Figure 1. Rapallo Notebook A, NLI 13,578, [22r], page numbered 17. This photograph shows the actual appearance of the page transcribed and discussed; the mark ⌜ indicates where the quotation "Sometimes my instructors . . ." starts. The original includes cancellations that are not transcribed, as well as illustrating some of the problems with deciphering Yeats's hand. Courtesy of NLI; photograph courtesy of Catherine E. Paul.

This image is magnified even further in *A Vision B*, to embrace "innumerable dials" all completing "their circles when Big Ben struck twelve upon the last night of the century," while he also offers "a symbol of the lesser unities that combine into a work of art and leave no remainder" (*AVB* 248, *CW14* 181), but, with the removal of the spiritual meaning for the individual soul, the import of these Platonic numbers is harder to appreciate in *A Vision*. Even if Yeats decided to reject the concept of the soul's liberation as an aesthetic act determined by Pythagorean integers, this vision of mathematical congruence provides a missing context—or the memory of one—that helps to explain a rather cryptic section of the published book.

Yeats consistently prefers mystical mathematics, where integers multiply into perfect numbers, to the messy fractional values of scientific reality. In terms of the harmony of cycles, he also makes the useful clarifying comment (see the last four lines of Figure 1):

> There are many clocks great & small, & nations, movements of thought & emotion of all kinds are all beings that incarnate, each incarnates a moment, a year, a miriad of years, & their clocks are [?innacurate /inncarnate] time keepers.[62] Christendom is now passing from phase 22 to phase 23, but a nation or individual or movement may be at any phase, though that phase must always work within the general phase &[,] even if opposing[,] express that phase.[63]

A consideration of the Great Year's relation to the precession of the equinoxes leads to observations about when the Great Year, and therefore the current *primary* dispensation, began. Hipparchus discovered equinoctial precession in the second century BCE (cf. *AVB* 252, *CW14* 184) and Yeats appears to see this as falling in some fated way at the opening of the eras:[64]

> XI
>
> My instructors have told me repeatedly without explaining it the Great Year began not at the birth of Christ when these diagrams seem to begin it. I think it probable, they hold that Hipparcus chose the Equinox place of the sun during his own life time as our 0 of ♈ [=*0° of Aries*], not because it was during his life time but for a more profound reason. The Alexandrian Greeks who founded Astrology as it has come down to us must have considered that the great year began during his life time, for their successors judged the positions of the stars not in relation to the constellations but to 0 of ♈ long after 0 of ♈ had ceased to coincide with the begging [=*beginning*] of the constelation Ares [=*Aries*]. They considered 0 of ♈ as the ascent [=*ascendant*] in the horoscope of the epoch
>
> { a point that remains fixed like the ascend of the individual horoscope }

& related all their calculations to it. Astrology does not rely as is generally supposed upon the ~~influence~~* [?devine] influence of stars but upon that of certain mathematic relation between stars & a point mathematically ascertained. My instructors spoke of ten generations from the start of the Great Year to Christ, & if I count 15 years for a generation that being the length according to Heraclitus one gets a date during the life time of Hipparcus.

Footnote

* Each astrologic aspect is the distance between two ancles [=*angles*] of one of the regular polygons, & their polygon must have some relation to those described in the Timeus, though the ancles of those in the Timeus [?lie] within a sphere not within a circle.

Plutarc thought so for he confused the twelve sided figure in the Timeus with the zodiac. Astrology had its theoretic foundation in some part of great mathematic philosophy that has been lost, but now
{ that Mr Wyndham Lewis can acuse Mr Bertram Russell of substituting Mr 4.30 in the afternoon for Mr Smith we may recover it. }[65]

This is a first draft toward *A Vision B*'s Book IV, section VIII, which endorses "the conviction of Plotinus that the stars did not themselves affect human destiny but were pointers which enabled us to calculate the condition of the universe at any particular moment and therefore its effect on the individual life" (see *AVB* 253; *CW14* 184).[66] Yet almost the only element of the draft that survived intact into *A Vision B* itself is Yeats's strange interpretation of *Time and Western Man* as presaging a return to an astrological sense of timing: "has not Mr. Wyndham Lewis accused Mr. Bertrand Russell of turning Mr. Smith into Mr. Four-thirty-in-the-afternoon by his exposition of space-time," giving the idea a cast that neither Lewis nor Russell—nor Bergson, who was actually the more immediate target in this excerpt—would have recognized (*AVB* 253n; *CW14* 184n).[67]

The final two pages of this section deal with the difference between *primary* and *antithetical* revelation, though in different terms from those used in *A Vision*, using Gautama Buddha as an *antithetical* contrast to Christ.[68] Through many reformulations, Yeats struggles with the expression of a distinction between *primary* and *antithetical* by considering representations of Buddha, the landscape art of China, and the sainted scholar-artist-official-engineer, Kōbō-Daishi, founder of Shingon Buddhism in Japan.[69]

As explained in the note on "Transcription Principles," I have omitted cancelled text in most previous quotations for the sake of readability; here, however, I include the cancellations (even though some readings are uncertain) in order to give an idea of the drafting process as seen in the notebook, with rephrasing, false starts, repetitions, and Yeats's clarifications of his own handwriting (Figure 2 shows the second page transcribed here). It may be difficult to follow (for a reading text, see note 71), but shows the mind turning over an idea and seeking its best expression, only for most of it to be rejected later on.[70]

(19

XII

They tell me that the primary revelation comes soon after the opening of the year, & the antithetical considerably before its close & that East & West are ~~a~~ Primary & Antithetical respectively, ~~two & that they~~ <each> one dying the others life living the others death. I do not know [*why*] the Primary revelation should not begin its year but image that the antithetical comes before its close, though it is the inspiration of ~~the~~ its successor because out of human intellect & not from beyond it & so needs a mature tradition. As antithetical Europe at the end of an antithetical year [?approached] primary revelation, primary Asia, at the end of a primary year brought forth antithetical revelation in Buddha. Christ speaks to & is born of the primary masses, but Buddha is a kings son & speaks to kings, & Buddhism grows by its effect upon kings courts. ~~Its appeal It offers nothing but long & audacious intellect no consoling god~~ ~~<the world is the separation>~~ ~~that all immortal souls each but a~~ if the world [?use] comes from the sepparation of the knower & the known, ~~if this can be united~~
~~birth itself~~ being born is the supreme crime, but after many incarnations ~~or after one life of incredible self denial~~ – we may escape into nothing, or into a ~~somet~~hing that the most [?po]
~~to the common man~~ No god no consoling heaven, ~~nothing for the common man, no [?on] & to even the most audacious intellect something that seems~~ so little common man can understand that generations ~~dispute whether its supreme reward is being or not being as to whether has promised anything~~

Nothing for the common man, no god no consoling heaven. ~~Generations must dispute before men are certain that its rewards for may [?reward]~~ men dispute as to whether it [?gnows] of any punishment but life any reward but extinsion. ~~It took <~~take> <Having taken> from the sculptor of Alexander the high bred ~~faces &~~ face of a god ~~&~~ it moulded ~~it not that of~~ <express> ~~the contemplative Buddha~~ from it ~~a face~~ the symbol of a solitude more terrible than that of Oedipus.

(20

~~Then it sings [=*sinks*] into the primary soul of Asia~~

When Christianity ~~was taken up into the Antithetical European soul~~ <lost its first character>, ~~when a~~ when eclesiastic became princes, but Buddhism ~~sa~~ as Buddha sank down <~~in Primary Asia, thus India, the sec sculpture faced became grew vague, & the bodies many armed~~ into Primary Asia, ~~the scu the Indian scultors gave their gods~~ the abstraction of the Vedas, that something that seems to disolve all form away coarsed into India ~~sculpt~~ sculpture, gave it vague pleasant faces & a multitude of arms. ~~Only in~~ <~~in China~~> In Japan <& China alone> could ~~it~~ <Buddhism> prolong its Antithetical nobility, ~~for~~

for there <it was> ~~its constant St Agustine its Sankara no abstract philosophy~~ <~~commissioner & saint~~>, ~~no primary~~ Sankara no abstract philosopher, but ? . . — Daishi, ~~painter & saint philosopher,~~ who was a great artist & commissioner <& saint>, united it to the common faith by making it thought centred, the inspiration & defe ~~with thought~~ <joined ~~it~~> to the common belief ~~by great artist & commissar, who made the inspiration~~ by great works of art ~~yet even there & created an art~~ where one can study ~~the antithetical~~ the primary <primary> soul in its antithetical moment. ~~The~~ Their style defines <defining> a ~~subject matter~~ theme rather than a personality ~~& it~~ passes ~~from generation to generation in~~ on, in the same family from generation to generation, or ~~will be~~ is taken up or laid down when the narrative selects a new ~~subj subject~~ theme, & it is ~~primary~~ <above all> an art ~~in~~ of landscape, ~~mountains & cloud great mountains without names, the mountains, th & cattaract~~ <~~mountains that have no names, cattaracts that plunge into holy descend from clouds~~> ~~that stream of mist~~ <~~great sheets of mist~~> ~~that old saint by the road side~~, ~~wrought its~~

{ great ~~namely~~ <nameless> mountains, ~~cattacts~~ <cattaracts> falling through cloud into cloud an old saint climbing to some mountain shrine, & all}

& all caught up <into> a ~~rythm~~ powerful <rythm>, that unlike the rythms of European art, carries <us> beyond ~~the work~~ <its scene> that we may share ~~Buddha~~ <the> contemplation of Buddha.

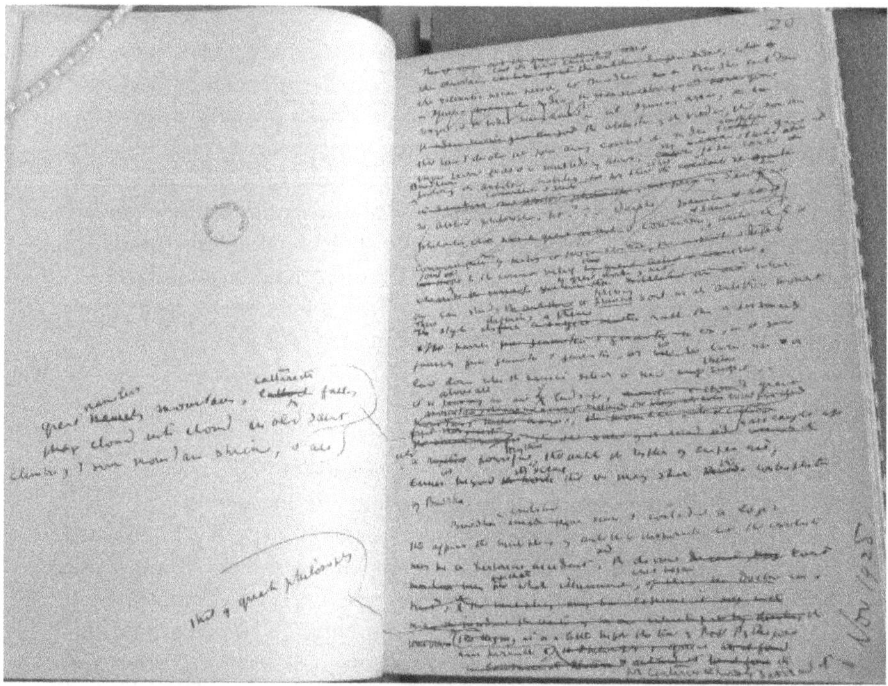

Figure 2. Rapallo Notebook A, NLI 13,578, [24v–25r], page numbered 20. Courtesy of NLI; photograph courtesy of Catherine E. Paul.

> Buddhas ~~single figure~~ <in isolation> seems to contradict a logic that affirms the multiplicity of antitethical inspiration, but that isolation may be a historical accident, <and> the devine ~~descent, may~~ event ~~may have been that all~~ that whole illumination <which began> ~~of which his doctrine was a part,~~ & <or> ~~the multiplicity may have expressed it self in the making the invidual that vents of his own salvation of it by desolving the universe, that beging~~ at or a little before the time of ~~Pith~~ Pythagoras ran parallell to
> { that of Greek philosophy }
> ~~the philosophy of Greece~~ ~~till it found in Sankara its Plotinus & outlived it [?but] it found its~~ for centuries & hardly survived it.
>
> [*vertically*] Nov 1928[71]

The exact thread of argument is difficult to follow. Indeed, even if there were less revision, the thinking would probably be rather incoherent, yet the gist is clear, as is the relation to the system. An inchoate mix of ideas, it was never intended for another reader, and, though very little is present in *A Vision*, elements adumbrate themes that appear later in the poetry—the old Chinese saint climbing to the mountain shrine in "Lapis Lazuli" (1936), the solitary meditator dissolving the universe in "Meru" (1934), and the *antithetical* proportions and sculpture of Greece related to the *primary* Asian sculpture of Buddha in "The Statues" (1938)—showing that these ideas remained with Yeats and ripened with time.

Much of the treatment seems to draw on Laurence Binyon's writings on Asian art, particularly "Some Phases of Religious Art in Eastern Asia," published in G. R. S. Mead's *Quest*. Elements, and even phrases, that Yeats seems to have borrowed include Binyon's focus on Alexander and Hellenistic influence on "the type of the Buddha which Gandhara sculpture evolved," "the Chinese genius for rhythm," "the effort to concentrate in figures, usually isolated, all that the self-liberated soul of man can conceive of loftiness and intellectual peace," and "paintings of mists and mountains."[72] One of Yeats's reasons for rejecting this material may have been doubts about whether Buddha, a figure of the fourth or fifth century BCE, or the Buddhism of China and Japan effectively bore out *A Vision*'s pattern of history.[73]

While the date "Nov 1928" is fitted into the bottom right-hand corner, there are three cancelled lines on the next recto, isolated in an otherwise blank spread. The fragments on [26r] appear to follow on from "that whole illumination which began at or a little before the time of Pythagoras ran parallel to the philosophy of Greece till it found," continuing: "~~Plotinus in Sankara, but a Plotinus~~ | ~~in Sankara its Plotinus~~ | ~~for so many~~ <~~a few~~ many> ~~centuries & survived hardly survived it.~~"[74] It seems likely that, realizing this line of thought did not go any further, Yeats decided to squeeze the concluding phrases into the space at the bottom of the previous page—"~~in Sankara its Plotinus~~ &

~~outlived it~~ ~~but it found its~~ for centuries and hardly survived it," before rejecting the connection between Plotinus and Sankara.

It also seems more probable that this material was added during the later revision, when Yeats knew that this was the end of the section, and so put his customary finishing date there in November 1928. After leaf [26] with the fragments on it, there are a further three blank leaves [27–29]. As the material that comes after this is from August, September, and October, Yeats evidently left a number of blank pages in the knowledge that he would be returning to revise and add to the *Vision* material, though in the end he did not need all of them.[75]

[30v–33r] "Censorship & Thomas Acquinas"

The next draft is the first of two articles in response to "The Censorship of Publications Bill," continuing Yeats's involvement in Senate business even though he had made his "last Senate appearance" on July 18, 1928, "A little speech of three sentences, [which] was followed by a minute of great pain," as he wrote to Lady Gregory on July 30 (*CL InteLex* 5137).[76] The following day James Fitzgerald-Kenney, the Minister for Justice, introduced the Censorship Bill to the Dáil, and it was read for the first time.[77] Yeats told Lady Gregory that he had "arranged two interviews & other things to fight the censorship so I am still in public life & shall be till I get to Rapallo" (*CL InteLex* 5137).[78] His opposition to the proposed bill was based on a mixture of reasons, and he was particularly suspicious of any attempts at legal definitions or criteria, which he addressed in the article, "The Censorship and St. Thomas Aquinas," which appeared on September 22, 1928 in the *Irish Statesman*, under the editorship of George Russell (AE).[79] Characteristically, Yeats contrasts "Byzantium & Platonic Theology,"[80] which separate and isolate the soul from the body, with the Thomist view that "the soul is wholly present in the whole body and in all its parts,"[81] and he sees Thomism as lying behind the emergence of Renaissance art and "that art of the body, that is an especial glory of the Catholic Church."[82] Though very much a first draft, with cancellations and insertions throughout, and gaps left to be filled later, it is almost complete and close to the final text used, showing Yeats honing his expression and adding focus to this short essay.

The article's final section gives a good example of the process involved in the drafting, which I try to reflect in the transcription here, though the accumulation of cancellations and insertions cannot be properly conveyed in print (see Figure 3).

III [=IV]

There is such a thing as immoral ~~art~~ <painting> & immoral literature, & ~~a criticism~~ <~~an historical~~> <~~critical~~> <~~method~~> <~~a criticism~~> <& a criticism always growing more profound> <establishes> ~~[?shaped] by~~ [?~~shaped] by~~ ~~the cen~~ ~~as ex~~ ~~evolved through centuries established that is as exact as a science has established~~ that ~~it~~ <they> is bad ~~art~~ painting & bad literature ~~but it cannot be defined in a senten~~.

{ ~~but unless one say that does not some [?sense ?gave] the~~

~~but though one can say of it, that~~

but ~~apart from~~ though it may be said of ~~it~~ <them that they> ~~does~~<~~do~~ sin ~~in some way~~> always ~~some how seem~~ <in some way> gainst "in toto corpore", ~~it~~ <they> cannot be defined in a sentence }

If you ~~find~~ <think> it neccary to exclude certain books or pictures, leave <it> ~~the church exclusi~~ to men learned in the ~~arts~~ <art & letters> & ~~if you can find them & if you cannot~~ <~~if you cannot find them in such will leave it to~~ if they will serve you & if they will not> <to> average educated men. ~~They will make may blunder & may be [?often ?in] the wrong [?after~~ each] ~~<whatever choice you make, your censors will often blunder>~~ ~~but a legal definition often~~ <choose what men you may they will make blunders> blunder but you need not compel them to by a definition.[83]

There were further modifications, but stripped to the undeleted material, this passage is very close to the final copy that appeared in the *Irish Statesman*, and indeed the essay kept the four sections and their concerns unchanged from this first rough draft.

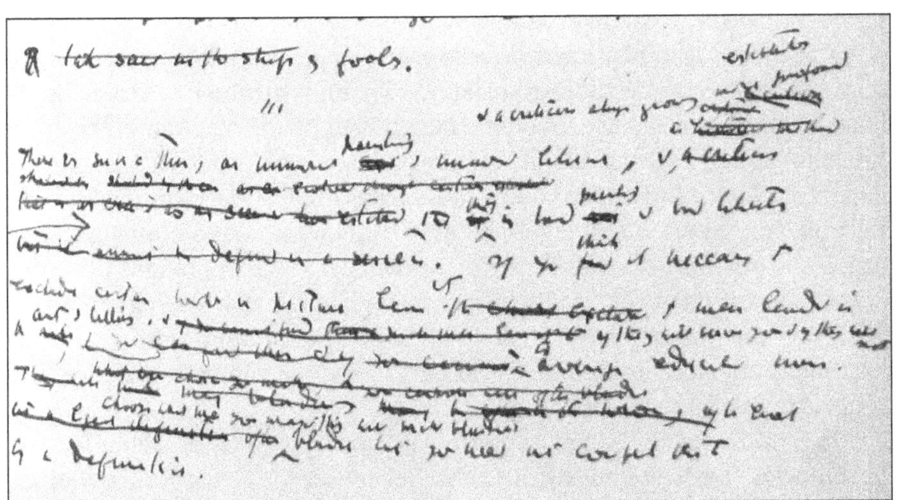

Figure 3. Rapallo Notebook A (NLI 13,578), [33r], page numbered 2; cf. *CW10* 213, *UP2* 479–80. The transcription is the passage starting "There is such a thing . . .". Courtesy of NLI; photograph courtesy of Catherine E. Paul.

Another stretch of three blank leaves [34–36] follows the end of this draft, before the next section (dedicated to *A Vision*), so it is possible that Yeats envisaged extending this essay or starting on the one intended for the *Spectator*. Whereas this *Irish Statesman* article (September 22, 1928) argued from Catholic doctrine as understood by Yeats, the *Spectator* was a London journal; in the article published there the following week (September 29, 1928), the argument took a different tack (see [66v–76r], below).[84]

[37v–48v] "First Things 12 pages (first page lacking)"

The first eight leaves of "First Things" evidently became loose because the leaves on the other side of the gathering—coming at the end of this bloc of draft—were torn out. This must have happened relatively early on, since the loss of the first leaf was already recorded by Yeats when he listed the contents [1v], though, as with other removed pages that can be ascertained, the folio numbering used here counts it, as leaf [38] (see Appendix). The remaining pages, though now secured in the rebinding, are visibly discolored and more damaged at the edges than the rest of the notebook. The verso of the undamaged preceding page [37v] also contains an insertion, and this appears to connect to a line with an arrow on the extant page opposite numbered "2" [39r], so is presumably a revision made after page "1" was lost.[85]

Apart from the missing opening, the text follows the draft in Rapallo Notebook B, incorporating the revisions and changes made there and with further additions, as outlined above in "The Sequence of Rapallo A and B." For instance in Rapallo B, Yeats wonders "why if the daimon is perfect ~~it was necessary to create man~~ man came into existence" and Rapallo A "why if each be perfect man should come into existence"; Rapallo B's "being a symbolist & no philosopher" becomes Rapallo A's "being a symbolist ^dramatist ~~& know no philosopher~~ ^~~logician~~ not a dialectician."[86] The diagram of the circle symbolizing the *Daimon* has no caption in Rapallo B, whereas it is given a line from *Hamlet* in Rapallo A and subsequent drafts: "Have you had a quiet watch? | Not a Mouse stirring."[87] A paragraph that was a late addition on a verso in Rapallo B ("Between this symbol and the next. . . .") is brought up to the beginning of Section III,[88] and there are major changes in phrasing and order. There are also corrections, such as Rapallo B's "Guido Valentanti" (the exact lettering is not clear) to "Guido Cavalcanti."[89] The exposition of the gyres and cones is revised at each step.

The presentation relies heavily on the pre-Socratic philosophers Empedocles and Heraclitus, with further references to "Greco-Roman Stoics," Plotinus, Proclus, Cavalcanti, and Grosseteste, in an approach that is broadly similar to that taken in the final version of *A Vision B*, though different in most particulars. Most importantly, this initial presentation of the gyres and cones is in terms of the *Principles*: *Spirit*, *Husk*, *Passionate Body*, and *Celestial Body*. Seeking to explain the relationship of the *Principles*, Yeats gives a fascinating insight into his reading of Berkeley and Coleridge, together with the symbolism of *The Cat and the Moon*. (In this case I transcribe cancelled material, but omit some as [~~. . . .~~], in cases where it is simply reformulated and repeated in the following text.)

> It is customary to deney or affirm a "substratum" behind the irrational film or smudge but we who begin all with the full & perfect daimon discover the substratum behind the ~~completed thing,~~ the picture as matured by the intellect, ~~not only behind~~ and [*not*] behind the picture only, behind fruit or tiger[,] but behind all their functions & capacities. This substratum, ~~the daimon itself~~ <Passionate or Celestial Body>, imeasurably exceeds our knowledge, for only what Husk desires ~~reflects itself as~~ <is transformed into> light or nature and only that so ~~reflected~~ <transformed> can arrouse our Spirit into contemplation. It must however be considered later whether in Spirit [~~. . . .~~] [,] which no longer lives, or living has been aroused by desire that [~~. . . .~~] exceeds our own[,] can, to use a metaphor employed by Betheus [=*Boethius*] to describe the intercourse of angels, cast its light into our Spirit as into a mirror.
>
> [~~. . . .~~] Some ~~old~~ Buddhist preacher of the first or second century described the ~~body~~ mind ~~depending upon the body as~~ in relation to the body as a lame man upon a blind mans back. That metaphor must have been Christian as well as Buddhist for the people of my ~~neighbours~~ Galway neighbours, say that our Holy Well, the Well of St Colman was discovered by lame man, ~~who had dreamed that night & found where~~ who had seen himself ~~[?cast] in a dream, & found the right spot, mounted~~ & ~~his friend~~ a blind man cured at a certain spot, & found it mounted on the blind mans back. I turned the story into a little comedy called "The changes of the moon" ~~for which I h~~ picturing as in some obscure & grotesque tapestry the ~~depends~~ dependence of ~~the Known Spirit & Celestial Body, the Knower & the Known, upo upon the Husk & Passionate Body, the Is & the Ought; & needing requiring for performance actors who can sing & dance and/to play a drum.~~
> ~~Spirit & Celestial Body, up Thought or Spirit & Celestial Body~~ upon one another of ~~Thought Spirit & Celestial Body & Will or Husk & Passionate Body~~ Will (~~Spi~~ Husk & Passionate Body[)] & Thought (Spirit & Celestial Body) [90]

Most readers will recognize the outline of *The Cat and the Moon*, though Yeats's memory of his own title was shaky and recalls the phrasing used by Owen Aherne, "Sing me the changes of the moon once more" in "The Phases of the Moon" (*VP* 373, *CW1* 164).[91] As the first version of the play was written in the summer of 1917, before the Yeatses' marriage and the beginning of the automatic script, the play was not created out of the system, but originally reflected the basic duality of mind and body, with some of the concerns about the mind seeking its opposite expressed in *Per Amica Silentia Lunae*.[92] The play had been published in magazine form and by the Cuala Press in 1924, and in the notes to the Cuala volume, Yeats connects the play with the *antithetical* and *primary tinctures* of *A Vision*, stating that "when the Saint mounts upon the back of the Lame Beggar he personifies a certain great spiritual event which may take place when Primary Tincture, as I have called it, supersedes Antithetical" (*VPl* 805, *CW2* 896). This refers to the transition from the third into the fourth quarter of the Wheel, described in *A Vision*, where "Before the self passes from Phase 22 it is said to attain what is called the 'Emotion of Sanctity,' and this emotion is described as a contact with life beyond death. It comes at the instant when synthesis is abandoned and fate is accepted," a description that Yeats actually places in his description of the culmination of this process in Phase 27, the Saint (*AVA* 114, *CW13* 92; *AVB* 181, *CW14* 134). Evidently in this image, the Saint mounting on the back of the Lame Beggar, or mind, expresses the attainment of "Emotion of Sanctity."

In Rapallo A's examination in 1928, this scene is now analyzed further and in terms of the spiritual *Principles* that Yeats was trying to integrate into the system: the solar pair—*Spirit* and *Celestial Body*—are associated with mind or spirit and the figure of the Lame Beggar, while the lunar pair—*Husk* and *Passionate Body*—are associated with incarnate life as the Blind Beggar. The lunar *Principles* are effectively the vehicle that makes incarnation possible—*Passionate Body* is the emotional matrix, *Husk* the link with the physical, and their light is nature—so that the Blind Beggar carries the Lame Beggar; meanwhile the solar *Principles* are mind, *Spirit*, and spiritual reality, *Celestial Body*, and their light is thought, so that the Lame Beggar directs the Blind Beggar carrying him (cf. *AVB* 190, *CW14* 140). The notebook also refers to them as Knower and Known, Is and Ought—*Spirit*, *Celestial Body*, *Husk*, and *Passionate Body* respectively[93]—exactly as in "A Dialogue of Self and Soul," which explored the same distinctions at the end of 1927. Like the Lame Beggar choosing the Saint's blessing, the mind or Soul can become one with the supernatural environment and "ascends to Heaven" (*VP* 478, *CW1* 239), while body, Will, or Self, like the Blind Beggar, chooses physical healing—and to have revenge on his companion—effectively pitching "Into the frog-spawn of a blind man's ditch, / A blind man battering blind men" (*VP* 479, *CW1* 240). However, as the Lame Beggar, by choosing blessing, is also healed,[94] the Self may "cast out remorse" and become in its turn "blest" (*VP* 479).[95]

The following page describes the *Principles* as finding a unity in the *Daimon*, an idea that reappears in Rapallo E but is present only as a shadow in the published version of *A Vision B*, where Yeats describes "the *Four Principles* in the sphere" (*AVB* 193, *CW14* 142).

X

> When the Four Principles are one in the daimon there is no greater or lesser, no decrease or increase because no time & space, & therefore but one of a form and no conflict between form & forms, & life in action lacking hope & memory because all but itself has been consumed. Some such thought passed through my mind when I wrote the last stanza of ["]the Withering of the Boughs" & described that King & Queen "so happy and hopeless, so deaf & so blind with wisdom, they wander till all the years have gone by"[.] But before the union the Celestial Body, still discordant, or undefined, it preserves all the acts of struggle in what my instructors have called the Record. The Record is accessible to Spirit but it is no memory for what comes into memory does so voluntarily or by association, in a context not its own, & is always abstract. When we are not content to say "so & so["] was dark or fair, round or long faced, & call up a concrete image that image, however like the old, is a new creation. The Record upon the other hand contains the actual event in its own context. When we are in Spirit & Celestial Body alone we must pass through these events in reverse order to that of Time, & it is this inverted life of the dead that in contemplation compells us to trace all things to their source.[96]

The association of the *Principles* in the *Daimon* with a timeless state of Platonic Ideas, with only the divine Idea, is significant, as is the way in which Yeats rereads earlier poetry in the light of his new ideas.[97] The explanation of the *Record* here may be no fuller than that of *A Vision*, but it is distinctly clearer in its description. By the time he writes of it in *A Vision B*, Yeats has brought in a quotation from Blake and a remembered sentence from an Indian writer that may express similar ideas but do so more obliquely.

Generally, the draft of "First Things" shows the tension between an attempt to be more methodical in the presentation of the system's central ideas and Yeats's naturally more discursive approach and allusive style. As ideas are added and links elided, the exposition becomes less disciplined and structured, and it ranges from enigmatic comments on the nature of the *Daimon* to pre-Socratic thought and the mechanics of the cones, then to the interactions of the *Principles* and *Faculties* and the avatars or incarnations associated with the start of a religious dispensation, as well as the symbolism of the Christian year, reminiscent of the erratic chain of loosely connected ideas that characterized the approach of much of "What the Caliph Refused to Learn" in *A Vision A*.

The last material in this section consists of two versions, both cancelled, of Yeats's attempt to use the idea that St. John the Baptist and Christ represent a form of opposition, with appeals to Coventry Patmore and Leonardo da Vinci.[98] These form part of a series of drafts, which will be considered more

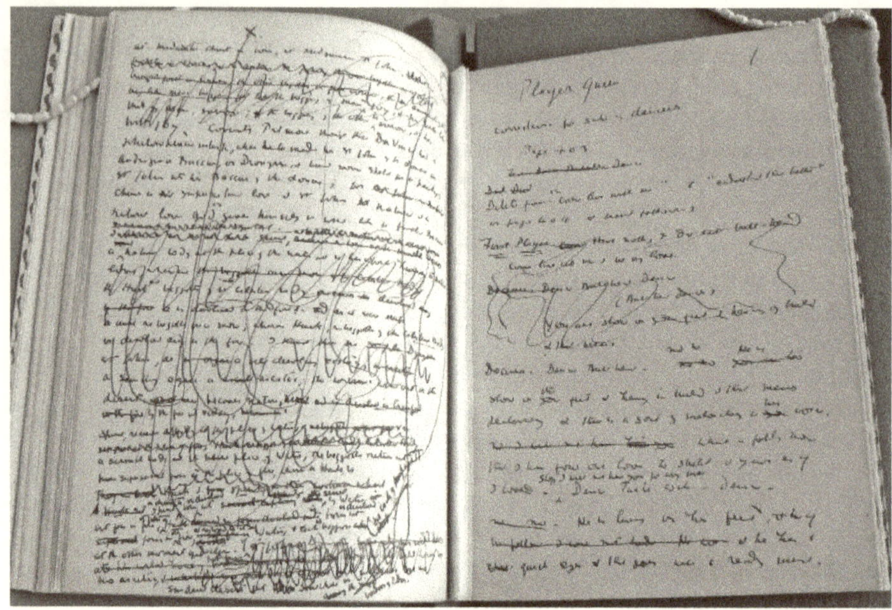

Figure 4. Rapallo Notebook A (NLI 13,578), [49v] and [58r], page numbered 1. Courtesy of NLI; photograph courtesy of Catherine E. Paul.

fully in the context of Rapallo Notebook B, but the final page here is so vigorously cancelled that its gestural energy brings it close to expressionist art (see Figure 4). This verso [49v] was probably not the last page of this section of draft, as some eight pages were removed from the book before the next section on *The Player Queen*, and at least one of the lines appears to indicate that text was originally to be inserted onto a facing recto that is no longer there.

[50–57] [8? stubs of pages]

The rebinding by the National Library of Ireland and the Delmas Conservation Bindery, carried out in 2006, includes eight stubs of Japanese paper used to bind in the loose pages on the other side in. These represent some of the leaves removed from the notebook that led to earlier pages of this gathering [38–45] being loose, as well as probably two in the following one [74–75].[99]

[58r–63r] "Player Queen (corrections) 6 pages"

The following pages, titled "Player Queen | corrections for sake of dancers," offer a stark contrast to the tangle of the preceding drafts, with well-spaced writing, albeit still with many changes and second thoughts (see Figure 4). These pages constitute "Draft 32" in Curtis Bradford's *The Writing of "The Player Queen"*—the last of the play's drafts and, because they were made after the play's publication, rather adrift from the rest of the material in Bradford's book. As such this is one of the only parts of this notebook that has been transcribed and published (see Appendix).[100]

A few questions that perplexed Bradford are clearer now with more evidence available, especially from letters. Bradford was puzzled as to why Yeats was revising and suggested that Yeats "may have made these changes, which he labeled 'corrections for sake of dancers,' for the revival of the play by the Cambridge Festival Theatre in the week beginning May 16, 1927."[101] The dating of the notebook makes this impossible, but the experience of the Cambridge production may well have inspired Yeats to make a necessary revision, though the immediate incentive was undoubtedly rehearsals for the Abbey's staging of the play in September 1928, when it was put on with ballets choreographed by and starring Ninette de Valois.[102] In his letter to George from Coole on August 17, 1928, Yeats wrote: "I have finished all my 'Player Queen' revision & now no dancer has to speak" (*CL InteLex* 5145; *YGYL* 194).[103] He also told Maud Gonne on September 6, 1928 that he was being held up in Dublin by, among other things, "a revival of my 'Player Queen' which I have so modefied that the new Abbey Ballet can dance abundantly in the middle & at the end" (*CL InteLex* 5158).

Another riddle for Bradford was that: "The page numbers to which Yeats refers in Draft 32 do not correspond to any printing of *The Player Queen*," leading him to speculate that they might have been the 1934 page proofs, noting that Yeats "included the substance of these but not too many of the actual words in the text of the play printed in *Collected Plays*, 1934."[104] However, these page numbers correspond exactly to the American printing of Macmillan's *Plays in Prose and Verse: Written for an Irish Theatre, and Generally with the Help of a Friend* (1924). Though not the most obvious printing of the play to have used, it was an appropriate volume to be using at the house of that very friend, Lady Gregory.[105]

[63v–66r] "Essay on Coinage 3 pages"

The draft of "Introduction to *The Coinage of Saorstát Éireann*" is an early one, starting with a version of what would be section IV—"What advice should we give the government. on the choice as artist? No good could come of a competition open to everybody"—and petering out after the first sentence of section VI—"We did not allow ourselves to see the designs till we saw them all together, the name of each artist, if the medal had been signed covered with a piece of stamp paper."[106] Writing to his wife from Coole, Yeats announced on August 28, 1928, "I have finished my coinage essay" (*CL InteLex* 5150), evidently referring to a version later than this one, which is incomplete, so this initial draft must date from earlier in the month. Yet, if the uncancelled text is extracted from the web of insertion and revision, the text that emerges is relatively close to the final version that was published, as is the case with the censorship essay.

II

> ~~To design sometimes~~ When ~~art~~ an artist takes <up> some task for the first time ~~his work he has~~ he must sometimes experiment before [??] he has mastered the new tecnique, we therefore advised that the artist himself should make every alteration necessary, & that if he had to go to London — ~~if by chance th must chose might to~~ his expenses should be paid & the Government accepted our advice. An Irish artist ~~had made~~ [?was asked &] had made an excellent design for the great seal of the <Dublin> National Gallery & that design founded [*upon*] the seal of a ~~medieval~~ Irish Abbey had been altered by the Mint, <& round> academic ~~design~~ <contours> substituted for the flat planes ~~& [?still] forms of~~ <of a> medieval design, & we felt ~~confident that the authorities of the London~~ confident that the [?adjunct] head of the London <Mint> recently appointed ~~as the rest of~~ to satisfy the [?critic] of art would think the better of us for protecting the ~~artist~~ artist, who ~~not seen may not seem not perhaps [?as ?mast ?of] not completely a craftsman from the craftsman who can be never be an artist~~.
>
> { quote Blake— }
>
> who many not ~~be~~ seem, or ~~may~~ as yet may not be a master of the craft, from the crafts man who never be an arttist.
>
> As the deputy master of the mint has commended, a precaution which protects the artist, who ~~may not seem, or as yet may not be a m who turning~~ set to a new task, & not as yet ~~its master from the~~ a craftsman from the crafts man who will never be an artist. One remembers the rage of Blake, when his designs for Blairs Grave came smooth & lifeless from the hand[107]

Yeats invests considerable care in finding the exact ordering of his phrases to express the need to protect the expression of the artist from the technique of the craftsman, turning over in his mind the progressive refinements, happily preserved on paper.

[66v–73r, 75r–76r] "Censorship 10 pages"

The following pages draft the article "The Irish Censorship" for the *Spectator*.[108] It is difficult to ascertain if Yeats returned to the subject of censorship after starting his draft on the coinage, but this seems more likely than his leaving blank pages and jumping to a point somewhere in the latter half of the book to start the article once he had finished the other essay on censorship and Aquinas. This version is more complete, though still very much a first draft.[109] Written for a London magazine, it has a rather different approach from the Thomist arguments of the article for the *Irish Statesman.* It starts with the scandal over "The Cherry-Tree Carol," a medieval song that the Christian Brothers deemed blasphemous because, when asked for cherries by the pregnant Mary, Joseph says "Let them gather thee cherries / That brought thee with child."[110] While saying that government ministers sponsoring the bill were "full of contempt for their own words,"[111] Yeats also notes that the law "will give one man, the Minister of Justice, absolute control of what we may or may not read," rephrased in the printed version as "control over the substance of our thought," removing the word "absolute" but going further than simple reading matter.[112] Thinking of what could be banned, he notes that the Government intends no general prohibition, but that "in legislation intention is nothing, & the letter of the law is everything."[113]

Two leaves, [74] and [75], became loose, with the removal of other leaves, and when the notebook was photographed for the microfilm held at Harvard in the late 1940s, leaf [74], containing notes on Indian ages, was placed as the final page of the notebook, though the cancelled first line of section VI of the *Spectator* article at the top of the leaf indicates its original position, which has now been restored. However, it was obviously already out of position when Yeats was numbering the pages, as [73r] is numbered "8," [75r] "9," and [76r] "10." Leaves [74] and [75] show characteristic damage to the edge of the page, whereas [76], the first leaf of the next gathering, secured by its sewing and corresponding folio, is undamaged.

[74r & v] [notes on Indian ages]

Interjected before the last two leaves of the censorship article is a leaf with notes on the great ages of Hindu tradition, "Indian ages of world," including various kalpas, mahayugas, and manvantaras. These notes were probably taken from H. Jacobi's article in Hastings's *Encyclopaedia of Religion and Ethics*—which Yeats had consulted for *A Vision A* and cites in Rapallo D—as the material follows the same order.[114]

[75r–76r] ["Censorship" continued]

At the head of [75r], before the start of section VI, there is a brief observation, which may continue the preceding section or be a note: "There is no remedy but better education, & taste for reading, & enough mature [?purpose] [?to] . . . ." a comment that Yeats leaves unfinished. At the end of section VI on [76r], Yeats has placed his signature to indicate that the work was completed, even if still in very rough form.

[77r] "letter in Reply to Miss H 1 page"

The *Spectator* article is followed by a single page with a draft of a letter to the editor of the *Irish Statesman* in response to A. E. F. Horniman's claim that Yeats's article on censorship and Aquinas displayed ignorance in suggesting the Palatine Chapel in Palermo as the inspiration for Richard Wagner's Chapel of the Grail in *Parsifal*. She had written to the editor on October 6, 1928, that, "It would be unreasonable to expect you to correct the mistakes of your contributors, but you may like to know that the Byzantium Chapel at Palermo, spoken of in the article on The Censorship and St. Aquinas, has nothing whatever to do with the Grail Temple scene in 'Parsifal' at Bayreuth,"[115] and accused Yeats of confusing Palermo with Pavia. Yeats's response was published on October 13 and dismisses Pavia as merely the inspiration for the painted scenery, while the people of Palermo would "~~tell her that Wagner~~ was there day after day seeking—unless local patriotism deceive it self—an idea powerful enough to call into his hearers mind the chapel of the Grail."[116]

[78r] [note on Coinage]

Page [78r] contains an isolated note for the essay on the coinage concerning the Croatian sculptor Ivan Meštrović, noting that he was away from the address to which they had sent their invitation to compete. This may well have been drafted at the stage of correcting galleys or proofs to be added to the pamphlet, and a version of it appears in the published text.[117]

[79r] [entry to be inserted in the 1930 diary]

Yeats appears to have returned to this notebook late in 1930 to use a blank page to continue his diary entry for October 20. The main entry was started on the penultimate leaf of his 1930 diary, where it is given the Roman numeral X in the diary (published in *Pages from a Diary Written in 1930*, it is grouped together with other entries as XL).[118] It considers the relations of Protestant Anglo-Ireland and Catholic Ireland, and starts by asserting that: "We have not an Irish Nation until all classes grant its right to take life according to the law & until it is certain that the threat of invasion, made by no matter who, would rouse all classes to arms" (cf. *Ex* 338). In the diary, the entry finished:

> Will the devout Catholicism and enthusiastic Gaeldom commit the error commited at the close of the close of [*sic*] the 18th century by dogmatic protestantism. All I can see clearly, bound as I am within my own limited art[,] is that every good play or poem or novel <that is characteristically> binds the opposing Irelands together.[119]

The rest of this page and the diary's remaining two blank pages contain an undated entry that opens with a comment on Seán O'Casey's *The Silver Tassie* (XI in the diary and XLI in *Pages from a Diary Written in 1930*), along with a further two sections dated "Nov 16" (not published) and, on "Nov 18," the final epigram: "Science, separated from philosophy[,] is the opium of the suburbs" (cf. *Ex* 340).[120] At some stage—presumably once the diary was already full—Yeats went back to the diary and wanted to extend the ideas leading to the conclusion of entry numbered X, so he cancelled the last sentence with a single line, adding the instruction to "see book D," the label on the cover of Rapallo A and evidently its designation in 1930.

Diary (Oct 20 continued)

> . . . . Dogmatic protestantism. Much of the emotional energy in our civil war came from the ~~refus~~ indignant denial of the right of the state, as at present established to take life in its own defense, whether ~~by~~ <by> arms or by process of law, and that right~~, & the~~ is still denounced by a powerful minority. Only when ~~both conditions all grant the right & when~~ all ~~that grant to the state the rxxx right to~~ permit the state to demand the voluntary or involuntary sacrifice of ~~xxx~~ ~~the lifes~~ its citizens lifes ~~wh~~ will Ireland prossess [*sic*] that moral unity to which England according to Coleridge, [?~~are awar~~] owes ~~so~~ a large part of its greatness. All I can see clearly, bound as I am within my own limited art is that <our moral unity is brought nearer by every> ~~evry~~ play or poem or novel that is characteristically Irish ~~binds classes into one~~ [?~~mass~~][121]

This addition was duly published in *Pages from a Diary Written in 1930*, but the paragraph that follows it was not. This latter continues from the entry on the *Silver Tassie* in the main diary, numbered XI, taking up the themes of "moral unity," of "the Irish Salamis" and Mallarmé's denunciation of the attempt "to build as if with brick and mortar within the pages of a book" (*Ex* 339).

(This follows XI)

XII

> ~~We seek~~ ~~We must~~ <It is not enough to> have moral unity; we must have unity of a particular kind. We must recognize that our Salamis has been fought & ~~one~~ won. An [*sic*] commercial empire can afford to build in brick & mortar with[*in*] the pages of a book, but a small <or week [*sic*]> nation must fall back upon its self, must encrease its ~~energy~~ <unity> that it may encrease its [?~~oness,~~] energy.[122]

In writing these final entries from 1930 in Rapallo A, Yeats was clearly using a blank page that was to hand, and they are fully integrated into the diary's thought, for instance repeating the final sentence "bound as I am within my limited art" with slight modifications. Both diary and notebook were probably with Yeats in Dublin, as Yeats returned to Dublin from London in mid-November.

[80–97] [blank pages]

Yeats was probably aware that there was plenty of space available at the end of this notebook as the final eighteen leaves of the notebook are blank. Yet in late 1928 there was considerable overlap in the use of different notebooks. Rapallo Notebook C was "begun. Sept. 23. 1928 in Dublin," just a day after the publication of the first censorship essay, and it was initially designated a "Diary of Thought."[123] Rapallo B's cover declares that it was "Finished, Oct 9, 1928," while Yeats was evidently also using Rapallo A, as the draft of the letter in response to Annie Horniman's letter of October 6 shows; he also returned to revising the material on the Great Year in Rapallo A as indicated by the date of "Nov 1928" at the close of that draft. Rapallo D was started at the end of 1928, in other words roughly as he was finishing that revision, and the two new notebooks (Rapallo C and D) probably account for the unused space at the end of Rapallo A. In fact, Rapallo D was put aside after a few pages, and Rapallo C was the main workbook for the first half of 1929 until July, after which Yeats took D up again in August.[124]

Although we usually value Yeats most for his poetic invention and genius, the prose style that he had developed over the years is vigorous and distinctive. Yeats was aware of Coleridge's "homely definitions of prose and poetry; that is, prose = words in their best order;—poetry = the *best* words in the best order."[125] Yeats's poem "Adam's Curse" explains the labor of poetry, but good prose is almost as demanding in the "stitching and unstitching" (*VP* 204, *CW1* 78) required to organize words into their best order. It has only been possible to show a few instances of the drafting process that is visible in Rapallo A, but no one who has examined these pages could doubt the attention that Yeats paid to the precise placing of words and phrases, to the movement of the argument, or his commitment to expressing ideas as effectively as possible.

The Appendix (following the treatment of Rapallo B) gives a tabular overview of the notebook, offering a slightly clearer idea of how the various pieces of work stand in relation to each other. And, as noted in the introduction and summary, part of the interest of Rapallo A in particular is seeing Yeats's obsession with *A Vision* running up against the demands of the public man—whether senator, involved in the controversies and the symbolism of the state, or man of the theater, addressing the practicalities of a new production.

Rapallo Notebook B

As far as we can tell, Rapallo B was the first notebook that Yeats started in Rapallo.[126] As outlined above in "The Sequence of Rapallo A and B," Yeats appears to have arrived in Rapallo with a leather notebook (NLI MS 30,359) that he was using for Crosby Gaige's commission of "16 pages to be privately printed in America" (to Frederick MacMillan, September 16, 1927, *CL InteLex* 5029). However, Yeats was already complaining to Olivia Shakespear in October 1927 that the "new poems interrupted my rewriting of 'A Vision'" (*CL InteLex* 5034; cf. *L* 730) and David R. Clark notes that the leather "notebook was probably to be devoted to *The Winding Stair*, but already on leaf 9 Yeats seems to have had enough of poems, and his occult investigations start to crowd the poetry out."[127]

Once he had fulfilled his obligation to provide the poetry—and quite probably before George Yeats dispatched the corrected typescripts to New York on March 13, 1928[128]—Yeats evidently felt at liberty to return to his "occult investigations." At some point after arriving in Italy in February, it seems that the Yeatses bought "those Italian MSS books,"[129] very possibly with the purpose of using them for the postponed work on *A Vision*.

The writing in this notebook is frequently a form of shorthand, with the endings of words in particular left as suggestions rather than actually written. Terminations such as -ly, -er, -tion, or -ment are sometimes even non-existent and their presence indicated only by syntax. Yeats was never overly concerned with spelling, and these are private notebooks intended for no one's eyes but his own or possibly George's, so that it is frequently almost impossible to be certain of a word except by context or, in some cases, from later, clearer versions of the same passages, or, even more helpfully but only occasionally, typescripts, often dictated from the manuscripts.

Contents: Overview

Initially, however, this first notebook was not focused on *A Vision*, at least not directly, stating on the title page that it was "Prose" and suggesting "? Siris," the title which also heads the prose on the following recto. This was originally intended, as he explained in a letter to Lennox Robinson on March 10, 1928, to be:

> a comment on a philosophical poem of Guido Cavalcantis, translated by Ezra Pound, which I hope to make a book of to follow your Anthology. I think of calling the book "Siris"; it is about Rapallo, Ezra & the literary movements of our time all deduced from Guido's poem, as Berkeley in his "Siris" deduced all from tar-water. (*CL InteLex* 5088)[130]

Destined for his sisters' press, to follow Robinson's *A Little Anthology of Modern Irish Verse* (1928), Yeats evidently hoped to create a work of philosophical and associative prose along the lines of George Berkeley's *Siris: A Chain of Philosophical Reflexions and Inquiries Concerning the Virtues of Tar-water, And Divers Other Subjects Connected Together and Arising One from Another.*[131] Yeats echoes the last phrase of that title when he describes the project to Lady Gregory as "a little book I am writing for Lolly, an account of this place, & Ezra & his work & things that arise out of that" (March 12, [1928], *CL InteLex* 5089).[132]

The poem Yeats refers to is Cavalcanti's "Donna Mi Prega," a work that has fascinated and baffled readers and critics for centuries. Yeats seems to have remembered the "obscure canzone upon the origin of things" as expressing a form of the antinomy of his own system's "opposing gyres" through the roles of "it may be Mars & Venus," both astrologically and mythologically, in Cavalcanti's poem.[133] He continued with the intention of using the poem until the summer of 1928, when he re-read Pound's translation, at which point he seems to have realized that his projected structure relied either upon a misunderstanding of the poem or that it would require too much explication to be elegant.[134] However, even in the spring of 1928, when the poem was still conceived of as the central element, Yeats deliberately started his chain of reflections with the setting of Rapallo and Ezra Pound himself.

The impressionistic vision of the Italian town and its bay in these opening pages very fittingly inaugurates the Rapallo notebooks, evoking this "indescribably lovely place—some little Greek town one imagines—there is a passage in Keats describing such a town," as he had rhapsodized to Lady Gregory shortly after their arrival ([February 24, 1928], *CL InteLex* 5081, *L* 738). The closeness of the notebook's prose to the descriptions filling his letters at the time show how immediate the inspiration was. After central sections covering most areas that he was rewriting for *A Vision* itself, the notebook concludes with a first draft of "Introduction to the Great Wheel" that would explain the truth about the "incredible experience" of the automatic writing.[135] In contrast to the sensuous presence of Rapallo, these other drafts for *A Packet for Ezra Pound*, coming at the end of the notebook, look backwards over the preceding ten years with a mix of autobiography, essay, and speculation, in a style that Yeats had been making his own since the unpublished journals, the *Reveries over Childhood and Youth*, *Per Amica Silentia Lunae*, and *The Trembling of the Veil.*[136]

As just noted, the remainder of the notebook is taken up with the material for the revised edition of *A Vision*. Yeats had already decided to retain the delineations of the twenty-eight typical temperaments ("The Twenty-Eight Embodiments" became "The Twenty-Eight Incarnations") and the survey of history ("Dove or Swan") largely intact (see [40r–41r] and [96v] below), and there is evidence that, at this stage, he also hoped to retain other sections with revisions (see [43v–44r] below).[137] However, the rest was to be recast, and this notebook contains examples of all the new material: two sections of introductory material, titled "First Things" and "Introduction," as well as sections on "The Soul in Judgement" and the Great Year in antiquity. Much of this is tentative, showing long passages revised, recast, replaced, and rejected, and indeed little of the material presenting the gyres and their movements or the afterlife was used in the form Yeats attempted here, so that its main interest is as a stage in the evolution of his thinking and his struggle with how to present the ideas most clearly and effectively. The drafts are frequently illuminating on problematic elements, such as the *Daimon*; other aspects are clearly intermediate and superseded by later reformulations, though even in these cases seeing the process by which Yeats reached the later presentation can clarify his general approach or specific details.

Rapallo Notebook B is thus of particular interest to those studying *A Vision*, including in this context *A Packet for Ezra Pound*, and the development of these writings. Perhaps because of its relative focus, it is the most complete of the Rapallo notebooks, with ninety-eight extant leaves, though there are still some pages torn out. Conversely, it shows little of the cross-fertilization that gives added interest to other notebooks, and rather bears witness to the frequently Sisyphean labor involved in the attempts to revise *A Vision*. Many of the drafts here are repeated in other versions both in manuscript (including Rapallo A) and typescript, some eventually reaching published form, but most abandoned. The more the drafts are explored, the clearer it is that the published version of *A Vision* itself, in either version, is only the visible tip of an iceberg, and that Yeats was not stretching the truth when he wrote that "this book has filled my imagination for so many years, that I can never imagine myself studying anything without in some [way] relating it or incorporating it with what is here."[138]

In Greater Detail

[Cover]

The notebook's cover declares that it was "Finished, Oct 9, | 1928," a date that seems to be borne out by the contents, though there is no specific date internally. Yeats noted in the contents that the notebook's final bloc of material—what would become "Introduction to the Great Wheel" in *A Packet for Ezra Pound*—was continued in a loose-leaf notebook. Certainly on November 23, 1928, he informed Ezra's mother-in-law:

> I am finishing a little book for Cuala to be called either "A Packet" or "A Packet for Ezra Pound". It contains first a covering letter to Ezra's (sic) saying that I offer

> him the contents, urging him not to be elected to the Senate of this country & telling him why. Then comes a long essay already finished, the introduction to the new edition of "A Vision" & telling all about its origin, & then I shall wind up with a description of Ezra feeding the cats ("Some of them are so ungrateful" T. S. Elliott says) of Rapallo & Ezras poetry — some of which I greatly admire. (to Olivia Shakespear, *CL InteLex* 5191; cf. *L* 748)[139]

Though this reverses the final order, the drafts in this notebook are often very close to the version that was published and show Yeats as an assured writer of prose for evocation, description, and autobiography, yet continually redrafting to achieve the desired finish.[140]

[1r–1v] [title page and "Contents"]

Titling the first page as "Prose" indicates that this was perhaps not, in the first instance, a book for *Vision* material, and the title "? Siris" indicates his model in Bishop Berkeley's chain of associations that starts with the medicinal qualities of water mixed with pine resin and ends with the ancient philosophers' conceptions of the divine. Having moved through the links of 368 sections, the final sentence admonishes: "He that would make a real progress in knowledge, must dedicate his age as well as youth, the latter growth as well as first fruits, at the altar of Truth";[141] for Yeats such a dedication was perhaps more important in "Decrepit age" than youth, as he wondered whether he must "Choose Plato and Plotinus for a friend" (*VP* 409, *CW1* 198).

Apart from the unsuitability of Cavalcanti's poem as a central text, Yeats may also have realized that part of the strength of *Siris* is the gradualness of the ascent from the mundane to celestial, entailing some length and some philosophical depth. At any rate, "Siris" was rejected as a title, and Rapallo itself was brought to the fore; the contents give two versions, as the rather flat "Note on Rapallo" is cancelled, and replaced with "Rapallo in Spring," the phrase which also replaces "Siris" on the following page, and this may indicate that the revision happened as Yeats was creating the list of contents.

Contents.

~~Note on Rapallo~~
Rapallo in Spring. 9 pages. First 4 to be used
First Things. 15 pages.
~~Book I "Great Wheel"~~
Additions ~~to Book I~~ & corrections of Vision Book II
7 pages (dated May 1928)
Great Year 21 pages. (early version)
Soul in Judgement ~~(first draft)~~ 10 pages
Introduction. 12 pages (continued in loose leaf book.

Rapallo A and B are the only Rapallo notebooks to have a list of contents, and Yeats's listing is relatively accurate, even to the point of indicating some false starts.

[2r–10r] "Rapallo in Spring 9 pages First 4 to be used"

This first draft of *A Packet for Ezra Pound*'s "Rapallo" opens with an evocation of the Riviera town before focusing on the resident of most interest to Yeats. As the contents page indicates, the first four pages were used with relatively little revision for the Cuala volume, making up the first three sections of "Rapallo." Both published versions—the Cuala Press edition and the prefatory material to *A Vision B*—continue this section with a consideration of Rapallo's English-speaking church and the finishing of *A Vision*, while the Cuala version also has a further section on Ezra Pound's poetry.

These are not included in the notebook, which instead has further sections that explore the "the literary movements of our time" (*CL InteLex* 5088) partly through Balzac's *Chef d'oeuvre inconnu* [5r–7r], and considerations of the nature of imagination and poetry. Since these drafts show a range of aspects of Yeats's drafting and how he worked on his material, I shall give particular attention to these few pages.

There are in fact three sections all numbered "V": the first one on [5r–6r] is brief and replaced by the second on [6r and 5v], which is itself completely rewritten on [7r], while the third one [8r–10r] is different material and appears to be a mistake for "VI," but none was used for publication. Elements touching on Balzac from the earlier versions were, however, salvaged and added to the earlier Section II, in a jigsaw of elements keyed for insertion from the facing versos. In the published versions of *A Packet for Ezra Pound*, the references to Balzac's short story are applied to Pound's *Cantos*.

As well as *Siris*'s chain of reason, Yeats's train of thought often seems to follow "the crooked road of intuition" that he symbolized as a butterfly (*VP* 827), zigzagging through a range of topics and references, often within the space of a sentence or two. The drafts, however, reveal that these allusive paths often started with a slightly more hawk-like "straight road of logic" and sequence as part of a more expansive treatment of the topic, which successive revisions gradually telescope into briefer forms that are often harder to follow. This process was seen with the symbolism of the sphere in relation to the *Daimon* in Rapallo A above, but, whereas those drafts never reached publication in recognizable form, with the treatment of Balzac's *Le chef d'oeuvre inconnu*, we can trace the evolution backward from the published version, through the drafts of insertions to Section II, to the original formulation in the abandoned Section V. Writing of what Yeats perceives as Pound's aim in the Cantos, the published version suggests that:

> There will be no plot, no chronicle of events, no logic of discourse, but two themes, the Descent into Hades from Homer, a Metamorphosis from Ovid, and, mixed with these, mediaeval or modern historical characters. He has tried to produce that picture Porteous commended to Nicholas Poussin in *Le chef d'œuvre inconnu* where everything rounds or thrusts itself without edges, without contours—conventions of the intellect—from a splash of tints and shades; to achieve a work as characteristic of the art* of our time as the paintings of Cézanne, avowedly suggested by Porteous, as *Ulysses* and its dream association of words and images, a poem in which there is nothing that can be taken out and reasoned over, nothing that is not a part of the poem itself.
>
> * Mr. Wyndham Lewis, whose criticism sounds true to a man of my generation, attacks this art in *Time and Western Man*. If we reject, he argues, the forms and categories of the intellect there is nothing left but sensation, "eternal flux" [. . . .][142]

It would seem that Yeats was citing from memory, substituting Balzac's Porbus with Porteous,[143] without checking his sources—but this is not quite true, as we shall see. He also appears to reshape several ideas related to painting in Balzac's story—of which more below—in much the same way that he had made a very personal interpretation of Pound's translation of "Donna Mi Prega," which had not stood up to rereading. At the same time, putting these considerations to one side for the moment, this short passage traces a rapid zigzag of thought and allusion where aspects of contemporary art jostle one another: the poetry of the *Cantos* is compared to a painting described by Balzac, the post-Impressionist painting of Cezanne,[144] and James Joyce's *Ulysses*—although the supposed "dream association of words and images" seems more applicable to Joyce's *Work in Progress*, which had started appearing in 1924. There is also a reference to Wyndham Lewis in a note. And yet Yeats conceives this "art of our time" as having "nothing that can be taken out and reasoned over, nothing that is not a part of the poem itself," showing an inner coherence, similar perhaps to that described by Balzac's Frenhofer, "the unity which simulates the conditions of life itself."[145] There are, however, a series of ideas and connections, elided or suppressed in this final version, that are clarified considerably by the drafts.

This passage first takes its published form in a pencil draft on the notebook's third recto, corrected in ink and with insertions from the verso of the second leaf, in four separate impulses of thought, a first treatment of hypnagogic visions, a second, on artistic unity, to be inserted in the first, and a third section on "Porteus," for insertion in the second, along with a footnote on Wyndham Lewis that refers to *Ulysses*, all to be inserted in the text on the recto.

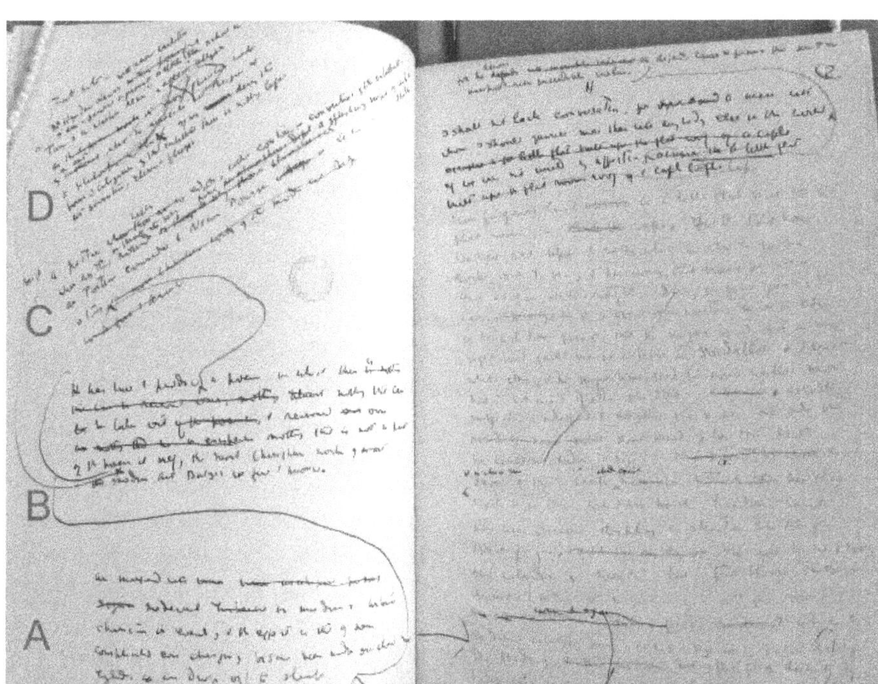

Figure 5. Rapallo Notebook B, NLI 13,579, [2v–3r]. The insertions on the verso are labeled here in probable order of composition. Courtesy of NLI; photograph courtesy of Catherine E. Paul.

The relevant text can be assembled as follows:

> [3r] There will be no plot, no calendar of events but two themes, the Odysse[*a*]n descent into Hades, the metamorphosis of a god from Ovid, ~~as repeated~~ <~~come~~> ~~& again~~ <[~~xxx xxxxx~~]> ~~in different forms, combined with certain medieval archetype mind—perhaps Sigismond, perhaps Lorenzo De Medici & this archetypal with reflection of descent of [?perhaps plan] as of archetype in the life of our own day~~.
>
> [2v]
>
> [**A**] and mixed with ~~various archetypal persons segments~~ modern ~~historical~~ or modern & historic characters or events, & the effect is that of some complicated even changing vision seen under our closed eyelids as we are dropping off to sleep.
>
> [**B**] He has tried to produce
>
> [**C**] <such> a picture ~~where there are no~~ without edges, without contours—conventions of the intellect—where everything rounds or thrusts itself from a splashing surge of tints or shades as Porteus commended to Nicolas Poussin in his story~~, the most characteristic work of the modern art Balzac was to first anounce~~

> [**B**] a poem in which there ~~is nothing that can be reasoned over, nothing almost~~ is nothing that can be taken out ~~of the poem~~ & reasoned over ~~and nothing that has an existence~~ nothing that is not a part of the poem itself, the most characteristic work of ~~an art~~ that *modern art Balzac was first to anounce.
>
>> [**D**] [*]Foot note
>> Mr Wyndam Lewis ~~in his powerful~~ <with whose criticism> <I am in general agreement attacks the school in> "Time and Western Man" ~~attacks "Ullyses"~~ ~~as the typical work~~ its most characteristic work of ~~a school~~ an art which he associates with Bergson & the philosophy of Time. If we ~~rxxxxx~~ deny that form & categories of the intellect there is nothing left but sensation, eternal flux. [146]

In layering these thoughts together, Yeats adds to the complexity of his treatment, suggesting many aspects of what he considered the art of his own time "at this 23rd Phase," though earlier in *A Vision A* he had appeared to see dissociation of "the *physical primary*" and "the *spiritual primary*" (*AVA* 211–12, *CW13* 174–75) as the modern characteristic, rather than works where there "is nothing that can be taken out" (draft and published text). With the cancelled reference to *Ulysses*, all the elements of the final version are included, except that to the painter Paul Cezanne, while the draft's hypnagogic vision is removed.

The contrast of a pencil draft [3r] corrected in ink [2v] suggests a later revision, and it seems likely that Yeats returned to section II after deciding to abandon section V ([5r–7r]), in order to reuse the elements he wanted to preserve. As outlined above, there are effectively three versions of the passage under discussion, and to continue tracing backward, I shall start with the last:

> (6
>
> A friend tells me that Cezanne deduced his art from certain passages in Balzac <u>Chef D'oeuvre Inconnu</u> & I discover in those passages what divivides [*sic*] the school most dominant today from that but which is now born. Nicholas Poussin an unknown art student called upon his friend the painter Porbus in the year 1612 & met in his studio a strange old man whose criticism [~~....~~] was by its effect upon the mind of Cezane to destroy impressionism & to be first word of all this discussion, which has establisht among the most audacious of a new generation a school of literature opposed to that I was born in.[147]

It is evident here that Yeats had gone to check the story, as the date, given in the story's first sentence, is correct, and the name Porbus appears to be spelled correctly—twice, including a cancelled instance—but Yeats's "b" is easily mistaken for an "l" or an uncrossed "t," so it seems that the mistake came from Yeats misreading his own handwriting later on. However, Porbus is not Poussin's friend at the start of the story, so it is unclear whether Yeats actually refamiliarized himself with the story or just checked details, and the immediate focus is an adaptation—possibly on the part of the "friend"—of an anecdote about Cezanne.

In Balzac's story, the fictional Frenhofer, the only pupil of Jan Gossaert (Mabuse), impresses the younger Frans Porbus and even younger Nicholas Poussin—all of whom are historical—with his fascinating theories about art and his brilliant retouching of Porbus's canvas. They learn that Frenhofer has been working on a canvas of surpassing mastery for over a decade, which he keeps secret while he perfects it. By offering Poussin's beautiful young girlfriend as a model, Porbus and Poussin are finally able to enter Frenhofer's studio and see the painting of *Catherine Lescault, La Belle Noiseuse*. Poussin "can see nothing there but confused masses of colour and a multitude of fantastical lines that go to make a dead wall of paint," though in a corner there is a beautifully realized "bare foot emerging from the chaos of colour, half-tints and vague shadows that made up a dim formless fog" that "had escaped the incomprehensible, slow, and gradual destruction."[148] Though they are horrified, Frenhofer seems unaware and asserts that he has "succeeded in softening the contours of my figure and enveloping them in half-tints until the very idea of drawing, of the means by which the effect is produced, fades away, and the picture has the roundness and relief of nature."[149] Porbus declares that "There [. . .] lies the utmost limit of our art on earth," but Poussin tactlessly lets drop that "sooner or later he [Frenhofer] will find out that there is nothing there."[150] Accusing them of jealousy, but thrown into dejection, Frenhofer drives them out, and that night he dies as his studio is destroyed by fire.

The story is, of course, full of ambiguities. Has Frenhofer's mad perfectionism led him to ruin a near-perfect masterpiece—as indicated by the remaining foot and the preparatory works on the walls—or has he simply gone beyond the conventions of his day to something so radical that his more orthodox colleagues fail to recognize its genius? Is the master, who is able to breathe life into Porbus's canvas with a few touches of the brush, unable to see where to stop, marring his own creation? Or is this truly the "utmost limit" of art? Frenhofer's work has been taken as the forerunner of the Impressionists, the post-Impressionists, or abstract art.

The story had particular resonances for Cezanne, and the ambiguities only multiply. A friend of his recorded how Cezanne once pointed to himself in a self-accusatory manner as Frenhofer, and in a questionnaire, Cezanne named "Frenhoffer" as the literary character he was most drawn to.[151] Yet when Cezanne identified himself with Frenhofer, was he identifying with genius ahead of his time, with failure, or both?[152] Critics vary. Yeats, however, understands the anecdote differently, seeing Cezanne as taking Balzac's descriptions as a guide or manifesto for his own artistic practice, turning self-accusation into a *modus operandi*. Cezanne is seen as the "first word" of a new school encapsulated in the words that Balzac puts in Frenhofer's mouth and those that describe his painting.

In Yeats's preceding draft, this idea followed an examination of "the art of my generation, 'pure art' as men have come to call it, with sentences the young Hallam wrote of the Tennyson of the Lotos Eaters and the early poems"—referring to Arthur Hallam's review essay "On Some of the Characteristics of Modern Poetry, and on the Lyrical Poems of Alfred Tennyson"—all of which was later cancelled.[153] Here, in the context of "pure art," Yeats comments:

> I am to day dissatisfied with <that> descri[*p*]tion & remember that Cezanne — or so I am told — turned his own art to Chef-d'oeuvre inconnu of Balzac....

This was cancelled and taken up again a few lines later:

> A friend tells that Cezzane deduced his art from some passage in Balzac's Chef-d'oeuvre inconnu & ~~Frenhofer's describing of what he has attempted~~ <that passage, if indeed I have found it>, ~~describes the words~~ describes the art to day more accurately ~~than those of Hallam~~ <that [=*than*] Hallam[*'s*] words>, which turn the soul into a mirror.[154]

Yeats was evidently looking to find a way to express the theme of schools and movements in art and time, which he was adapting from final pages of *A Vision A*'s "Dove or Swan" to his projected "Rapallo in Spring."[155] Alighting on Cezanne as the expression of a modern spirit, inspired by a novella written more than half a century earlier,[156] Yeats wrestled with how to express the connection of ideas with elegance and economy. And he was consulting Balzac's story in search of the passage alluded to by his friend.

The very first draft of the material actually starts with Cezanne—cancelled—moving, on second thought, to Wyndham Lewis and the Modernists, cancelled in its turn:

> V
>
> ~~A friend tells that Cezanne traced art the his most characteristic his art painting to his reading to Balzacs Chef-d'oeuvre inconnu~~
>
> Sometimes I have discussed with Pound those ~~powerful mighty~~ books in which Mr Wyndham Lewis ~~has attacked him confounds to geth describes him, as of the same school as Jame Joyce, Gertrude, Stein, Charly Chaplin & Henri Bergson & Ezra Pound~~
>
> (5
>
> ~~confounding all together in his powerful invective symbols according to powerful rhetoric invect invective, of an anarchic sexual emotional art~~

> chooses him ~~out for analys~~ & James Joyce, & ~~as the two most representative of a an~~ to represent a whole school ~~—Gertrude Stein, Henri B Lawrence, &~~ which seem to him emotional & anarchic.[157]

This, then, is the first expression of the idea that was finally published as the footnote. Yet that footnote is no afterthought, being rather the tip of an iceberg of thought and labor, which so often underlies even minor elements within the published work.

The references to Frenhofer's words and his work were also salvaged, though mixed together and assigned to Porbus/Porteous instead. If modern readers have created some of the ambiguities in Balzac's story, Yeats's misremembering blurs things further. While Yeats has Porteous commend a picture "where everything rounds or thrusts itself without edges, without contours—conventions of the intellect—from a splash of tints and shades,"[158] in Balzac's story it is Frenhofer who says:

> there are no lines in Nature, everything is solid[. . . .] So I have not defined the outlines; I have suffused them with a haze of half-tints warm or golden, in such a sort that you can not lay your finger on the exact spot where background and contours meet. Seen from near, the picture looks a blur; it seems to lack definition; but step back two paces, and the whole thing becomes clear, distinct, and solid; the body stands out; the rounded form comes into relief; you feel that the air plays round it.[159]

And it is not "Porteous' disastrous picture,"[160] as Yeats writes, but Frenhofer's that shows "a bare foot emerging from the chaos of colour, half-tints and vague shadows that made up a dim, formless fog. Its living delicate beauty held them spellbound."[161] It is all the more surprising that Yeats occludes the role of Frenhofer—who is mentioned in these drafts—since in some respects he is a *daimonic* artist: while Frenhofer is adding his masterful touches to Porbus's painting, "it seemed to the young Poussin as if some familiar spirit inhabiting the body of this strange being took a grotesque pleasure in making use of the man's hands against his own will" and later, when Frenhofer falls into abstraction, Porbus comments "he is in converse with his *dæmon*."[162]

There is a subterranean element to Yeats's use of Balzac, with his forgetfulness enabling greater freedom and serving his own purposes better. In using the art of Frenhofer and Cezanne to write of Pound and his younger contemporaries, Yeats is perhaps able to enjoy the ambiguity of the story: the *Cantos* may be at the "utmost limit" of art, unrecognized as yet in their genius, or maybe Pound is like Frenhofer and "sooner or later he will find out that there is nothing there."[163] Certainly *A Packet for Ezra Pound* contains comments that could be subtle barbs; as Catherine Paul remarks, when Yeats advised Pound not to "be elected to the Senate of your country,"[164] "there are few things Pound would have preferred to having his own government require his expertise."[165]

Although there is no sign in the drafts in Notebook B that "Rapallo in Spring" was yet conceived of as material directly associated with the new edition of *A Vision*, connections were inevitable, and indeed at the back of this notebook Yeats would create a first draft of the introduction itself, declaring, as already cited: "I can never imagine myself studying anything, without in some [way] relating it, or incorporating it with what is here" in *A Vision*.[166] Thus, his examination of recent movements in art and literature inevitably relates to the treatment of the current period that he had outlined in *A Vision A*, extending and building on those earlier perceptions.

The rest of the notebook is dedicated to the new material for *A Vision*, rethinking the initial presentation, the descriptions of the afterlife, the expanded material on the concept of the Great Year, and an account of the automatic script and its origins.

[10v–33r] "First Things 15 pages"

"First Things" is a projected introductory text for the revised system of *A Vision*, and it would later be redrafted in Rapallo Notebook A. As mentioned earlier, elements of the first page or so had already been outlined in the leather notebook that Yeats had brought with him to the south of Europe,[167] where he titled a brief treatment of "the daimon" "suggested first paragraph of system."[168] There he had inserted a sentence at the beginning—"all that can <need> be said of the daimon in this place can [be] put into a few sentences," and the new opening in the Rapallo B draft is an elaboration of this theme:

> I begin with the daemon & of the daimon I know little, but comfort [*myself*] with this saying of Marc[*i*]on's "neither can we think, know, or say anything of the gospels'['], & with this cry from the Indian sage Behold the exposition of God – the lightening fills the sky – ah – ah – my dazzled eyes are shut – ah – ah – the exposition of god is finished & that cry of the Japanese attaining Nirvana "You ask me what is my religion & I hit you on the mouth". At the same time I remember that an Arian theologian once wrote "I know God as he is known to himself" & write out with confidence what my teachers have said, or what I have inferred from their messages [*and*] diagrams.[169]

As commented already, Yeats's rapid delivery of gnomic fragments here both dazzles and befogs. The quotations may illustrate the problem of speaking about the ineffable but would do little to help the reader at the start of a complex exposition, except that they are characteristic of Yeats's range of reference. This group of quotations was retained through a long series of drafts, and the two Eastern examples—one Japanese and one Indian, both taken from

Daisetz Suzuki's *Essays on Zen Buddhism*—were retained into the published version, though moved to the end of the exposition of "The Completed Symbol" (*AVB* 215, *CW14* 158).[170] Critics have commented more on Yeats's references to Eastern thought than his knowledge of Christian thinkers, but this is nonetheless impressive, if usually focused less on the writers themselves than their heretical targets. The two examples from early Christianity were used again the following winter in Rapallo C in a short examination of what "Ezra Pound bases his scepticism upon. . . ."[171] Again they form a contrasting doublet of "a Church father [who] said 'we can never think or know anything of the gospel'"—a vaguer but rather more credible attribution than Marcion, whose views about the gospels were very decided—and "some Arian [who said] 'I know god as he is known to himself,'"—referring to Eunomius, Bishop of Cyzicus, who scandalized the Church Father John Chrysostom: "A mere human has the boldness to say: 'I know God as God himself knows himself.'"[172]

Even though Yeats may have little in common doctrinally with the Church Fathers, he shares something of their approach to philosophical questions and abstract reasoning, and, as the Pre-Raphaelite Brotherhood identified Raphael as the beginning of a deterioration in art, Yeats treats René Descartes as the pivotal figure in a detrimental shift in thinking. This is adumbrated in a new opening section that he sketches on the opposite page to be inserted as the very first section of the new presentation:

> I
>
> ~~This book de cannot~~ help
> ~~What I have to say,~~ This book ~~cannot~~ would be different if it ~~did not come from if if were not founded upon the words~~ had not come from those, who claim to <have> died many times, ~~& so begin~~ & & ~~did not assume must assume their~~ in all they say assume their own existence. In this it resembles ~~not some ancient books of philosophy, xx but none no book no modern book, but some that are ancient no book xxxxx~~ nothing since Decartes but much that is ancient.[173]

This is both a clear statement of the central role of the automatic script and yet a scrupulous distancing from any declaration about what or who the voices are—they "claim to have died many times" and "assume their own existence," but Yeats withholds giving greater credence to their claims than is strictly warranted. They may assume their own existence yet still be the figures of dream, appearing as projections or dramatizations from the medium's mind.[174]

After these preliminaries, which include the initial presentation of the *Daimon* as outlined earlier in "The Sequence of Rapallo A and B" [11r and 12v], Yeats moves on to explain the gyres. The redrafting was far from clear and the process of composition of the following twenty pages is particularly complex. Right at the outset, three pages have been torn out prior to section III [12–14], so that this page [15r], numbered "2," is clearly already a reworking of rejected material, and the following pages are a thicket of cancellations at various levels, with the page numbering, evidently added at a relatively late stage, moving forwards and backwards (through verso revisions; see Appendix) and on to recapitulations or substitutions: for example, the exposition of how Plotinus supplies a connection between the *Daimon*'s sphere and the double vortex, first drafted on [15v], is repeated or moved into a new arrangement on [26v].

The treatment shows some of the features of the distinctive presentation in *A Vision B*, including a drawing of a cone with "Time" and "Subject" at its apex and "Space" and "Object" at its base ([15r], cf. *AVB* 71, *CW14* 52). At the same time it seeks to frame the dualism in terms of a "universal self, or daimon of daimons, consciousness itself [?presenting] through time & mirroring space & a separate self set in the midst of space & struggling for room to live & mirroring the Daimon passions. Thought is from the first movement, emotion & sensation from the second."[175] These categories and formulations were not included in *A Vision* itself, yet the ideas are present in further formulations, including the Seven Propositions ("Astrology and the Nature of Reality" in Rapallo D),[176] and they clearly underlie Yeats's deeper understanding of the system.

After presenting the opposing gyres in terms borrowed from Proclus, Cavalcanti, and Heraclitus, Yeats proceeds to introduce their movements in terms of the *Four Principles*: "To the Two in the unshaded cone we give the names Husk & Passionate Body.... The Two gyres In the shaded cone, which are called Spirit & Celestial Body have an exactly corresponding movement."[177] This contrasts with both versions of *A Vision*, which present the movement of the gyres in terms of the temporary *Faculties*. As Yeats stated further on in this notebook, his understanding of the *Principles* as the permanent spiritual forms of the *Faculties* had come after he wrote "The Twenty-Eight Embodiments" of *A Vision A*,[178] and evidently he was seeking to remedy this misunderstanding by presenting the material related to the gyres in terms of the *Principles*.

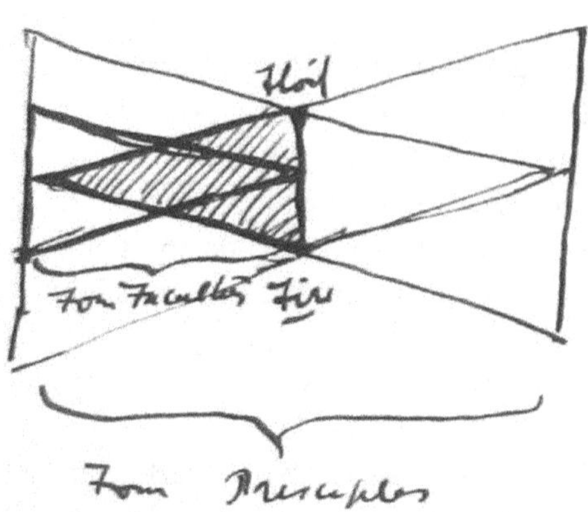

Figure 6. Detail from Rapallo Notebook B, NLI 13,579, [29v]. The cones of the *Four Principles* contain the cones of the *Four Faculties* (here on the left). The two crisis points are "Flood" (top) and "Fire" (bottom), mirroring the two manners of destruction of the universe. Courtesy of NLI.

In the end, this approach was not adopted, however, with the result that many readers have found the *Principles* unnecessary duplicates and insufficiently clarified or differentiated.[179] Some of the material that Yeats outlines here—such as the *Principles* in relation to light and to "their unity in the daimon"[180]—was included in *A Vision B*, not in the initial presentation as envisaged here, but delayed until the second "book," "The Completed Symbol," where it is treated so summarily that readers have not found it very illuminating. Yet the ideas here, worked through as part of the system's technicalities, still underlie imagery and poetry. The following draft, for instance, suggests the foundation of the poem "Chosen," while Yeats also recalls the transcendent close to "Among School Children" understood as Unity of Being:

> It was a Greco Roman fancy, that the soul could at ~~the po~~[*int*] where the zodiac is crossed by the Milky Way turn aside from its path & become a sphere; & the whole aim of the soul is to become a sphere, to allow such a harmonious confluence of all the principles & faculties, that the whirling ends for ever, & all return into the daimon. Some shaddow of its final achievement is found at every point of the vortex, but only complete union at one or other extreme limit, either when Husk may be absorbed in Passionate Body & all be beauty, or when Spirit may be absorbed in Celestial Body & all be Truth, and then only to the supreme Soul. Because Spirit & Celestial Body are human life alone when united to Husk & Passionate Body, & so nourished by particular reality; because all search is through the Four Faculties the union of the Faculties must accompany that of Spirit & Celestial Body. Once that supreme union is attained, Celestial Body & Passionate Body, the known & the ought are our body, the Spirit & the Husk, the knower & the Is our soul, & body & soul are one "How shall we know the dancer from the dance?"[181]

At the same time, the symbolisms involved in the relationship between the sexes, the church calendar, and the Great Year jostle in the treatment, as Yeats's attraction to favorite ideas draws him into characteristic streams of association. One that first appeared in *A Vision A* and is repeated in more than one context in Rapallo A and B is the idea of John the Baptist and Christ as complementary opposites. In *A Vision A*, John's midsummer birth is contrasted with Christ's midwinter nativity, and their conceptions placed at the respective equinoxes nine months earlier, an idea attributed to St. John Chrysostom (*AVA* 164, *CW13* 133). Yeats compares Leonardo da Vinci's painting of John the Baptist to a Dionysus, as he is conceived when the grapes are picked and born when the wheat is harvested. Each of these points is elaborated in the new treatment:

> At midwinter—"the generation of all things with water" Porphyry wrote—Christ is born, at summer St John, Christ begotten in Spring, & in the Autumn

St John, one begotten in joy & brought forth in sorrow, one begotten in sorrow & brought forth in joy.

[. . .]

Coventry Patmore called St John "Natural love" & so a preparation for "supernatural love" following doubtless some father of the Chuch, & did some member of the Platonic Academy of Florence first suggest to Da Vinci a St John with the likeness of Dionysus a form emerging perhaps, not from ~~a sandy desert but~~ some wilderness like that of Eden. The Spirit—supernatural love—begotten a [?new] at the midpoint, receives a natural body when the year brings round the Water – the natural flux; the Husk anew self, instinct, natural love, begotten at the opposing point receives a supernatural body when the year brings round the fire – the purifying ecstacy. Did [?early] Christian [?revery] turn Dyonysus into a saint & mistake his wild honey for the food of an ascetic.

{ ~~Christ is always antithetical to man~~

The God, "boundless love" the universal self is always the antithetical portion of the vortex, but when the year or month of the Faculties is primary it is antithetical, & when antithetical primary; & escaped from the whirl of month or year, the soul born in purifying in flame, rebegotten in the [?su[*pe*]rcelstial] body is Nature itself. }[182]

This draft brings in the cataclysms of flood and fire, which Yeats had read about in Duhem's *Le système du monde* and Plato's *Timaeus*,[183] along with the regeneration of the *Principles*, as well as the transformed body purified in flame, that recalls the spirits "on the Emperor's pavement" of fire in "Byzantium" (*VP* 498, *CW1* 253). The introduction of Coventry Patmore looks forward to the treatment that survived into *A Vision B*, where Patmore is said to have "claimed the Church's authority for calling Christ supernatural love and St. John natural love, and took pleasure in noticing that Leonardo painted a Dionysius like a St. John, a St. John like a Dionysius" (*AVB* 212; cf. *CW14* 156, which corrects the misspelling of "Dionysus"). Yeats attributes to Patmore much that he had already found elsewhere or thought himself: "The Precursor" does speak of St. John and Christ as natural and supernatural love, but none of the essays in *Religio Poetæ* mentions Leonardo's painting, though Walter Pater's *Renaissance* does.[184]

Yeats returns to this group of ideas later in this same notebook in the context of the Great Year, presenting God and man as two wheels that oppose each other, with the spring of one being the autumn of the other (see below).[185] And, in another version later in this notebook (see below, p. 133) and redrafted in Rapallo A, Yeats goes so far as to include a quotation from Patmore—"Christ is supernatural love & St John natural & in natural love God 'gives himself in wine like the fabled Baccus [sic]'"—using a phrase wrenched from a completely different essay and context.[186] This last addition was dropped, but, whether the conflation was consciously contrived or not, Yeats evidently found it convenient to ascribe his own mythopoeic mix to the Catholic convert Patmore.

Yeats's repurposing of this idea in different contexts within the construction of the book and its arguments is a larger-scale version of the way he moves clauses around in a sentence and rephrases the elements. Just as he evidently wanted to include the material on Balzac's *Le chef d'oeuvre inconnu* somewhere in "Rapallo in Spring," he seems to have been set on putting some version of the knot of ideas about Christ and John somewhere in *A Vision*. Eventually he included it among a variety of "the symbols of the relations of men and women and of the birth of children" (*AVB* 211, *CW14* 155), but immediately after presenting the contrast between Jesus and his cousin, Yeats cuts off further exploration: "But I need not go further, for all the symbolism of this book applies to begetting and birth, for all things are a single form which has divided and multiplied in time and space" (*AVB* 212, *CW14* 156).

Rapallo B's draft of "First Things" ends with the question "How are we different at the years end from what we were at its beginning?" answering in terms of Blake's illustrations to the Book of Job. I include cancelled material for clarity:

> What in his designs to the book of Job ~~represents~~ showing that begin & end shows of a necessity a year. At the begging [=*beginning*] is Job surounded by his children ~~xx all have~~ que [*?=quiet*] at prayer, their stringed instruments hanging on the tree[,] their faces, ~~gentle,~~ passive, <timid> emotional, like the faces of good children who attend to their duties, do what they are told never open a book but in the two last pictures, his new family is about him their faces more beautiful, because full of intellect & daring & in the last of them they stand in triumph playing upon many instruments.
>
> { At first we are subject to Destiny, ~~or Husk and~~ or Passionate Body, to ~~Husk Fa Fat~~ Fate or Cellestial Body, but in ~~the end we attain~~ that ~~that state~~ we may escape from the constraint of our nature, & from that of external things, by entering upon ~~that condition~~ <a state> ~~where there is nothing but the condition itself~~ where all fuel has become [*flame*], & where ~~seeg~~ seeing that there is nothing outside the state, nothing to constrain it[,] flame is eternal. We attain <it ~~for a moment~~> in the creation, or enjoyment of a work of art but the moment ~~passes, because its circle~~ though eternal in the daimon passes from us, because it does not contain our whole being. Philosophy has always explained this in some such way & yet the mystery remains, }
>
> ~~Do we not at first rebel without~~ [?~~meaning~~] <~~a purpose~~> & [?~~obey~~] ~~the universal self without understanding . But however one explain it, & the philosopher & the misty~~ <[?~~the mustery~~]> [?~~remains~~] that the daimon is alone real, & that nothing can be added to it, nothing taken away; that ~~change & progress are~~ <all ~~progression is~~ progressions> are allusion [=*illusion*]; that all things have been born from it like a ship in full sail.
>
> March 1928[187]

At the end of the year or after a series of incarnations, Yeats contemplates a transformation from a dutiful innocence to vigorous experience, like the children of Job, which implies a form of progress. Yet paradoxically, it seems, nothing is added, as the later self rather approaches closer to its own archetype or *Daimon*. There is a momentary intimation of this *daimonic* eternity in creating art, where the numbers fold in on themselves, and the integrity can be seen in the modern art he had contemplated in "Rapallo in Spring," where "there is nothing that can be taken out & reasoned over nothing that is not a part of the poem itself, the most characteristic work of that modern art Balzac was first to anounce."[188] It is also—as Yeats writes at the end of Rapallo B—like *A Vision* itself, in which the value of the "single thought has expressed it self as if it were a work of art," with the clarity of "a smokeless flame" and a unity that "lies in the daimon."[189]

Little of this construct finds direct expression in *A Vision* itself, however, but, as mentioned earlier, there are clear echoes in the poetry. Purifying fire and "escape from the constraint of our nature" had been a theme in "Sailing to Byzantium,"[190] and the hard-worked struggle with words here would also feed later into in the fuelless flame of "Byzantium" (see Rapallo Notebook D) and the opening of "Old Tom Again": "Things out of perfection sail / And all their swelling canvas wear. . . ." (*VP* 530, *CW1* 274).

This treatment is dated March 1928 and, as Yeats usually seems to have dated his work after revising it, these drafts were probably created during the Yeatses' earliest days in Rapallo.

[34v–43r] "Additions & corrections of Vision Book II | 7 pages (dated May 1928)"

The folios from [34v–38r] contain various fragmentary paragraphs, including two or three false starts to the revised version of "Book II | 1. The Great Wheel." To some extent these seem to rework "First Things," containing some of the same material, but mainly seek to build on the exposition of the double vortex, or interpenetrating cones, moving on to the more flexible symbol of the Great Wheel.

Though brief and fragmentary, even these *disjecta membra* contain insights into Yeats's thinking and how he viewed his material, and Yeats numbered the pages, which generally indicates that he saw the material as useful. In the first introduction, he heads the paragraph, "~~Religio Poetae~~ | Book II | I. The Great Wheel"; since he had just quoted Coventry Patmore's *Religio Poetæ* on John the Baptist, this may be no more than a note that was rejected, but its size and position make it look like a title, so he might have been considering borrowing the title for some less than orthodox musings. Certainly, the opening paragraph he drafts below it focuses on the double vortex and the wheel (confusing Empedocles with Heraclitus, as he often did):

> The double vortex of Heraclitus was too simple, we know of it from a metrical fragment & when Heraclitus spoke to his pupils, he may have used some form that showed more of actual history. Things do not move gradually in one direction & then as gradually in another, as the narrowing & then expanding gyres suggest.[191]

Yeats evidently recognizes that the gyres might seem inadequate to "An Explanation of Life," as offered by the subtitle of *A Vision A*. Even if he considers that his instructors' version of the "double vortex" is more complex than that of Empedocles, many readers presented with *A Vision*'s single supreme diagram may well have felt that, however much it is modified by epicycles of complexity, the scheme is "too simple."

On the opposite verso, so probably later, Yeats also drafts one of his recurrent disclaimers, explaining, perhaps more clearly than elsewhere, what he means by the metaphor of the *dramatis personae*, a phrase which became the working title for these opening sections through a series of drafts:

> I am a dramatist & symbolist & often content with such definition or describtion [*sic*] as one can in list of Dramatis Personae, ~~preffering that "Principles" or "Faculties" "Daimon" "[?emotion]" "thought" "man" "God" or Da~~ ~~that my matters to reveal them selves in action~~ leaving my matter to display itself in action.[192]

The analogy does not seem particularly sound, as there is relatively little action within which to observe how these various actors behave, but it does show that Yeats's sparse definition and "character sketch" of his players is a deliberate choice. Again, many readers find the lack of delineation of *Faculties*, *Principles*, *Daimon*, man, or God something of a barrier to understanding.

In the following opening, the recto shows again "Book II | I. The Great Wheel," but preceded by two rejected titles, "~~Siris~~ | ~~A Foundation~~." Like "Religio Poetæ," the cancelled title "Siris" at the head may hint that Yeats considered embarking on more literary and discursive writing, which was then pushed aside by the expository material of "A Foundation," a title repeated on the following recto too. The text describes how the instructors gave the Great Wheel before the double vortex, explaining how it "is a pictorial ~~simpl~~ representation of a form of the Double Vortex" and presents the *Principles* with their corresponding *Faculties*, "Husk and P[assionate] B[ody] or Will and Mask" in an initial section that runs out of steam on the second page.[193] The text continues from the diagrams and explication of the preceding page, yet, at the top of the page, Yeats has cancelled “~~A Foundation~~ | ~~I~~| ~~This book would be different~~,” evidently using the new opening that he had drafted for “First Things.”

Though these two rectos, [36r] and [37r], are numbered, Yeats’s numbering skips the following recto, which has only a few abandoned efforts:

> ~~When for many weeks, after~~
> ~~When my instructors first taught me, they~~
> ~~For~~
> ~~For the first <couple of> years my instructors based the greater part of their instruction upon what “The Great Whel Wheel”, & some weeks of that time had bassed before I connected with it, certain gyres & cones used~~[194]

The rest of the page is blank. Though completely fragmentary, these false starts—and the more substantial one before—appear to show something like a practice run-up to a jump or pitch, and the following pages launch into a sustained exposition, drawing on these feints at starting.

> I. Introduction
> ~~When my instructors began I was taught to measure character & emotion by the movements of what I have called “The Great Wheel” movements that seemed as arbitrary as those in some game of chance [. . . .]~~ The Great Wheel is a circle of 28 lunar phases, or of 27 phases and a moonless night, each symbolized by a circle & a crescent, the circle for the convenience of an arbitrary symbol representing the sun, but for convenience of representation and symbol alike made dark.[195]

The exposition is presented now almost exclusively in terms of the *Faculties*, as the focus is on the character of the various incarnations, and the material is a variation on the presentations that would appear in the published version of *A Vision B*. Yeats had clearly decided to repeat the descriptions of *A Vision A*’s “The Twenty-Eight Embodiments,” explaining:

> When I first wrote my second Book for the first edition of this book I had not mastered all the geometrical symbolism & was so persuaded of its difficulty that I tried [*to*] interest my reader as I had been interested in the Great Wheel, as something unexplained but yet explaining the world. Somewhere in the Arabian Nights an Arab boy becomes a Zizier [=*Vizier*] & explains his wisdom by saying “O brother I have taken stock in the desert sand and of the sayings of antiquity”; & compelled to my great regret as I have explained to invent for my symbols an imaginary origin I thought I could draw attention to [*the*] most important of them by pretending this was the marks made upon the sand by certain enigmatical men & women, dancing to amuse & instruct

> a tyrant of Bagdad. What I had been told about the Four Principles meant nothing to me, because the geometry that explained it was still unintelligible, so I gave to each Faculty the quality of the corresponding Principle together with its own. Had I understood that the Principles are value & attainment, & the Faculties process & search I could not perhaps have done other without innumerable cumbersome explanatory sentences. During embodied life the Principles are brought into existence by the Faculties, & only when we speak of the state after death is it necessary to constantly distinguish one from the other. I wrote this book in my first excitement, when it seemed that I understood human nature for the first time, & leave it unchanged except for a few passages crossed out because their matter is somewhere in book I & three or four sentences added to sharpen a definition or correct an error.[196]

The repetition of the quotation about the Vizier and desert sand that he had used in *Per Amica Silentia Lunae* (*Myth* 343, *CW5* 17)—different from any of the translations but with exactly the same wording as the 1917 essay—shows how essential a part of Yeats's mental stock it was,[197] and how clearly he connected the ideas of that earlier essay with the Arabian fantasy of *A Vision A*, the diagrams made in the sand by the Judwalis, and Kusta ben Luka's young bride in "The Gift of Harun-al-Rashid or Desert Geometry."[198]

Yeats also admits that the descriptions of the twenty-eight incarnations should in fact be more complex and labored in explanation, as he is only including half of the relevant elements, yet many readers probably find even that half difficult enough to accommodate when they read about the different types. It is, indeed, unlikely that the description of the incarnations corresponding to the phases of the moon would gain any clarity or insight by adding the more spiritual layer of the *Principles*, though it would probably have helped readers to grasp how the two groups of his *dramatis personae*—*Faculties* and *Principles*—interacted on the stage in action, instead of the relatively abstract accounts of the *Principles* that are given in "The Completed Symbol" of *A Vision B*. Yeats clearly recognized that the description of "the 28 types of incarnation" was among the more approachable and attractive sections of the book, so worth keeping without alteration, even as he was attempting to integrate the *Principles* more fully into the system elsewhere.

He also admits to the many shortcomings of his presentation, only some of which are mentioned in the published version:

> As each gyre of 28 incarnations is succeeded by another of an opposite, & creates itself, by a struggle with predecessor or successor, it is impossible [*to*] explain any particular incarnation without knowing which among the twelve gyres it belongs to and this I cannot do. Again & again my instructors spoke of some man or woman, as belonging to the 4 or 5th or 6th, let us say, but my imagination has not been able to follow. I cannot even master in its detail the single type of

> gyre of this book. The list of attributes in "The Table of the Four Faculties" or "character in certain phases" [*is*] not my work, nor could I replace it if it was lost. It was dictated nine or ten attributes at a time, & all I have done is to change two or three words for reasons of style, after I had asked permission, or to fill a blank space with that somewhat vague description "Player on Pans pipes".
>
> A phase or type recurs until the soul has attained a proximate unity of being — unity of Spirit and Celestial Body "nourished" by that of the Faculties & the moment of this possible attainment "could be fixed mathematically" had I the power of abstract thought.
>
> May 1928 [199]

The dating of May 1928 shows that a few months had passed since he had started on "First Things" and two since revising it. This date also appears on a typescript that appears to have been dictated from this, while the corrections are dated July 1928,[200] and both appear to pre-date the equivalent material in Rapallo A.

Folios [44–50]

These folios are not accounted for in Yeats's table of contents. The spread of [43v–44r] gives notes for amending pages 12, 13, 14, and 15 of *A Vision A*, "The Great Wheel" (the last in fact relating to page 14). Clearly, in 1928, when presenting the concept of the Great Wheel, Yeats still intended to modify parts the presentation of *A Vision A* rather than rewrite the material completely, as eventually happened.

While [44r] repeats the page number of the preceding recto [43r]—"7"—the following three leaves, [45–47], have been removed, and the numbering on [48r] follows with the number "8." However, the following two rectos, [49–50], are unnumbered and, on these three pages, all the material is cancelled. The figure "II" at the beginning of the draft appears to relate to section II of the Great Wheel, and these pages outline rejected considerations of the Wheel, the latter parts relating to civilizations and the birth of Christ.

Following a diagram where Christ is placed at the center of a gyre (see Figure 7), the final line, which Yeats struck through along with the rest, ominously states that "My instructors have preferred a more complicated symbol,"

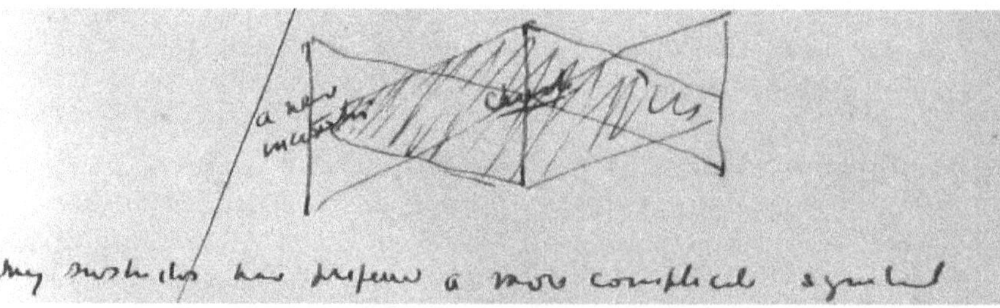

Figure 7. Rapallo Notebook B, NLI 13,579, [50r]. The annotations read "a new incarnation" and "Christ." Courtesy of NLI; photograph courtesy of Catherine E. Paul.

no doubt referring to the double cone that precedes "Dove or Swan" in both versions of *A Vision*.

[51r–74r] "Great Year 21 pages (early version)"

Although the next page appears to follow its predecessors as rejected text, it marks the beginning of the book that Yeats was preparing for the new version of *A Vision* on the Great Year of the Ancients, and the text is recognizably that of the published version: "'By common custom,' Cicero wrote in the Dream of Scipio 'men measure the year merely by the return of the Sun, or in other words by the revolution of one star. . . .'"[201] The following page is numbered as the first of the new section, which continues over the next twenty-two folios (numbered 1–8, one blank page, 8[bis]–21). Yeats attributes the 26,000-year period of the Great Year to his instructors, noting that with respect to the astronomical details involved, "I got this all wrong in the first edition of this book thinking that it must have begun between Taurus and Ares," rather than Aries and Pisces.[202] Personally, his purpose appears to include providing a framework that makes Christianity a phenomenon of a particular time and combination of cycles rather than a revelation for all time. (Part of the treatment here was reworked in the first section of Rapallo Notebook A: see the transcription from [8r] above, p. 84.)

> I myself seek a symbol that can thrust Christianity back into the crises where it arose, and there display it not as an abstract ideal but united to its opposite, or thrust it forward into the crisis where the actors must change robes & the defeated Tincture triumph in its turn. ~~An abstract ideal is lyrical.~~
>
> ~~VI~~
>
> ~~An ideal separated from its opposite is lyrical~~ ~~acquires a~~ ~~is lyrical;~~ ~~has a phantastic imobility like that of the Greek figures in Keats Ode & palls upon us po,~~ ~~has a phantastic imobility like that of the gr figures Keats saw upon the Urn & therefore xxx palls upon us, the exceptional moment past;~~ ~~whereas but an idea united to its opposite is tragic & stays always like the poetry of Dante~~
>
> ~~VII~~
>
> ~~and like the poetry of Dante needs no exceptional moment & always stays like the poetry of Dante.~~
>
> I am tired of Shellean Christianity. An ideal separated from its opposite is lyrical, & its phantastic imobility palls upon us, but an ideal united to its opposite is tragic & stays always like the poetry of Dante.[203]

It seems strange for a lyric poet to decry lyrical poetry, and to characterize it by an "imobility like that of the figures Keats saw upon the Urn," especially when he had referred to the very same poem and image in his evocation of Rapallo, which had brought "to mind the little Greek town described in 'An Ode to a Grecian Urn.'"[204] Yet evidently he sought to attain the grandeur and movement of drama, and to place religion within this context, by uniting *primary* Christianity to its *antithetical* counterparts.

The treatment includes a schematization that links the months of the Great Year to the signs of the zodiac, the months of the year, and the phases of the moon, as well as the seasons and points of the compass. He would continue to struggle with these schemes when he reworked this material in Rapallo A, and though he eventually abandoned all but a vague identification of the months of the year with the twelve "gyres" of the lunar phases, these correspondences evidently informed how he approached and thought about the process of development in time and history.

The treatment of history presents God and man as two wheels that oppose each other, spring to autumn and *Mask* to *Will*, in cancelled material that was reworked and incorporated into "The Completed Symbol" (cf. *AVB* 210; *CW14* 154) rather than "The Great Year of the Ancients." The seasonal contrast brings Yeats back to the opposition of St. John's Day on June 24 and Christmas on December 25, while Blake's "Mental Traveller" is invoked in both contexts. A cancelled page elaborates idea further, though with some jumps of thought that only make sense if one knows the earlier treatments. Some of the associations appear in the material already examined, but, yet again, Yeats elaborates ideas that do not appear in *Religio Poetæ*, connecting "natural love" to the desire for a transcendent object, the *Mask*, or more unexpectedly God as woman. He again alludes to the lush background of the St. John/Bacchus at the Louvre and to his use of St. John Chrysostom in *A Vision A*.

> I am puzzled by a symbolism which Patmore must have thought that of the medieval church unless I can understand "natural love" as all man does for a transcendant object, God is woman, an accepted discipline, a self lacerating ecstacy. I cannot transform a sun dried desert into the wilderness of eden. I do not know Chrisostom accept [=*except*] from what other[*s*] quote of him he has perhaps some passage, that explains what the early church ment by the Four Seasons. My instructors have warned me, not to consider theirs as the only possible symbolism.[205]

This last sentence forms something of a complement to the statement Yeats would include in *A Packet for Ezra Pound*—"but then there are many symbolisms and none exactly resembles mine"[206]—replaced in the version in *A Vision B*.

[66v]

In the following pages, amid exposition of the movements of the gyres of the solar diamond and the lunar hour-glass, and of how to read the positions of the *Faculties* in the cones preceding "Dove or Swan," there is a fragment of a plan for a lecture or an essay on a blank verso (Figure 8), possibly the only page in the notebook not directly connected to *A Vision*, though even here the line "My philosophy" may indicate the connection.

[?General].

? Materlinck do not touch me.
? what about Lang Etc

Influence from Sligo.
folk & faery
Lady G s book
} Origins

Chance Choice – | difference from other | ? [?~~desire~~] [?~~of~~] [?~~dicipline/deception~~]
Pater. V de l Adam ([?contrects]

Michel R & Mathers

Cambridge Neo Platonists

My philosophy

plays & self dicipline & public work
Castiglione[207]

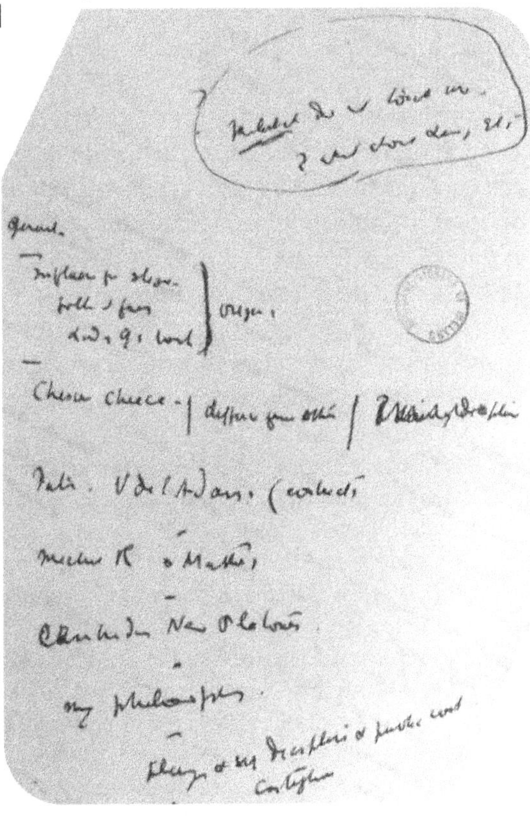

Figure 8. Rapallo Notebook B, NLI 13,579 [66v]. Courtesy of NLI; photograph courtesy of Catherine E. Paul. Image has been rotated 26° to align with the transcript above.

Despite some doubtful readings, the plan appears to outline a presentation or lecture. Much of it seems to relate to the growth of the poet's mind, recognizing important influences in Sligo's folklore and Lady Gregory's work on Irish myth, as well as his reading of Walter Pater and Auguste Villiers de l'Isle Adam's play *Axël.*[208] Chance and Choice, fate and destiny, had become an important element of the duality inherent in the system of *A Vision*, while the pairing of Michael Robartes with MacGregor Mathers points to what the fictional Robartes owes to the former leader of the Golden Dawn. *Per Amica Silentia Lunae* gives some indication of the significance that the Cambridge Platonists such as Henry More and Ralph Cudworth held for him, and the category of "My philosophy" could be as extensive or brief as Yeats chose. The inclusion afterwards of the theater work seems to imply that the "philosophy" was not the sole or even main focus, as it looks outward to Yeats's public work, citing the influence of Castiglione's *The Book of the Courtier*.[209]

The circled queries above these notes are even more enigmatic. In Maeterlinck's *Pelléas and Mélisande*, Mélisande's first words on stage are "Do not touch me," a phrase she repeats through the play, but it could be applied here in any number of ways, depending entirely on what aspect caught Yeats's interest.[210] His Deirdre also uses the phrase twice to King Conchubar after Naoise has been killed (*VPl* 383, 384), and it was a theme repeated in nineteenth-century literature, particularly drama, with both biblical and sexual connotations.[211] Andrew Lang had written on many folkloric themes, including taboos, which may indicate a possible approach. However, there is no clear relation with the more personal focus of the other notes.

[67r–74r] ["Great Year" continued]

The following pages continue the treatment of the Great Year uninterrupted, turning to more technical considerations of all the cycles coming together and how art partakes of the whole, as was redrafted in Rapallo A.[212]

> My instructors sometimes talk as if all were calculable, & then again insist upon mans freedom[,] though only at the moment [?some] reaches its climax[.] I have sometimes thought there were two parties among them[,] more often that there is one that can free themselves from the Kantian antinomy. Some times they compared the sphere to a number made of integer numbers whose multiplication make that number with no fraction over, & contrasted it to those others which are like the separate phases, made up of numbers that never constitute a whole, of clocks that do not chime when the central clock strikes midnight or strike some other hour. They compared the first kind of number to a work of art, because in the work of art each separate line, color or thought is related to whole, is as it were multiplied into it, & called both a "sequence", as the second kind they called a "recurrence" meaning I think that the units multiplied themselves but did not constitute a whole. Every phase, every act of the Four Faculties was such a "recurrence", & every such "recurrence" began with an "allusion" an unrelated fact or image which is like the 0 which precedes 1 & is the thing multiplied.
>
> { In pure "sequence["] there is no "allusion," no 0[,] all is from the whole & flows back into the whole. The spirits at phase 1, who are wholly passive, percieve [*sic*] "allusion" only. Others think & create through them but they themselves have neither "recurrence" nor sequence. }

> The subject however was never developed, owing to my mathematical incapacity, I touch upon it here because it echoes Platos perfect numbers, & because the anxiety of my instructors, as to the date of my childrens birth—I speak of that elsewhere—reminds me of the passage in the Republic, where when the rulers forget the perfect numbers, the wrong children come to birth.[213]

Again, the significance of symbolic or Pythagorean number seems to connect to slightly more practical numbers, with the birth of children and Yeats's sense that there is a mystery he has not penetrated. These thoughts are included at the end of "The Completed Symbol" in *A Vision*:

> There are certain numbers, certain obscure calculations in Plato's *Republic* meant to suggest and hide the methods adopted by the ruling philosophers to secure that the right parents shall beget the right children [. . . .] Will some mathematician some day question and understand, as I cannot, and confirm all, or have I also dealt in myth? (*AVB* 212–13, *CW14* 156–57)

Such eugenic concerns—both esoteric and more political—are also evident in "Under Ben Bulben" and *On the Boiler*.

After further consideration of the complementary wheels of Europe and Asia, Yeats addresses the question of his similarity to Spengler's historical scheme, material that was, in the main, eventually published in *A Packet for Ezra Pound* rather than *A Vision* itself.

> I have left what follows, except for the changes of Fountain into Phoenix on page [*blank*] exactly [*as*] it was when first published in 1925, some two or three months before the publication of an English translation of Spenglers ["]decline of the West". When the diagram on which it is founded came in 1917 while Spenglers book, was still at the german printers, & that was unfinished. I read no German, I knew nothing of Spengler except something about his general scheme of thought [?as was first/an Irish priest] told me during a [?comity] <in 1922 or 1924>, & his outline of European civilization resembles so closely that I have read him in astonishment. Not only are our dates & their significant [?contours] the same but we have both used the drilling of the eyes of <statues> at the time [*of*] Hadrian to prove the same contrast between Greek and Roman character, & described the staring eyes of Byzantine icons in almost the same sentence – I have "staring at miracle" he or his ~~English~~ translator has "staring at the infinite" & we both draw the same conclusion from how the portrait heads [*of*] Roman sculpture screw on to stock bodies. ~~I certainly though I wrote~~ The dates were from my diagram but I certainly thought I wrote those sentences myself. Yet why should I say "astonished"[:] that mind can know of mind without the intervention of speech or print does not astonish me; it has been my familiar thought, sometimes my experience, these many years.[214]

As is often the case, this final declaration is deflected away from personal disclosure in the published version, though possibly made more magical:

> I knew of no common source, no link between him and me, unless through
> 'The elemental things that go
> About my table to and fro'.[215]

The remaining three pages of this section consist of rewriting of the material already included in *A Vision A* about the Etruscan year and Hipparchus's observation of precession. They are headed by the instruction "insert at A," evidently earlier in the section, though that insertion point and symbol seem to have been lost with the removal of a page or pages.[216] They are followed by a completely blank leaf, [75].

[76r–90r] "Soul in Judgement ~~(first draft)~~ 10 pages"

The drafts next move on to a new version of the section dealing with "Life after Death," the cancelled title that is replaced with the ambiguous but more satisfying "Soul in Judgement." Though the section is new, Yeats again repurposes the treatment of St. John as Bacchus and natural love juxtaposed with Christ as supernatural love, though the idea has become so familiar perhaps that the writing is rather careless:

> Coventry Patmore thought Da Vinci had a philosophical intention when he painted a St John like a Baccus [*sic*], a Baccus like a St John, for Christ was supernatural, & Baccus natural love – "God give[*s*] him[*self*] in wine like the fable[*d*] Baccus["]. He had doub[*t*]less some tradition of the Church in his head, for he was an orthodox Catholic and no doubt remembered that early church symbolism attributed to Christ an annunciation at the Vernal Equinox, & a birth at midwinter, & to St John an autumn conception & a birth at midsummer, the one begotten in joy brought forth in sorrow, the other begotten in sorrow brought forth in joy.[217]

The pairing is now interpreted as a rather strained allegory of the *Principles'* cones of life and death, with St. John mirroring the *Husk* and Christ *Spirit*. In many ways, though, this obsessive repurposing of ideas (almost none of which ever crossed Patmore's mind) illustrates how Yeats views the myth of *A Vision*'s geometry: it is the underlying structure rather than the final form, the skeleton rather than the living bird, which "signifies truth" when it goes through the processes of life (*AVB* 214, *CW14* 158). It is perhaps to be regretted that Yeats did not include more of the mythic vision which seems to match the associative movement of his thought between supernatural Christ and the natural Bacchic Baptist:

> I do not quarrel with Patmores thought but must restate it. I read in the cones of the Four Principles & identify St John to Husk: for Husk is begotten when at Lunar North Solar West, when in the middle moment between Life & Death it is called back into life to reject a Celestial Body and find some new Celestial Body the antithesis of the old, as the new Celestial Body is born at the summer solstice or with the death of man; & identify Christ to Spirit for Spirit [*is*] begotten, or announced, when in the middle moment between birth & death, it rejects Passionate Body, & seeks some new Passionate Body the antithesis of the old, & the Passionate Body comes with phisical birth at the winter solstice. Christ, Spirit, identifies himself with the new body as an act of will, being of the Sphere, not of the gyre, the [*point?*] where Creative Mind, at its corresponding moment is en forced, Husk upon the other hand, perhaps given the cup of oblivion Porphyry talks of, intoxicates the soul[.][218]

This passage appears on leaf [77r], which is numbered "2." Although the treatment in the following four pages moves on to the processes involved in death, all are cancelled with a vertical line and are unnumbered, so that the page numbered "3" is actually [82r]—and even then most of the text is scored through. Yeats sets out to explain the movements of *Faculties*, representing the period between birth and death, and *Principles*, representing the whole circle from birth to birth—or death to death.

> Only the cones between Will & Mask represent our present life in them move the Four Faculties as well as the Four Principles, & within the other cone something more unexplained & mysterious. When the twelve cicles that began as Will reached 8 upon the circle reach their end with Will at 22, life will pas into the cone, to which we given the main[=*name?*] of the 13th cone. This is the same change that takes place with the Faculties, when the consciousness is transferred from the Will to the Spirit & the change from the bright fortnight to the dark; & The 13th spere [*sic*] is the present dwelling place of those [*who*] are set free from life.[219]

The *Thirteenth Cone* was an idea that evolved significantly between the two published versions of *A Vision*, and here Yeats seems to be moving away from the earlier idea of three further cycles beyond incarnation to that of a single state or being, the *Thirteenth Cone* or *Sphere*.[220] Calling it a "dwelling place" implies that it is, in this context at least, closer to state than being.

Since Yeats's thought works by analogy, and since he was still trying to clarify his thought about the nature of the *Principles*, at least in draft he seems to see an analogy between the *Principles* and the *Thirteenth Cone*. He also enters into significant speculation on the nature of mind, seeing waking consciousness as a relatively limited portion of a greater whole, both individually and as part of a unified whole. Some of the sentences run on and appear to shift from one construction to another, without making clear sense—as private notes they are part of the process of discovery, not an end in themselves—so I have not attempted to punctuate beyond the very basic level. (Handwriting is also a factor, so it is not always clear whether verbs or nouns are singular or plural.)

> That the Principles contain in their complete movement life and the state between lives means, if I understand my symbol[,] that they limit consciousness, which contains within it but is not contained by that of the Faculties. I have learned from Plotinus to consider the universe as a consciousness, & that the individual man is a movement—or change of quality—within it but not in himself conscious. My instructors tell me that to every phase, at a moment mathematically calculable[,] a man has the opportunity of unity of being—unity of Spirit & Celestial body "nourished" by unity of the Faculties, but that even if attained Antithetical man knows nothing of it or has at best a momentary knowledge; I admit that I am in my Principles a living conscious being of whose acts I know little for my Faculties are limited by memory. Beyond the limit of the Principles are yet greater limits up to that being that has none & contains all. The Principles themselves are related to the thirteenth cone, as the Faculties are to the Principles, the Faculties are a process not a value, a method of discovery not a beauty or truth, & Spirit though separated [?power/from] the Faculties bring to us always, if they bring anything, what comes from beyond themselves, what descends perhaps through Spirit after Spirit [—] only those in the 13 cone need no intermediaries. This was shown to me by a symbol. I was told that a Spirit of the 13 Cone was present I was asked to notice that whereas when other Spirits [*were there*] the house often smelt of some light scent, or of garden flowers, or some scent produced by burning church incense or the sweet or fragrant odour of some burnt wood or brack[,] it smelt now sea water. They would use always I was told such symbols, selected from our memories, as did not suggest artificial preparations.[221]

Part of these speculations inform "The Completed Symbol" of *A Vision*, while some of the account of the smells associated with spirits was used in *A Packet for Ezra Pound*. The more extended meditation upon how consciousness relates to the various aspects of being is never really given in the published versions, replaced by oblique references to Valéry's "*Le cimitière marin*," Iseult dancing on a beach in Normandy, and the Upanishads (*AVB* 219–23, *CW14* 159–62). However confused these musings of this draft may be, they genuinely illuminate an important aspect of how Yeats viewed the nature of mind.

After three sections of introduction, Yeats finally broaches the subject of the afterlife, only to admit that he will not really broach it.

> IV
>
> The first edition of this book contains a long section called the Gates of Pluto that now fills [*me*] with shame. It contains a series of unrelated statements, inaccurate deduction from the symbols, & was little but notes [*I*] [?have] recorded for my own future use. I postpone the theme till my instructors come to me again or my own thought take fire, & for the moment content my self with a few rambling comments.
>
> My instructors declare that soon after death the Spirit seeks to separate it self from the Husk & Passionate Body that should disapear, & to unite itself to the Celestial Body but that it is continually drawn back into the Passionate Body which compells it live over & over again the events of life that have most moved it or the delusion of its terror. It is the Homeric contrast between Heracles moving through the night bow in hand, & his happy spirit,
>
> "And Heracles the mighty I saw when these went by;
> His image indeed, for himself mid the gods that never die
> Sits glad at the feast, & Hebe fair-ancled there doth hold,
> The daughter of Zeus the mighty & Here shod with gold."[222]

Here, the ideas are already approaching the form that Yeats would publish in 1937 (*AVB* 226; *CW14* 164–65), contrasting the *Spirit*'s attraction to the memories of mortal life and to a more transcendent life (which would become the subject of a poem in Rapallo C, "Imagination's Bride").[223] This exposition does not use the anatomy of six stages that Yeats evidently developed later, nor the related terminology,[224] focusing on the processes of dreaming back—without using that term—and gradual separation from the previous life, but relatively cursorily in the course of a few pages. At the conclusion of this draft, the final stages of the afterlife (what would later be called *Beatitude*, *Purification*, and *Foreknowledge*) are then summarized in a few sentences:

> Then comes ~~a state of freedom~~ ~~states of~~ a condition I have been told little of, & I have learned little of unity, & brief beatitude, corresponding to phase one, followed by a long period when the soul [?~~can move] its own life~~ can take what form it please — one thinks of the shape-changers of folk lore — live a life planned by itself — being a Priest in its own house as Blake said — & await birth.
>
> { While so waiting it can foresee its future & through the living prepare for it, I was told by an an [*sic*] instructor who compared [*it*] to one of my Canaries at that moment [*it*] gathers down, grass & moss for its nest, ~~& be at such moments full of love & hate beyond anything known to the living. Porphyry spoke of such souls as drunk with the honey of generation~~. }
>
> In all these states, except that of union with the [?shade] the <u>Spirit</u> may become a messenger of the 13th cone to the living. Some few souls saints or sages may break away at the Beatitude[,] like a gyring bird that has seen its prey[,] & return to life no more.[225]

Though some readers of *A Vision* may feel that the treatment of the afterlife, particularly the latter stages, is rather scant, it is at least fuller than this outline would have given, though the final image provides the most striking feature, implying that the widening gyre may lead to escape from the constraints of nature when the falcon swoops through the center.

[91r–102v] "Introduction. 12 pages (continued in | loose leaf book[)]."

The final block of writing in the notebook is entitled "Introduction" and is the first—or a very early—draft of the "Introduction to the Great Wheel" of *A Packet for Ezra Pound*.[226] In fact, the first paragraph about Lady Gregory commenting that he was "a much better educated man," appears in an earlier version on the final recto of the notebook [102r], titled "Beginning for account of origin of system," implying that Yeats started this at the back of the notebook and then realized he would have rather more material than he had originally thought and might need more space, so moved back further into the book.[227] The text throughout is remarkably close to the final published version, though the paragraphs that explain the first automatic writing show some telling changes and second thoughts in the writing process, especially over the initial motivation or plan for attempting automatic writing.

> ~~Four days after my marriage~~ On the afternoon of October the 24, four days after my marriage[,] my wife ~~& I were~~ my wife ~~suggested~~ ~~said~~ ~~proposed that~~ said she would like to ~~try & do~~ attempt automatic writing. She told me afterwards that she ~~intended to amuse me by some invented message~~ had meant to make up messages & having amuse me for an afternoon say that what she had done. She wrote ~~one or two vague~~ did invent a few lines, some name & some imaginary addres when her hand was, as it were, grasp[*ed*] by another & there came ~~in an almost unintelligible~~ ~~in disjointed sentences & in~~ in disjointed sentences & in almost illegible handwriting ~~certain [?]startling sentences~~ ~~disjointed sentences that excited my imagination~~ ~~that were~~ what was at first a ~~development &~~ comment upon my ~~essay~~ little book ["]Per Amica Silentia Lunae", but so passed far beyond my thought ~~We sat gave up~~ From that on we gave some part of every day, when ~~my wifes strength permitted~~ ~~my wife felt that she that she could bear~~ what ~~was soon a heavy drain upon her vitality~~ my wife had strength enough for such a drain upon her vitality. ~~This~~ ~~We returned to Ireland & lived generally in solitary places absorbed in this task~~. We spent ~~much~~ part of 1918 ~~& part of 1919~~ then at Sligo Glendalough, & our house Thur Ballalee, Coole solitary places ~~absorbed in this task. At the begging of 1919~~ my wife bored & fatigued by her almost daily task I think & talking of little else. ~~Whe we had returned to England~~ Early in 1919 the communicating spirit said they would shortly change the method ~~to words~~ from the written to the spoken word as that would be less exausting for my wife, but The change did not come however ~~until late~~ until

> [*gap for date*] while I was on an american lecture tour. We had one of those little compartments on the train with two beds, & one night my wife began to talk in her sleap. ~~From At once it began became the principal & soon the only means of [?delivery] a little later the automatic writing ceased altogether, & the communicating spirits spoke [?talking for] my wife [?talking through] my wife while a sleap~~.[228] When ever they wished to ~~do so~~ <talk ~~in her sleap~~> in this way they would ~~give me an~~ signal ~~to me sometime during the day~~ ~~that~~ during the day — I will explain later what these signals were — & I would have pen & paper & my questions ready.[229]

In the course of revision, Yeats honed certain phrases and added more detail and anecdote—most notably the "metaphors for poetry"—but also glossed over George's idea of playing a game with invented script. Though this aspect was evidently true, and matches what George Yeats told Richard Ellmann,[230] Yeats was clearly aware of the impression that it would create. He himself was comfortable enough with the fictions surrounding mediumship, which he viewed as aspects of dramatization by the medium, but, perhaps suspecting that this would be seized on by skeptics to dismiss everything that followed, he eventually omitted it.[231] In contrast the simple phrase "what was at first a comment upon my little book [']Per Amica Silentia Lunae'. . . so[*on?*] passed far beyond my thought" is expanded to give a characterization of *A Vision*'s system of phases and cycles of history in relation to *Per Amica Silentia Lunae*, with allusions to Browning's Paracelsus and Goethe's Wilhelm Meister.

The continuing exposition follows a similar pattern, so the communicators' direct speech becomes indirect and a phrase such as "they said I must not read philosophy until they had finished their exposition" becomes "they asked me not to read philosophy until their exposition was complete," and "They were always in a hurry, because as they explained before long they must leave, & there were others who knew this, who tried to confuse us or in some way to waste time & were called Frustrators"—"Because they must, as they explained, soon finish, others whom they named Frustrators attempted to confuse us or waste time."[232]

His account of the genesis of *A Vision A* has a few variations of interest, particularly his refusal to publish it as his own work and the suggestion that the Instructors forbade the use of dialogues between Robartes and Aherne as a method of exposition.

> When I prepared for publication the first confused inconsistent edition of this book I had to invent a phantastic setting about one Robartes, the hero of an [?early] story of mine[,] bringing the philosophy from Arabia because I could not tell the real origin. My wife hated the idea of its origin becoming known, & I could not, though the spirits urged me, permit it to seem my own work, I had begun to write it as a series of

> diaglolgs [*sic*] between Robartes & other [?vaguer] characters, but that they forbid lest some one or other of them should mistake an imaginary person for himself. They had compelled me to write, though my thought was still confused, & a hasty arangement with a publisher compelled me to publish [?early] in 1925. Had I delayed no one would have believed that much of the section "Dove or Swan"—repeated in this book without alteration[—]was not a plagiarism from Spenglers "Decline of the West" of which an English translation appeared later in the year.[233]

He implies that the Instructors contrived a rather premature publication because they foresaw that the translation of Spengler would fatally undermine *A Vision* otherwise.

Writing about the communicator that came when they were in Cannes, just before they moved to Rapallo, Yeats notes that the visits were "almost nightly" and explained the circumstances in which these renewed sessions came.

> In Ireland I had rewritten a good deal of the "Vision", but there was a whole section of [*it*] that deals with the "Four Principles["] which I could not understand[.] I had put it aside to finish a book of verse "The Winding Stair["] & had worked at this at intervals through my illness, & by [?luck] I had I had [*sic*] taken it up again. He made me read what I had written to my wife that he might hear it, & now while my wife slept he went over it bit by bit. I had forgotten how powerful in thought was the communicator, how completely master of a system in its minute details, which I could but hope to master in outline[.] [A]s my embarrassment was increased by his irritability—some term from Plato, & a phrase from a modern realist enraged him—why was I not satisfied to get my tecnical term from him. He & his he explained were not always at their best—anger I had long noticed was a signal that [*they*] were at their best but that made it no pleasanter at the moment—presently some communicator not at his best would accept some false reasoning from me & all would be confused.
>
> { It was [?obvious], that though he tolerated my philosophical studies out of respect for freedom, he hated it, & later on}
>
> he was to tell me my present illness & another that preceeded it, were the result of my preoccupation with abstract thought. [?Altho] these quarrels within[=*with him?*] [?alarmed] me, & made my question[*s*] vague & confused I gained for the first time ~~an understanding of the Principles, which enabled me to get the geometry correct~~ to distinguish between the "Principles" between all [*that*] comes in Thomist philosophy from "revelation", & "Faculties" which construct it supporting Will & abstracting reason. I felt that I had known nothing & began that study which tests even Buddhist philosophers, the contemplation of the void, & struggle to substantiate the last conception which made the Japanese saint say of himself after the supreme experience of his [?riglen (=*religion?*)] "He comes no more from behind the embroidered

> screen, amid the sweet incense clouds, & goes among his friends & among the lute players: something very nice has happened to the young man but he will only tell it to his sweet heart.["][234]

This passage is relatively close to the version in *A Packet for Ezra Pound*'s section XI,[235] though in *A Vision B* the reference to the Zen poem was moved to the end of "The Completed Symbol," placed together with the other material drawn from Suzuki's *Essays in Zen Buddhism.*[236]

As mentioned, the suggestion that the reason for abandoning the Robartes–Aherne dialogues was not creative difficulties or problems with the framing fictions but because the instructors feared that they might identify with these characters underlines the closeness between the voices that spoke through George Yeats and the figures of W. B. Yeats's personal "phantasmagoria" of fictions (*VP* 821): both are dramatizations, names attached to certain words spoken that create the illusion of character. On the following page, Yeats continues exploring this theme in a different sense, stating how, "When I try to understand the means of communication I am struck by all it has in common with dreaming."[237] As in the published version of section XII, he recounts an incident of George's meaningless sleep-talking, which yet evinced "tricks in speach used by one or other of the philosophic voices," and, comparing the experience of the communications to a shared dream, he comments that "I feel that the 'spirits' would prefer such an explanation to one attributing all to themselves," which allows for the fact that the "spirits" can be allowed a preference and yet that dreaming is also a valid explanation.[238]

In further sentences dropped from the final version, he questions what benefit the communicators might derive from the intercourse, citing one answer that the spirit would have "'a short life', but what[*?=why*] that reward, if reward it can be called[,] for serving me."[239] Looking at the exchange from another angle, he notes that:

> One indeed ~~said~~ explained that I brought my questions & that though the answers came through them they were as startling ~~to them as much as~~ as greatly as they did me, but then seeing they have daimons of their own, are indeed being dead in a sense those daimons, why do they need my questions. The answer lies somewhere within the statement made in different forms, that all creation comes from the living.[240]

The idea that creation comes from the living is in fact a theme that Yeats had formulated in *Per Amica Silentia Lunae*, distinguishing the simplicity of the condition of fire, where selfhood is possessed in a single moment, from the heterogeneous complexity of earth, yet emphasizing that "All power is from the terrestrial condition" (*Myth* 356, *CW5* 25). And the dead, as he later explained in the introduction to *The Words upon the Window-pane*, "can create nothing, or, in the Indian phrase, can originate no new Karma. Their aim, like that of the ascetic in meditation, is to enter at last into their own archetype, or into all being: into that which is there always" (*VPl* 968–69, *CW2* 720, *Ex* 366). Increasingly, and certainly by the time he wrote these lines in 1931, Yeats came to identify that archetype, "that which is there always," with the *Daimon*.

Rapallo B closes with the first of many drafts in which Yeats sought to express his attitude towards the system of *A Vision* and how far he believed in it, the precursor of the Introduction's different final sections in *A Packet for Ezra Pound* and *A Vision B*. As the contents at the beginning of the notebook indicate, this draft is "continued in loose leaf book," yet the contours of the whole "Introduction" are already here. The nine sections would become fifteen, as the points were elaborated and illustrated further, but the introduction itself is already substantially formed and, whether Yeats yet saw this introduction being put together with "Rapallo in Spring" or not, the outlines of *A Packet for Ezra Pound* are clearly discernible.

There are at least five or six different versions of Yeats's statement of belief about *A Vision*, which vary and elaborate different aspects, and the version that appeared in *A Vision B* casts the coolest eye on the nature and possibility of belief.[241] This first outline is not necessarily the most committed, but it is the most inward-looking. Most of the later versions start with the phrase "Some will ask. . ." or a variation on it, focusing on what others will think, but this draft is a question of his own attitudes, as Yeats struggles to understand his own reluctance to speak of belief and the act or state of believing.

> IX
>
> Sometimes I have asked my self do I believe all this book, or only some part of it; ~~or do I believe different parts with different degrees~~ or do some parts of it seemed ~~ser~~ certain & some parts probably, & I always find my self loth to answer. ~~What I write in future, will~~ This book has filled my imagination for so many years, that I can never imagine myself ~~reading or xx~~ studying anything, without in some [*way*] relating it all incorporating it with what is here, & yet I do not want to answer because what ever else ~~it is~~ may be it is a dream. A single thought has expressed it it self as if it were a work of art, whether man or centaur, & I have tested each detail by its relation to the whole, each completed movement, by its reflection of the whole, ~~& though I am always conscious that there is a unity beyond that which I have found, a smokeless flame that I cannot reach~~, & the value of that single [*thought*], & therefore of the whole, lies in the daimon, which I can express but cannot judge.[242]

He acknowledges the time and commitment that the project has involved, and the impact it has had on his thinking, yet, as if discovering his feelings, he *finds* himself "loth to answer." Whatever else it "may be[,] it is a dream," shared with his wife and others and peopled by the *dramatis personae* of the spirits and fictions of their shared phantasmagoria. *A Vision* and its system has for Yeats the integrity of the numbers that multiply into the whole, the work of art not of science. The hybrid figure of the centaur may represent an impossible fusion, stand for mythic imagination, or symbolize wisdom,[243] but it has a unity born of integrity. Ultimately the work's value "lies in the daimon" and is therefore not a matter of believing but of being. The phrasing and expression of this declaration is perhaps too personal to be understood readily, and later versions remove both centaur and daimon, yet this is a fascinating glimpse of the personal ambiguity that Yeats grappled with. It is also an aspiration, for not only the poem but also the poet—"reborn as an idea, something intended, complete" (*E&I* 509, *CW5* 204)—aspires to the *daimonic* state, where the "flame is eternal. We attain it in the creation, or enjoyment of a work of art but the moment though eternal in the daimon passes from us, because it does not contain our whole being."[244]

The final work of art or system may be like a perfect number "where every thing is a part of everything, flows back as it were into the whole,"[245] aiming for the simplicity of fire, the smokeless flame, but the notebooks have much of the heterogeneity of the terrestrial, the "mound of refuse or the sweepings of a street" (*VP* 630), where opposites meet and there is choice, a fluidity of form. While Rapallo B may have a certain consistency of theme and purpose, the other notebooks do not even have that, but they all provide that essential creative meeting of things that are not already alike. The details are not related to the whole, because what form and order they may have are provided only by the physical form of the notebooks. That is, of course, what makes them unique.

Notes

1 Having arrived in Rapallo in February 1928, the Yeatses took a five-year lease on an apartment in via Americhe in March. They then spent the winters of 1928–29 and 1929–30 there, as well as time in April and June 1930. In their absence, the apartment was burgled in 1931, and they only returned to Rapallo in June 1934 to clear it out. See John S. Kelly, *A W. B. Yeats Chronology* [hereafter *ChronY*] (Basingstoke: Palgrave, 2003), 258–88, and *Life 2* 356–501.

2 See letter to George Yeats [hereafter GY], [August 17, 1928] (*CL InteLex* 5145; cf. *YGYL* 194), cited p. 83.

3 They measure 30 × 22 cm. (ca. 12 × 8.5 in.); the paper is unruled, unwatermarked, and about 20 lb. weight; see David R. Clark, ed., *'Words for Music Perhaps and Other Poems': Manuscript Materials* (Ithaca, NY: Cornell University Press, 1999), xvi–xvii. Uniform with Rapallo C and D is the notebook which W. B. Yeats [hereafter WBY] used to draft *Stories of Michael Robartes and His Friends* (National Library of Ireland [hereafter NLI], Dublin, MS 13,577); see Wayne K. Chapman, *W. B. Yeats's Robartes-Aherne Writings* (London:

Bloomsbury, 2018), 167ff. This notebook was further "mounted inside a heavy, ornately embossed, leather attaché cover with enlaced edges" (167).

4 Rapallo A (NLI 13,578) has a large "D" on the cover but an "A" on the first recto; Rapallo B (NLI 13,579) has "Finished Oct. 9. 1928" on the cover and "B" on the first recto; the cover of Rapallo C (NLI 13,580) is labeled "DIARY" and "Diary of Thought" is on the first recto; Rapallo D (NLI 13,581) has nothing on the cover and "Diary" on the first recto; Rapallo E (NLI 13,582) has a large letter "E" on the cover along with a cancelled three-line caption and no title on the first extant recto.

5 Neil Mann, "Yeats's Rapallo Notebooks," *YA22* (forthcoming 2022). I use a capitalized "Notebook" when it acts as the title of a particular book or books, as in "Rapallo Notebook A" and "the Rapallo Notebooks"; the lower-case "notebooks" is used where it is simply a descriptive term. However, the shortened forms of "Rapallo A," "Rapallo B," etc. are the main forms used to refer to the five notebooks in the essay for reasons of clarity and brevity.

6 As the presentation that follows shows, Rapallo B contains drafts that pre-date versions in Rapallo A. Rapallo A was originally labeled "D" on the outer cover in the same way that E is labeled (they are the only two with external letters). A large number of pages have been removed from the beginning of E, and the cancelled, barely legible caption on the cover bears no relation to its current contents.

7 *A Vision A* is dated 1925 but was actually released on January 15, 1926 (see Wade item 149, p. 152).

8 "Our most precious stone is thrown in the dung heap, most dear, cheap, and most vile," "Tractatus aureus," *Ars Chemica . . . Septem Tractatus seu Capitula Hermetis Trismegisti, aurei* ([Strasbourg]: [Emmel], 1566), 21.

9 The relevant volumes are: Clark, *"Words for Music Perhaps and Other Poems": Manuscript Materials*; Mary FitzGerald, ed., *"The Words Upon the Window-Pane": Manuscript Materials* (Ithaca, NY: Cornell University Press, 2002); and Jared Curtis and Selina Guinness, eds., *"The Resurrection": Manuscript Materials* (Ithaca, NY: Cornell University Press, 2011).

10 The Cornell volumes are inevitably selections of the manuscript material and the editorial approach varies across the series, so that some editors prioritize the process and the untaken roads, while others are more focused on the final versions. See Robin Gail Schulze, "The One and the Many: Reading the Cornell Yeats," ed. W. Speed Hill, *Text: An Interdisciplinary Annual of Textual Studies 10* (Ann Arbor: University of Michigan Press, 1997), 323–37.

11 There is one partial exception, in that a fair copy of "Byzantium" (now NLI 13,590 [17]) on two sheets of loose paper was kept at the back of Rapallo D and was photographed there for the Harvard microfilms, probably in the late 1940s; see Wayne Chapman, "Yeats's White Vellum Notebook, 1930–1933," *International Yeats Studies* [hereafter *IYS*] 2, no. 2 (2018): 58 n18.

12 These other sources include transcriptions by Richard Ellmann in *The Identity of Yeats* (1954; London: Faber and Faber, 1964), 239–40; David R. Clark, "Yeats: Cast-offs, Non-starters and Gnomic Illegibilities," in *Yeats: An Annual of Critical and Textual Studies* 17, 1–18; and Matthew Gibson, "Yeats's Notes on Leo Frobenius's *The Voice of Africa* (1913)," in *Yeats, Philosophy, and the Occult*, eds. Matthew Gibson and Neil Mann (Clemson, SC: Clemson University Press, 2016), 310–12. The Cornell manuscript series contains no material from Rapallo A and B, as they contain very little poetry or drama.

13 This leather-bound notebook is NLI 30,359.

14 WBY, *The Winding Stair* (New York: Fountain Press, 1929). See David R. Clark, ed., *'The Winding Stair' (1929): Manuscript Materials* [hereafter *WS29*] (Ithaca, NY: Cornell University Press, 1995). He proposes: "All drafts probably written between September 1927 . . . and March 13, 1928" (xviii); the starting date is suggested by WBY's letter to Olivia Shakespear of 2 October [1927] (*L* 728–29, *CL InteLex* 5034) explaining the arrangement

with Crosby Gaige (see *Life2* 350), and the end date is that of GY's letter (*WS29* xxv–xxvii) accompanying the typescript sent to New York (*WS29* xiii–xiv).

15 Leather notebook, NLI 30,359, [19r]. The sleeps are the version of "communication" from the instructors of *A Vision* that superseded automatic script in 1920. GY spoke in sleep or trance, while her husband listened, questioned, and noted the exchanges.

16 Leather notebook, NLI 30,359, [9v]. This sentence is inserted from the opposite verso; above "can" WBY has written "need" without cancelling the first. And the word transcribed as "put" may be "fit," but the form of the letter is closer to the surrounding p's than the f's.

17 Leather notebook, NLI 30,359, [10r].

18 The date comes on [30r]; as "First Things" takes up forty-one pages of large format paper (Rapallo B, NLI 13,579, [9v]–[30r]), it would likely have taken many days, and probably weeks, to draft.

19 Leather notebook, NLI 30,359, [19r]–[20r].

20 Rapallo B, NLI 13,579, [11r], page numbered 1. This appears in typescript form in NLI 36,272/11.

21 Rapallo A, NLI 13,578, [1v].

22 Typescript NLI 36,272/18 is based directly on Rapallo A, however, and it repeats Rapallo B's convoluted disclaimer largely intact. The typescript numbers the section quoted here "II"; this section precedes section "III" in the notebook.

23 Rapallo A, NLI 13,578, [39r], page numbered 2. The typescript NLI 36,272/18 corrects the Shakespearean quotation.

24 Another (probably later) manuscript draft explains the enigmatic quotation at least partially. See n87, below.

25 An even later typescript draft titled "Principal Symbols" telescopes this introduction, suppressing a useful connecting sentence: "All begins with what my instructors have called, probably taking the term from PER AMICA SILENTIA LUNAE the daimon. ~~Each Daimon is unique and perfect and has for its symbol the sphere.~~ One thinks of those words of Parmenides Plotinus has incorporated in his own system 'it is complete on every side equally poised from the entire in every direction like the mass of a rounded sphere' and of those of Empedocles 'so fast was the God in the close covering of harmony, spherical and round, rejoicing in his circular rest.'" It then gives a succinct description of the *Daimon*. (NLI 36,272/13, [1]).

26 Given WBY's handwriting, it is possible that "final version" could be read as "first version." It does not make sense in context, unless WBY made a mistake about priority (which might also explain the labeling of A and B on the fly-leaves), but the evidence points to Rapallo A's version coming after Rapallo B's "early version." It would, however, be dangerous to stake much on either reading.

27 Section V of Rapallo A ([12r] ff) is a direct redrafting of Section IV of Rapallo B ([61r] ff), clarifying and simplifying the earlier formulation. For example in Rapallo B, WBY writes: "Hitherto we we [sic] have had ~~two~~ three symbols of change ~~a double cone what I have called the double cone of Heraclitus~~ that of ~~the~~ a double cone, ~~when or where we can right [?subje] Antithetical at the one side Primary of the at the other,~~ that of the wheel formed from a double cone, & we can write Antithetical at one side Primary at the other of ~~both x~~ each. There ~~is a third symbol~~ are however two other symbols found from the ~~whel~~ wheel. . . across whose center we can write Primary or Antithetical. One is a figure like an hourglass. . . passes through centre of the wheel & joins Will & Mask representing Nature [. . . .] The other is a diamond shaped figure which passes through the centre of the wheel ~~& unites the~~ joins Creative Mind & the Body of Fate, ~~& represents xx the~~ all that is ~~the supernatural or spiritual.~~" (NLI 13,579, [61r–62r], pages numbered 8 and 9). In Rapallo A, this becomes: "~~Hitherto~~ we have ~~had three two three~~ four symbols of change, ~~that of~~ the

double cone, ~~that of~~ the wheel formed from the double cone {the two cones like an hour glass or like a diamond that cross the centre of the wheel uniting the Faculties to its centre [. . . .]}" (NLI 13,578, [12r], page numbered 8, and [11v]).

28 The date appears at the end of the draft of "Introduction," Rapallo B, NLI 13,579, [43r]. Some notes amending the printed text of *AVA* follow, and then the draft on the Great Year. There is no later date except the one that appears on the cover, "Finished Oct. 9, | 1928."

29 The reason for hesitancy in declaring it unambiguously the second notebook to be started is the label "D" on its cover, which may indicate lost notebooks.

30 WBY, *Uncollected Prose by W. B. Yeats*, vol. 2 [hereafter *UP2*] (New York: Columbia University Press, 1976), 477–85; cf. *CW10* 211–18.

31 *UP2* 485–86.

32 The diary kept in 1930, NLI 30,354, served as the basis for WBY, *Pages from a Diary Written in Nineteen Hundred and Thirty* (Dublin: Cuala, 1944).

33 The notebook has ninety-five leaves, counting nine removed leaves and twenty-three that are blank on both sides, so that sixty-three of them are used. Twenty-three leaves [4–26] are devoted to the Great Year and eleven leaves [39–49] to the new beginning of *A Vision*.

34 WBY was spurred on particularly by reading the early volumes of Pierre Duhem's *Le système du monde*, 10 vols. (Paris: Hermann, 1913–59); vols. 1–5 appeared between 1913 and 1917 and the remaining five volumes appeared posthumously between 1954 and 1959. Also important was WBY's discovery of Spengler and his further reading of Hegel. See "Editors' Introduction," in *CW14* xxvi–xxvii, and notes, 433 n59; Matthew Gibson, "'Timeless and Spaceless'?—Yeats's Search for Models of Interpretation in Post-Enlightenment Philosophy, Contemporary Anthropology and Art History, and the Effects of These Theories on 'The Completed Symbol,' 'The Soul in Judgment' and 'The Great Year of the Ancients,'" in Neil Mann, Matthew Gibson, and Clare Nally, eds., *W. B. Yeats's "A Vision": Explications and Contexts* [hereafter *YVEC*] (Clemson, SC: Clemson University Press, 2012); Matthew Gibson, "Yeats, the Great Year, and Pierre Duhem," in *Yeats, Philosophy, and the Occult*, eds. Matthew Gibson and Neil Mann (Clemson, SC: Clemson University Press, 2016), 171–224.

35 See *Life2* 373. His final appearance, without speaking, came a week later on July 25, 1928; *ChronY* 261.

36 See n79 and n109 below. These drafts take up twelve of the notebook's sixty-three written leaves: three leaves [31–33] and nine leaves [67–73, 75–76].

37 The draft occupies a single page, [77r].

38 These take up more than three leaves [63v–66r] and a fragment on [78r]. On August 12, 1928, WBY told Olivia Shakespear that he was going to Coole and had his "notes upon the new coinage to write" (*CL InteLex* 5142; *L* 746); on August 25, 1928, he was dictating part of the essay to Augusta Gregory at Coole (*ChronY* 262) and on August 26, had a "first draft of my coinage essay" (to GY, *CL InteLex* 5148; *YGYL* 196); and on August 28, he told his wife that he had finished the essay (*CL InteLex* 5150; *YGYL* 198).

39 These take up most of six leaves [58r–63r].

40 These come specifically between the material on "The Great Year" and the article on censorship and Thomas Aquinas (leaves [31–33]) and between that article and "First Things" for *A Vision* ([38v–49v]), with a single blank page also left at the beginning of the notebook, [3], between the Contents and notes on Plotinus and "The Great Year."

41 Sixteen blank leaves remain at the end of the notebook (80–95), with two more added during conservation.

42 The date comes from GY's covering letter, cited in *WS29* xxvi–xxvii; see n14 above.

43 The descriptions are divided into the book's natural sections, many of them indicated by Yeats's own list of contents. Descriptions taken from the contents are given in quotation marks; other supplied details are given in brackets.

44 The 1930 diary, NLI 30,354, [64r].

45 The "D" on the cover of Rapallo Notebook A (NLI 13,378) and the "E" on Rapallo E (NLI 13,582) are both drawn with multiple lines to create a thicker, wider capital letter.

46 See Mann, "The Rapallo Notebooks," (*YA22*) Two loose bifoliums associated with Rapallo E have an early draft for *The Resurrection* and also a brief line of personal material from the first month in Rapallo in 1928, though these pages could have come from another notebook.

47 The "new" ordering of the other three notebooks is roughly chronological, though Rapallo C and D have no explicit labels.

48 The missing page "1" of "First Things" (Rapallo A, NLI 13,578, leaf [38]) could indicate that the page numbering was done as Yeats wrote; however, if he was numbering later, he may well have omitted this number deliberately to remind himself of the missing material. Rapallo C and D have no page numbering by Yeats, while in Rapallo E only the *Vision* material and the draft of *The Resurrection* have numbered pages.

49 They had returned from Rapallo in mid-April; see *ChronY* 259. It is, however, also possible that he had made the notes earlier in Italy, traveling with the Plotinus; two years earlier, referring to an earlier volume of MacKenna's translation, he had written from Thoor Ballylee: "I have brought but two books Beadelaire, & Mackenna's Plotinus" (to Olivia Shakespear, May 25, [1926], *CL InteLex* 4871).

50 *Plotinus: The Divine Mind, Being the Treatises of the Fifth Ennead*, trans. Stephen MacKenna (London: Medici Society, 1926), 12.

51 Rapallo A, NLI 13,578, [5r], page numbered 2. Cf. "a Greatest Year for whale and gudgeon alike must exhaust the multiplication table" (Notes on *The Resurrection* [*VPl* 934, *CW2* 724]). The corresponding sentence in Rapallo B declares that "Aristotels Annus Maximus . . . is incalculable, because as Proclus thought we cannot reckon the life cycles of all living things, man, whale and gudgeon" (NLI 13,579, [73r], page numbered 20).

52 Rapallo A, NLI 13,578, [8r], page numbered 5. See below for the earlier treatment in Rapallo B, NLI 13,579, [53r–54r], including the image of Keats's Grecian Urn (see p. 128).

53 Jon Stallworthy, *Between the Lines: Yeats's Poetry in the Making* (Oxford: Oxford University Press, 1963), 9–10, emphasis in Stallworthy's original. See Mann, "Yeats's Rapallo Notebooks," (*YA22*).

54 Rapallo A, NLI 13,578, [14r], page numbered 10. The cones are presented in the form of the hourglass and diamond in most instances.

55 Rapallo A, NLI 13,578, [17r], page numbered 12.

56 Rapallo A, NLI 13,578, [19r], page numbered 14.

57 Rapallo A, NLI 13,578, [20r], page numbered 15. The serpent struggling with the eagle is an important symbol from Shelley's *The Revolt of Islam* (*Laon and Cythna*), Canto I. The figure of Demogorgon rising from earth in Shelley's *Prometheus Unbound* is used in connection with the *Thirteenth Cone* in *AVB*, Book II, Section XIV (*AVB* 211, *CW14* 155). WBY's use here of "immanent" (clearly written) in opposition to "transcendent" helps to confirm the correction that most commentators have felt warranted in *AVB* of substituting "immanent" for "imminent" when WBY contrasts "a *primary* dispensation looking beyond itself towards a transcendent power," with "an *antithetical* dispensation [which] obeys imminent power" (*AVB* 263, *CW14* 192); see Neil Mann, *A Reader's Guide to Yeats's 'A Vision'* [hereafter *ARGYV*] (Clemson, SC: Clemson University Press, 2019), 321 n16; 353 n12.

58 See *ARGYV* 169 and Neil Mann, "Plotinus and *A Vision*, Part II," in *The Widening Gyre* (March 1, 2020), yeatsvision.blogspot.com/2020/03/plotinus-and-vision-part-ii.html, addressing WBY's conflation of the hypostases and "Authentic Existants," an error from which several critics have tried to rescue him.

59 This diagram shows the solar diamond (associated with *Spirit* and *Celestial Body*), with two complete zodiacs running clockwise around the edge. Starting at the right-hand side at the top is the symbol for the first sign, Aries ♈, with the sixth and seventh signs, Virgo ♍ and Libra ♎, at the right-hand point, and the twelfth, Pisces ♓, at the base; the same sequence then ascends on the left-hand side from Aries to Pisces again.

60 Rapallo A, NLI 13,578, [21r], page numbered 16. Though omitting cancellations in general in this transcription, I leave one of the deleted phrases to show how the syntax originally worked.

61 Rapallo A, NLI 13,578, [22r], page numbered 17. Although cancelled text is omitted, one stricken phrase is included to make the remaining text comprehensible. I have not tried to reproduce the letters on the page exactly, as a number of words are even more gestural than is usual for WBY—"information as distinguished from knowledge" is actually closer to reading "ınfomalxn as dılıgxxd fxxx knowlxge," with "t's" uncrossed and "i's" undotted, and the "x" standing for an indeterminate character (see Figure 1).

62 The phrasing here may recall the closing song from *The Resurrection*—"Everything that man esteems / Endures a moment or a day. . . ." (*VPl* 931)—or the play's notes, in which WBY writes of "these souls, these eternal archetypes, coming into greater units as days into nights into months, months into years" (*VPl* 935). Also relevant are *AVB*'s observations that the "wheel is every completed movement of thought or life, twenty-eight incarnations, a single incarnation, a single judgment of act of thought" (*AVB* 81, *CW14* 60), and, "It is as though innumerable dials, some that recorded minutes alone, some seconds alone, some hours alone, some months alone, some years alone. . . ." (*AVB* 248, *CW14* 181).

63 Rapallo A, NLI 13,578, [22r–23r], pages numbered 17–18.

64 For the discovery, Pierre Duhem gives a date of 129 BCE in *Le système du monde* 2:182, though Emmeline Plunket, in *Ancient Calendars and Constellations* (London: John Murray, 1903), refers to the "Initial Point of the Grecian Zodiac fixed by Hipparchus at equinox 150 B.C." (Plate III, facing p. 40). Plunket's volume was in the Yeatses' library, see Wayne K. Chapman, *The W. B. and George Yeats Library: A Short Title Catalog* [hereafter *WBGYL*] (Clemson, SC: Clemson University Press, 2019), item 1608, and Edward O'Shea, *A Descriptive Catalog of W. B. Yeats's Library* [hereafter *YL*] (New York: Garland, 1985), item 1596. O'Shea records that WBY annotated a correction on this page, but WBY seems to have taken Plunket's date; he also appears to view Hipparchus's whole lifetime (c.190–c.120 BCE) in a more symbolic sense in the draft cited here. The precession of the equinoxes is a consequence of Earth's extremely slow wobble, whereby the sun's position at the year's two equinoxes drifts backwards in relation to the constellations, going through a complete circle of the zodiac in some 26,000 years. At the vernal equinox the sun was located in the constellation of Aries in Hipparchus's day, but is in Pisces in our day—yet the equinoctial point retains the name "The First Point of Aries" (WBY's "0° of Aries") despite the drift.

65 Rapallo A, NLI 13,578, [23r], page numbered 18, and [22v]. One cancelled word is included as the anchor for WBY's footnote, and the first sentence of the footnote is moved from its position in the text to the note, as indicated by WBY's balloon and arrow. WBY appears to confuse polygons and polyhedra. Plutarch, in "The Platonic Questions," speculates that Plato related the solid "dodecahedron to the globe," as, like "globes made of twelve skins, it becomes circular and comprehensive" and, by the subdivision of its faces, "it seems to resemble both the Zodiac and the year, it being divided into the same number of parts as these"; *Plutarch's Morals*, 5 vols., ed. W. W. Goodwin (Boston: Little, Brown, 1878), 5:433. Like WBY, A. E. Taylor commented on Plutarch's mistake, which was to see "a circular band" rather than the "twelve angular points" of the solid, in Taylor, *A Commentary on Plato's 'Timaeus'* (Oxford: Clarendon Press, 1928; *WBGYL* 2121, *YL* 2107), 377. According

to the half-title page, WBY's copy of Taylor's commentary was "Read Sept 1929 etc," so WBY either knew the objection already, or he came back to make the note later.

66 Claudius Ptolemy (c. 90–168 CE) had sought to establish a rational Aristotelian basis for astrology, with a chain of cause and effect working through the inflow of stellar "influence"; Plotinus (c. 204–270 CE) argued against this, stating that the stars were signs not causes in *Ennead* 2:3 "Are the stars causes"; see Stephen MacKenna's translation, *Plotinus*, vol. 2 (London: P. L. Warner, 1921; *WBGYL* 1602; *YL* 1590), 159–77. WBY's treatment here also prefigures some of the aphorisms in "Astrology and the Nature of Reality" in Rapallo D (later called Six or Seven Propositions); see Neil Mann, "Seven Propositions," (revised September 2008, corrections April 2009), www.yeatsvision.com/7Propositions.html.

67 Wyndham Lewis, *Time and Western Man* (London: Chatto and Windus, 1927; *WBGYL* 1136, *YL* 1126). See *CW14* 430–31, n43; see also Katherine Ebury, "'A new science': Yeats's *A Vision* and Relativistic Cosmology," *Irish Studies Review* 22, no. 2 (2014): 167–183; 170.

68 Rapallo A, NLI 13,578, [24r], page numbered 19. WBY had contrasted the Buddha and the Sphinx in "The Double Vision of Michael Robartes" but was told that he "should have put Christ instead of Buddha, for according to my instructors Buddha was a Jupiter-Saturn influence" (*AVB* 208, *CW14* 153); i.e., Buddha was *antithetical*, like the Sphinx.

69 The passage leaves a question mark and blank in front of "Daishi," indicating that WBY partially remembered and partially forgot Kobo Daishi, the title given posthumously to Kukai (774–835); see *E&I* 236 (*CW4* 173 adopts a mispunctuation from *Essays* [1924] that originates in the Cuala volume, putting a comma between Kobo and Daishi). The passage contrasts Kobo-Daishi with the eighth-century Indian teacher Sankara (Adi Shankaracharya), whose works are the foundation of Advaita Vedanta in Hinduism, and the third-century Neoplatonist Plotinus, whose works influenced both Christian theology and pagan philosophy.

70 The material about the differing lengths of *primary* and *antithetical* dispensations is used in modified form in *AVB*, Book II, Section XII (*AVB* 208, *CW14* 153–54).

71 Rapallo A, NLI 13,578, [24r–25r], pages numbered 20–21. *Reading text*: "They tell me that the primary revelation comes soon after the opening of the year, & the antithetical considerably before its close & that East & West are Primary & Antithetical respectively, each one dying the others life living the others death. I do not know [why] the Primary revelation should not begin its year but imag[in]e that the antithetical comes before its close, though it is the inspiration of its successor because out of human intellect & not from beyond it & so needs a mature tradition. As antithetical Europe at the end of an antithetical year [?approached] *primary* revelation, primary Asia, at the end of a primary year brought forth antithetical revelation in Buddha. Christ speaks to & is born of the *primary* masses, but Buddha is a kings son & speaks to kings, & Buddhism grows by its effect upon kings courts.

"Nothing for the common man, no god no consoling heaven. Men dispute as to whether it [?grants] of any punishment but life any reward but extinxion. Having taken from the sculptor of Alexander the high bred face of a god it moulded from it the symbol of a solitude more terrible than that of Oedipus.

"When Christianity lost its first character when eclesiastic[s] became princes, but Buddhism as Buddha sank down into Primary Asia, the abstraction of the Vedas, that something that seems to disolve all form away coarsed [=*coursed?*] into Indian sculpture, gave it vague pleasant faces & a multitude of arms. In Japan & China alone could Buddhism prolong its Antithetical nobility, for there it was joined to the common belief by great works of art where once can study the primary soul in its antithetical moment. Their style defining a theme rather than a personality passes on, in the same family from generation to generation, or is taken up or laid down when the narrative selects a new theme, & it is above all an art of landscape, great nameless mountains, cattaracts falling through cloud into cloud an old saint climbing to some mountain shrine, & all caught up into a powerful rythm, that unlike the rythms of European art, carries us beyond its scene that we may share the contemplation of Buddha.

"Buddha in isolation seems to contradict a logic that affirms the multiplicity of antitethical inspiration, but that isolation may be a historical accident, and the devine event that whole illumination, which began at or a little before the time of Pythagoras ran parallel to that of Greek philosophy for centuries & hardly survived it."

72 Laurence Binyon, "Some Phases of Religious Art in Eastern Asia," *The Quest* 2, no. 4 (1911); the four quotations are found on pages 657, 662, 662 (again), and 666, respectively. The essay mentions Kobo Daishi and a painting of him as a child, which is generally regarded as anonymous but, in *Painting in the Far East*, 2nd ed., (London: Edward Arnold, 1913; *WBGYL* 201; *YL* 194), Binyon attributes it to Nobuzane, and WBY repeated this in "Certain Noble Plays of Japan" (*E&I* 236, *CW4* 173). See Louise Blakeney Williams, *Modernism and the Ideology of History: Literature, Politics, and the Past* (Cambridge: Cambridge University Press, 2002), especially chapter six, "'Our own image': the example of Asian and non-Western cultures."

73 WBY potentially saw them as comparable to fifth-century Athens (Buddha and Confucius were also active in this century) and the period from Justinian's Byzantium (in which Chan Buddhism developed in sixth-century China and moved to Japan as Zen) to Charlemagne, whose dates (748–814) make him a little older than Kobo Daishi (774–835).

74 Rapallo A, NLI 13,578, [25r]. On Sankara and Plotinus, see n69.

75 There is no point in the drafts where WBY is obviously restarting after a considerable break.

76 See *Life2* 373. His final appearance, without speaking, came a week later on July 25, 1928; *ChronY* 261.

77 See www.oireachtas.ie/en/debates/debate/dail/1928-07-19/16/ (accessed July 2019). The bill reached its Second Stage and was debated in October 1928. It was enacted on July 16, 1929; see www.oireachtas.ie/en/bills/bill/1928/41/ . This is explored extensively in Warwick Gould, "'Satan Smut & Co': Yeats and the Suppression of Evil Literature in the Early Years of the Free State," *YA21* (2018), 123–212, which focuses particularly on "The Cherry-Tree Carol," dealt with in WBY's second essay.

78 WBY was interviewed for the *Manchester Guardian* by the paper's Irish Correspondent, and "Censorship in Ireland. The Free State Bill. Senator W. B. Yeats's Views" appeared on August 22, 1928 (p. 5); see Appendix to Gould, "'Satan Smut & Co.,'" 203–05. The next day, in rejoinder, the *Irish Independent* published "Censorship: Mr Yeats's Peculiar Views" (August 23, 1928), 5.

79 WBY, "The Censorship and St. Thomas Aquinas," *Irish Statesman* (September 22, 1928), 47–48 (*CW10* 211–13, *UP2* 477–80). There are two typescript versions in NLI: NLI 30,170 and another typescript, NLI 30,867, dated September 1928.

80 Rapallo A, NLI 13,578, [32r], unnumbered page; cf. "the Platonizing theology of Byzantium," *CW10* 212.

81 *CW10* 212, *UP2* 478. The draft does not include this text as it gives: "Cardinal Mercier writing in his 'Manual of Modern Scholastic philosophy,['] vol I; page 314, English Edition | ' (quote marked passage) [']"; Rapallo A, NLI 13,578 [31r], page numbered 1. The volume is in the Yeatses' library (*WBGYL* 1318, *YL* 1305), with the passage marked as indicated.

82 Rapallo A, NLI 13,578, [32r], unnumbered page. Cf. *CW10* 212, *UP2* 479.

83 Rapallo A, NLI 13,578, [33r], page numbered 2, and [32v].

84 WBY, "The Irish Censorship," *The Spectator* (September 29, 1928), 391–92 (*CW10* 214–18, *UP2* 480–85).

85 On the loose pages, see n99. The cancelled and unfinished paragraph on [37v] appears to relate to the formulation of "being a symbolist <dramatist> ~~& know no philosopher~~ <~~logician~~> <not a dialectician>" on [39r]. The sentences on [37v] read: "In obedience to their will I remain a dramatist and if I define a thing my definition is summary and casual as in a list of a dramatis personae. I wish it to unfold itself as the actor unfolding, & no more expect, & seeing that . . ." where it breaks off (this transcription ignores earlier cancellations, which repeat the same material).

86 Rapallo A, NLI 13,578, [39r], page numbered 2, and Rapallo B, NLI 13,579, [11r], page numbered 1. The spelling of "know" for "no" may indicate that someone—perhaps GY?—was dictating from the earlier draft.

87 Rapallo A, NLI 13,578, [39r], page numbered 2, and Rapallo B, NLI 13,579, [11r], page numbered 1. Later drafts correct the quotation to "Have you had a quiet guard?" (*Hamlet* I:1). Its application is rather enigmatic, but partly explained in a stray sheet of loose-leaf manuscript developing this draft: "I accept his [*the instructor's*] thought, & being a symbolist & dramatist not a dialectician, apply to the daimon ~~the words~~ Parmenides description of the universe. 'It is complete on every side, equally poised from the centre in every direction like the mass of a rounded sphere'[.] But as ~~he~~ Parmenides ~~applies the~~ means some kind of philosophical object & I some kind of a ghost add the opening words 'Have you had quiet guard? Not a mouse stirring'" (NLI 36,272/3). Its significance seems personal, probably alluding to the time he spent on watch or waiting for GY's "Sleeps" to start.

88 Rapallo B, NLI 13,579, [15v], and Rapallo A, NLI 13,578, [39r].

89 Rapallo A, NLI 13,578, [39r] and [42r], pages numbered 2 and 5; and Rapallo B, NLI 13,579, [15v] and [16r] unnumbered verso and page numbered 3. A line or two earlier on in Rapallo B, NLI 13,579, [16r], WBY had cancelled a more correctly spelled "~~Guido Cal Cavilanti~~."

90 Rapallo A, NLI 13,578, [47r–48r], pages numbered 10–11. The manuscript has been interpreted with the help of a typescript, probably dictated from this draft (NLI MS 36/272/18/1, page numbered 13, section IX).

91 The dictated typescript (see previous note) has the correct title. Andrew Parkin observes that the connection of the play to its title is not immediately obvious and had baffled "that doggedly faithful Dublin playgoer, Joseph Holloway: 'What the name given to the piece had to do with it, I could not fathom,'" in *"At the Hawk's Well" and "The Cat and the Moon": Manuscript Materials* (Ithaca, NY: Cornell University Press, 2010), xlvii. The poem "The Cat and the Moon" follows "The Phases of the Moon" in WBY, *The Wild Swans at Coole* (London: Macmillan, 1919), but was first published in *Nine Poems* (privately printed by Clement Shorter, 1918).

92 See A. Norman Jeffares and A. S. Knowland, *A Commentary on the Collected Plays of W. B. Yeats* (London: Macmillan, 1975), 172. Parkin gives the full reasoning behind this dating in *"At the Hawk's Well" and "The Cat and the Moon": Manuscript Materials*, xlix.

93 In these Rapallo notebooks, all of WBY's presentation was expressed in terms of the *Principles*, but in *AVB* these descriptions are applied to the counterpart *Faculties* (*Husk–Will*; *Passionate Body–Mask*; *Spirit–Creative Mind*; *Celestial Body–Body of Fate*): "It will be enough until I have explained the geometrical diagrams in detail to describe *Will* and *Mask* as the will and its object, or the Is and the Ought (or that which should be), *Creative Mind* and *Body of Fate* as thought and its object, or the Knower and the Known, and to say that the first two are lunar or *antithetical* or natural, the second two solar or *primary* or reasonable"; *AVB* 73, *CW14* 54.

94 The Lame Beggar's cure is far more clearly indicated in the revised version of 1934, apparently written in 1930 or 1931; see *"At the Hawk's Well" and "The Cat and the Moon": Manuscript Materials*, 241ff.

95 For an examination of how "A Dialogue of Self and Soul" draws on the categories and thinking of *A Vision*, see Neil Mann, "Yeats's Visionary Poetics" in Matthew Campbell and Lauren Arrington, eds., *Oxford Handbook of W. B. Yeats* (Oxford: Oxford University Press, forthcoming).

96 Rapallo A, NLI 13,578, [49r], page numbered 12.

97 "The Withering of the Boughs" dates from 1900; *VP* 203–04.

98 Rapallo A, NLI 13,578, [48v] and [49v], section X. *AVA* had made the connection (*AVA* 164, *CW13* 133), but it was developed in *AVB* (*AVB* 212, cf. *CW14* 156).

99 The Harvard microfilm appears to indicate that seven leaves of "First Things," numbered 2–8 [39–45], were loose, as were [74], the leaf with Indian kalpas on it, and [75], the penultimate page of the *Spectator* article draft, numbered 9. Together with the missing leaf [38], these total ten leaves, but the paper anchors used in restoration appear to number eight (my thanks to Jack Quin for checking this in a time of COVID-19 restrictions). I have chosen the lower number as more clearly verifiable, but recognize that the counting of phantom leaves is somewhat arbitrary, especially as we are uncertain how many leaves each notebook originally contained.

100 Curtis Bradford, *The Writing of "The Player Queen"* (DeKalb: Northern Illinois University Press, 1977), 447–51.

101 Bradford, *The Writing of "The Player Queen,"* 447; see WBY's letter to GY of [May 23, 1927], *CL InteLex* 4999.

102 The play opened on September 24, 1928, for seven nights, and was directed by Lennox Robinson, with Sara Allgood as Nona and Arthur Shields as Septimus; see the Abbey Theatre website, www.abbeytheatre.ie/archives/production_detail/3227/, accessed March 2020. Various ballets were performed alongside *The Player Queen*; see www.abbeytheatre.ie/archives/production_detail/8363/, accessed March 2020.

103 This is the letter, written shortly after arriving at Coole, in which WBY apologized to GY for making her search for notes on Plotinus in the wrong notebook; it is possible that he stumbled on the notes when he reached for Rapallo A to sketch out the revisions.

104 Bradford, *The Writing of "The Player Queen,"* 447.

105 Wade item 137; the second impression (1928) had some variations of pagination, but these do not affect *The Player Queen*. There were two copies in the Yeatses' library, the first with the notes and music torn out (*WBGYL* 2425; *YL* 2399) and the second from a limited edition of 250 (*WBGYL* 2425a; *YL* 2399A).

106 Rapallo A, NLI 13,578, [64r], page numbered 1, and [66r], numbered 3.

107 Rapallo A, NLI 13,578, [65r–66r], cf. section V of the final version, *CW6* 168–69.

108 WBY, "The Irish Censorship," *CW10* 214–18, *UP2* 480–85.

109 There are three typescripts in NLI 30,105, and a fourth in NLI 30,116.

110 See *English Folk-Carols*, collected by Cecil J. Sharp (London: Novello, 1911), 8 (first version). Gould, "'Satan Smut & Co.'" reproduces the center spread of the carol in *Pears' Annual* 1925, illustrated by Richard Kennedy North (127). The carol draws on chapter twenty of the apocryphal *Infancy Gospel of Matthew*, popular in the Middle Ages, where Joseph chides Mary for pining for dates, but the infant Jesus makes the tree bow.

111 Rapallo A, NLI 13,578, [67r], cancelled, numbered 1, and *CW10* 214.

112 Rapallo A, NLI 13,578, [71r], numbered 6, and *CW10* 215.

113 Rapallo A, NLI 13,578, [72r] and *CW10* 216.

114 Hermann Jacobi, "Ages of the World (Indian)," in *Encyclopaedia of Religion and Ethics*, ed. James Hastings (Edinburgh: T. & T. Clark, New York: Charles Scribner's Sons, 1908), vol.1: 200-01. Jacobi's article is referred to in notes on the same topic in NLI 13,581 [10r–12v], along with Sepharial's book, *Hebrew Astrology* ([6v] ff.).

115 Cited *UP2* 485.

116 Rapallo A, NLI 13,578, [77r], cf. *UP2* 486, *CL InteLex* 5176.
117 See *CW6* 297 n10.
118 The 1930 diary, NLI 30,354, [63v]. WBY, *Pages from a Diary Written in 1930* (Dublin: Cuala, 1944), reprinted in *Explorations* (London: Macmillan, 1962).
119 The 1930 diary, NLI 30,354, [64r].
120 The 1930 diary, NLI 30,354, inside back cover [65r].
121 Rapallo A, NLI 13,578, [79r], with cancellations omitted; cf. *Ex* 338–39.
122 Rapallo A, NLI 13,578, [79r]. The entry for November 16 was also omitted, passing directly to November 18; see Mann, *ARGYV* 298–99.
123 Rapallo C, NLI 13,580, [1r].
124 See Mann, "The Rapallo Notebooks."
125 Samuel Taylor Coleridge, in his *Table Talk* of July 12, [1827]; the edition in WBY's library is Coleridge, *Table Talk, and the Rime of the Ancient Mariner* (London: Routledge, 1884; *WBGYL* 417, *YL* 406), 63.
126 A formerly loose double bifolium, bound in what is now Rapallo E, contains some material that could be as early, or even earlier, but its original source is unclear.
127 *WS29* xxvi.
128 *WS29* xxvi–xxvii.
129 Letter of [17 August 1928], *CL InteLex* 5145; cf. *YGYL* 194. The same letter refers to a "leather bound book I put you looking for," which could have been NLI MS 30,359.
130 The reference to Lennox Robinson's *A Little Anthology of Modern Irish Verse* (Dublin: Cuala Press, 1928) shows that the book was conceived with the Cuala Press in mind.
131 George Berkeley, *Siris: A Chain of Philosophical Reflexions and Enquiries Concerning the Virtues of Tar Water, and Divers Other Subjects Connected Together and Arising One from Another* (London: C. Hitch; C. Davis, 1744; Dublin: R. Gunne, 1744).
132 This was repeated some weeks later: the "essay . . . . takes a poem of Guido Cavalcanti's for text & discusses the latest movements in contemporary literature"; WBY to Augusta Gregory, April 1, [1928], *CL InteLex* 5097; *L* 739.
133 Rapallo B, NLI 13,379, [15r].
134 See Catherine E. Paul, "Compiling *A Packet For Ezra Pound*," *Paideuma* 38 (2011), 29–53, for everything touching *A Packet for Ezra Pound*. In a note on WBY's letter of April 1, 1928 to Lady Gregory, Allan Wade claims that "Yeats wrote [the essay] and then destroyed it, finding it, he said difficult to make clear or even readable" (*L* 739n). Whether Wade was relying on personal information from WBY or upon letters he did not publish, the situation that emerges in the letters appears a little more complex. Writing from Coole on August 26, 1928, WBY told Ezra Pound, "I came down here some ten days ago to complete that essay begun in Rapallo on you and your work. I toiled away at it and then . . . I got suddenly the thought I wanted. I went at it again and all was going beautifully until George sent me your Cavalcanti translation which I hadnt looked at since I left Rapallo. I read it and it was almost clear to me, but the meaning I found had no relation at that time. I dare not risk it without a whole apparatus of learning, for they would either accuse you of bad translation, or me of bad scholarship. If I am to use my essay about you I must use it without the Cavalcanti which uninterpreted would be without meaning to the Cuala readers and interpreted would get me out of my depth at the best" (*CL InteLex* 5147). A month later, he seems to imply that Pound's translation, with its deliberate archaisms, was not direct enough for him to use: "I worked hard until I found myself plunging into solutions that seemed impossible for the period, & realised that as I could not read the Italian & even if I could lacked historical knowledge, nobody would accept me as interpreter. On the other hand your verse translation is far from explaining itself, & people would want to know why what they regarded as a work of art — verse translations are always so regarded — was

not sufficient to itself. I wish you could make yourself do another & purely conjectural version which was clear. I would delight to comment upon it in this strain 'Whether this is Cavalcanti or not I neither know nor care — it is Ezra & that is enough for me.' I would then go on, all out of my own head & without compromising you in any way, & say that it was your religion, your philosophy, your creed, your collect, your nightly & morning & prayers, & that with it F and Buckler you faced a Neo-thomist, Wyndam-Lewis, Golden Treasury World in Arms"; September 23, [1928], *CL InteLex* 5161. Pound did not rise to the bait.

135 Rapallo B, NLI 13,579, [87r]; see also *AVB* 8, *CW14* 7.

136 *Reveries over Childhood and Youth* (London: Macmillan, 1916), *Per Amica Silentia Lunae* (London: Macmillan, 1918), and *The Trembling of the Veil* (London: T. Werner Laurie, 1922).

137 "I wrote this book in my first excitement [. . .] & leave it unchanged except for a few passages crossed out because their matter is somewhere in book I & three or four sentences added to sharpen a definition or correct an error" ([41r], p. 126, n196); "the section 'Dove or Swan'—repeated in this book without alteration" ([96v], p. 139, n233); cf. [71r], page numbered 18, n214); and the changes proposed for pages 12–14 of *AVA* ([43v–44r], p. 127).

138 Rapallo B, NLI 13,579, [102v], see p. 141, n242.

139 *CL InteLex* reads "the Senate of this country" (which would imply Italy); though WBY's handwriting may well suggest "this," the reading in Wade's *Letters*, "the Senate of his country" (the United States), makes more sense and agrees with the published version, "Do not be elected to the Senate of your country," in WBY, *A Packet for Ezra Pound* [hereafter *PEP*] (Dublin: Cuala, 1929), 33.

140 See Paul, "Compiling *A Packet For Ezra Pound*."

141 Berkeley, *Siris*; the work passed through some six editions in just six months in 1744. The word σειρίς "*siris*" is a diminutive or variant of "*sira*," meaning cord or chain, and Berkeley notes it is applied to the Nile; see A. A. Luce, "The Original Title and the First Edition of 'Siris,'" *Hermathena* 84 (1954): 45–58; 52.

142 *AVB* 4, *CW14* 4; cf. *PEP* 2.

143 Frans Pourbus the Younger was the last of three generations of painters surnamed Pourbus or Porbus, the spelling favored by Balzac and used in the translation owned by WBY; Honoré de Balzac, *The Unknown Masterpiece (Le Chef d'oeuvre inconnu) and Other Stories*, trans. Ellen Marriage, vol. 37 in the Temple edition of the *Comédie humaine* (40 vols.), ed. George Saintsbury (New York: Macmillan, 1901; *WBGYL* 109, *YL* 109).

144 Paul Cezanne's surname did not have an acute accent in his native Provence, though Parisian orthodoxy added one, which was customarily used through most of the twentieth century. The Société Paul Cezanne and surviving family, however, advocate the Provençal spelling; see Anna Brady, "Drop the accent? Cézanne's acute dilemma," *The Art Newspaper* [London and New York] (January 9, 2020), www.theartnewspaper.com/news/drop-the-accent-cezanne-s-acute-dilemma. While WBY's publishers tend to give the accent, his own manuscripts omit it (albeit probably through inattention), so the unaccented spelling is used here.

145 Balzac, *The Unknown Masterpiece*, 7.

146 Rapallo B, NLI 13,579, [2v] and [3r], page numbered 2. In the text on page 3r is written in pencil, there are a few cancellations in ink in the last lines (double strikethrough here), and two vertical ink strokes cancelling all four last lines (single strikethrough here), to be substituted by the text from the opposing page.

147 Rapallo B, NLI 13,579, [7r]. This is just the uncancelled text, omitting several sentences relating Balzac to Keats, Tennyson, and Hallam; see below.

148 Balzac, *The Unknown Masterpiece*, 29–30.

149 Balzac, *The Unknown Masterpiece*, 30.

150 Balzac, *The Unknown Masterpiece*, 31.

151 Émile Bernard visited Cezanne in 1904: "One evening, when I was talking to him about the *Chef-d'œuvre inconnu* and Frenhofer, the hero of Balzac's drama, he rose from the table, stood up in front of me, and, striking his chest with his index finger, pointing to himself without a word, but repeating this gesture, indicated in a self-accusatory manner that he was that very character from the story" (my translation); Bernard, "Souvenirs sur Paul Cézanne et lettres inédites," *Mercure de France*, 69 no. 247 (October 1, 1907), 403, https://gallica.bnf.fr/ark:/12148/bpt6k105566f/f19.item. As reshaped by Joachim Gasquet, this anecdote took the form that became more current: "Frenhofer, he declared one day with a silent gesture, pointing a finger at his own chest, while the *Chef-d'œuvre inconnu* was being discussed, Frenhofer is me" (my translation); Gasquet, *Cézanne* (Paris: éditions Bernheim-Jeune, 1921), 42–43, https://gallica.bnf.fr/ark:/12148/bpt6k1521407h/f83.item. The French, "*Frenhofer, c'est moi*," recalls Gustave Flaubert's statement "*Madame Bovary, c'est moi*," but with very different implications. Both articles, with the questionnaire, "Mes Confidences," are collected in P. M. Doran, *Conversations avec Cézanne* (Paris: Macula, 1978). For full consideration of the theme, see Bernard Vouilloux, "«Frenhofer, c'est moi»: Postérité cézannienne du récit balzacien," in *Tableaux d'auteurs: Après l'*Ut pictura poesis (Saint Denis: Presses universitaires de Vincennes: 2004), https://books.openedition.org/puv/6183. See also Dore Ashton, *A Fable of Modern Art* (Berkeley: University of California Press, 1991), especially chapter two, "Cézanne in the shadow of Frenhofer," http://ark.cdlib.org/ark:/13030/ft8779p1x3/ .

152 Bernard contrasts Balzac's Frenhofer with Claude Lantier, a painter based on Cezanne in Émile Zola's *L'Œuvre* (Paris: G. Charpentier, 1886): "Oh—there is a huge distance between this Frenhofer, impotent through genius, and this Claude, impotent by nature, that Zola unfortunately saw in [Cezanne]!" (my translation); Bernard, "Souvenirs sur Paul Cézanne," 403.

153 Aspects of this material echo what WBY had written on Hallam, Tennyson, and the Romantics in his 1913 essay "Art and Ideas," especially section II (*E&I* 346–55, *CW4* 250–56).

154 Rapallo B, NLI 13,579, [6r].

155 The material in *AVA* dealing with contemporary art and the near future (*AVA* 210–15; *CW13* 174–78) was not used in *AVB*, and WBY had projected another ending, rather more focused on politics and society, which was never used; a relatively final version dated "September 1932" is given in *CW14*'s Appendix II, 293–98. The artists mentioned in *AVA* had included Lewis, Pound, and Joyce, taken up in these drafts.

156 It first appeared in 1831 in a periodical, *L'Artiste*, in two parts, before being published in book form later that year. Influenced by Théophile Gautier, it was heavily revised for inclusion in Balzac's *Études philosophiques* (1837), gaining more detail and artistic theorizing, and it was incorporated into the grand scheme of *La Comédie humaine* in 1845. A further version with a minor variations appeared in 1847 in *Le Provincial à Paris* (vol. 2), while Balzac's personal copy of the story in *La Comédie humaine* has corrections. See René Guise, introduction to Balzac, *Le Chef-d'œuvre inconnu*, in *La Comédie humaine*, vol. 10, Pléiade edition ([Paris]: Gallimard, 1979), 399 ff.; see also Ashton, *A Fable of Modern Art*, chapter one. WBY would have known the version published in *La Comédie humaine* in Ellen Marriage's translation, which bears the date 1845 (*The Unknown Masterpiece*, 1).

157 Rapallo A, NLI 13,578, [5r–6r].

158 *AVB* 4, *CW14* 4; cf. *PEP* 2.

159 Balzac, *The Unknown Masterpiece*, 16.

160 *AVB* 5, *CW14* 5; cf. *PEP* 4.

161 Balzac, *The Unknown Masterpiece*, 30.

162 Balzac, *The Unknown Masterpiece*, 12, 16.
163 Balzac, *The Unknown Masterpiece*, 31.
164 *PEP* 33, *AVB* 26, *CW14* 19.
165 Catherine E. Paul, "A Vision of Ezra Pound," in *YVEC*, 263. Pound could have retorted that WBY was never elected.
166 Rapallo B, NLI 13,579, [102v]. See n138 and n242.
167 Leather notebook, NLI 30,359.
168 Rapallo B, NLI 30,359, [9v]. This sentence is inserted into [10r] from the opposite verso. See above, p. 76.
169 Rapallo B, NLI 13,579, [11r], page numbered 1.
170 See Daisetz Suzuki, *Essays in Zen Buddhism*, first series (London: Luzac, 1927; *WBGYL* 2045; *YL* 2033), 230, 242n. The metaphor of lightning actually comes from the *Kena Upanishad* (IV:29), while "Chōkei (Chang-ching, died 932)" was the author of the short poem: "'How deluded I was! How deluded indeed! / Lift up the screen and come see the world! / 'What religion believest thou?' you ask. / I raise my hossu and hit your mouth" (233–34). The author is given as his master, Seppo (822–908), in the original article *The Eastern Buddhist* 1, no. 3 (Sep.-Oct. 1921), 213, https://archive.org/details/in.ernet.dli.2015.283162/page/n223/mode/2up.
171 Rapallo C, NLI 13,580, [6r], dated "Jan 1929," cited by Ellmann, *The Identity of Yeats*, 239.
172 St John Chrysostom, *On the Incomprehensible Nature of God*, Homily II, §17, in *The Fathers of the Church*, vol. 72, trans. Paul W. Harkins (Washington, DC: Catholic University of America Press, 1984), 77. There are several nineteenth-century sources from which WBY might have gleaned the saying, though none is more obvious than another.
173 Rapallo B, NLI 13,579, [10v].
174 See *ARGYV* 32–34.
175 Rapallo B, NLI 13,579, [15v].
176 For a summary of the four versions of the propositions, see Mann, "Seven Propositions." Concerning the Seven Propositions, see *ARGYV* 81–84 and 323 n5. See also Neil Mann, "'Everywhere that antinomy of the One and the Many': The Foundations of *A Vision*," *YVEC* 8–9 and Margaret Mills Harper, "Words for Music? Perhaps," *IYS* 1 no. 1 (2017), 3–5.
177 Rapallo B, NLI 13,579, [16v]–[17v].
178 See Rapallo B, NLI 13,579, [40r–41r], numbered 4 and 5 (p. 126, n196) and [100r–101r], numbered 10 and 11 (p. 139–40, n234).
179 See *ARGYV* 94.
180 Rapallo B, NLI 13,579, [17r], page numbered 6.
181 Rapallo B, NLI 13,579, [30r–31r], pages numbered 11 and 12. Cf. "It was a Greco-Roman phantasy that at a point in the Zodiac where it was crossed by the Milky Way the vortex changed into a sphere, and when man and woman turn from domination and surrender to love their vortex becomes a sphere, the union of spirit and celestial body fed by that of the faculties, and all things are at an end. Because the two passive faculties are the reflection of the two active principles Guido Cavalcanti is justified in finding in the beloved his body of science, and every lover of a beautiful woman in that form drawn as with a diamond, the symbol or image of his undiscovered wisdom." NLI MS 36,272/18/4(f), pages 24–25.
182 Rapallo B, NLI 13,579, [32r–33r], pages numbered 13 and 14, and [32v]. Most cancelled text is omitted, except for two instances that are included for clarity. The last paragraph's opposition to the cone of the month or year alludes to the opposition of the *Thirteenth Cone* explained in *AVB* 209–10, *CW14* 154–55.
183 The destruction of the world by conflagration when the planets are all in Cancer and by deluge when they are in Capricorn goes back to some of the earliest astrological writings, the *Babyloniaca* of Berossus (fl. 280 BCE); see Duhem, *Le système du monde*, vol. 1, 70, 276.

Stanley Mayer Burstein, *The Babyloniaca of Berossus*, Sources from the Ancient Near East, vol. 1, fasc. 5 (Malibu, CA: Undena, 1978), 15.

184 Coventry Patmore, "The Precursor," in *Religio Poetæ* (London: George Bell, 1898; *WBGYL* 1553, *YL* 1542), 17, refers to Renaissance painters only to point out that John the Baptist is paired with John "the Divine." Walter Pater comments on "the so-called Saint John the Baptist of the Louvre" and its "strange likeness to the Bacchus, which hangs near it" in Pater, *The Renaissance* (London: Macmillan, 1873), 111–12, though the observation about the lush wilderness may well indicate that WBY was drawing on his own viewing of the paintings too.

185 Rapallo B, NLI 13,579, [60r], entirely cancelled, unnumbered page.

186 Rapallo A, NLI 13,578, [49v]. The version later in Rapallo B is very sketchy: "Christ was supernatural, & Baccus natural love – 'God give him in wine like the fable Baccus[']"; NLI 13,579, [76r], page numbered 1. Patmore's actual formulation is: "When God makes Himself as wine to the Beloved, like the fabled Bacchus, the one thing He resents is inattention, and when she [the Soul] has fallen into this offence, she has to recover her favour with Him by tears and prayers"; Patmore, "Dieu et Ma Dame," in *Religio Poetæ*, 171.

187 Rapallo B, NLI 13,579, [34r], page numbered 15, and [33v]. The word "flame" is missing following "where all fuel has become" but is supplied from a typescript closely based on this MS and dated "May 5, 1928," NLI 36,272/18/4, pages numbered 25 and 26. Similarly, although "allusion" has a special meaning in the system of *A Vision*, the typescript gives "illusion."

188 Rapallo B, NLI 13,579, [2v], cf. *AVB* 4, *CW14* 4; cf. *PEP* 2.

189 Rapallo B, NLI 13,579, [102v]. See p. 141, n242.

190 Warwick Gould convincingly suggests inspiration in the Stella Matutina's ritual for 7=4 Initiation, which required the aspirant to repeat a meditation, "Earthborn and bound our bodies close us in"; Gould, "Byzantine Materiality and Byzantine Vision: 'Hammered Gold and Gold Enamelling,'" in *Yeats 150*, ed. Declan Foley (Dublin: Lilliput, 2016), esp. 111–13. WBY made at least two attempts at rewriting the poem, one in the PIAL Notebook, dated to November 1915 (NLI 36,276, [36v]) and another on writing paper headed "18 Woburn Buildings," which was inserted in a copy of *Responsibilities and Other Poems*; see *YL* 356 for a very inaccurate transcription. Volume 2 of Wayne Chapman's forthcoming "*Something that I read in a book": W. B. Yeats's Annotations at the National Library of Ireland* (Clemson, SC: Clemson University Press) will provide a better version. See also Nick Farrell, *King Over the Water: Samuel Mathers and the Golden Dawn* (Dublin: Kerubim, 2012), 139–40. R. W. Felkin's original version reads: "Planets encircle with their spiral light, / Stars call us upward to our faltering flight – / Thus we arise. / Sun-rays will lead us higher yet and higher / Moon-beams our souls scorch with their purging fire, / Thus we arise," while WBY cuts this back to "The stars & the planets sumon [sic] us / The sun calls the moon is a purging fire" (writing paper) or even more concisely "The stars call & all the planets / and the purging fire of the moon"; PIAL Notebook, [36v].

191 Rapallo B, NLI 13,579, [35r].

192 Rapallo B, NLI 13,579, [34v].

193 Rapallo B, NLI 13,579, [36r–37r], pages numbered 1 and 2. The cancelled "simpl" seems to indicate WBY baulking at the word "simplification."

194 Rapallo B, NLI 13,579, [38r].

195 Rapallo B, NLI 13,579, [39r], page numbered 3.

196 Rapallo B, NLI 13,579, [40r–41r], pages numbered 4 and 5. Cancellation omitted. Cf. a corrected typescript dated May 5, 1928: "What I had been told about the Four Principles meant nothing to me because the geometry that explained it was still unintelligible, so I gave to each Faculty the quality of the corresponding Principle together with its own. Had

I understood that the Principles are value and attainment, the Faculties process and search, I could not perhaps have done otherwise without innumerable cumbrous explanatory phrases." "Book II: Introduction," NLI MS 36,272/18/4(f), pages numbered 4 and 5. A few minor variations may indicate it was dictated from Rapallo B; WBY sometimes introduced minor changes during dictation.

197 The tale "King Wird Khan, his Women and his Wazirs" (in Richard Burton's translation), is not included in all collections, but rather than WBY's vague wording about "sayings," the translations specify a particular "saying of the ancients." Burton gives, "The boy replied, 'O brother, I know this from the sand wherewith I take compt of night and day and from the saying of the ancients, "No mystery from Allah is hidden; for the sons of Adam have in them a spiritual virtue which discovereth to them the darkest secrets."'" *The Book of the Thousand Nights and a Night*, 16 vols., trans. Richard Burton (London: Kamashastra Society, 1885–87), 9:117. In John Payne's version: "'O brother,' answered the boy, 'I know this from the sand wherewith I tell the tale of night and day and from the saying of the ancients, "No mystery is hidden from God;" for the sons of Adam have in them a spiritual virtue which discovers to them hidden secrets."' *The Book of the Thousand Nights and One Night*, Cashan edition, 13 vols., trans. John Payne (London: privately, 1901), vol. 8, 276.

198 See Warwick Gould, "'A Lesson to the Circumspect': W. B. Yeats's two versions of *A Vision* and the *Arabian Nights*," in *The "Arabian Nights" in English Literature: Studies in the Reception of "The Thousand and One Nights" into British Culture*, ed. Peter L. Caracciolo, (London: Macmillan, 1988), 245–46.

199 Rapallo B, NLI 13,579, [42r–43r], pages numbered 6 and 7. The typescript NLI 36,272/8/4 gives "'could be fixed automatically,'" but that is probably because WBY or the person dictating misread the handwriting.

200 NLI 36,272/8/4, the date appears on page numbered 6.

201 Rapallo B, NLI 13,579, [51r], cf. *AVB* 245, *CW14* 179.

202 Rapallo B, NLI 13,579, [53r]. WBY repeatedly writes "Ares" (the Greek name for the planet that rules Aries) for "Aries." He also consistently writes about the sun "rising" at the Equinox, which shows remaining confusion about the meaning of the Equinoctial Point, which is unconnected with any time of day.

203 Rapallo B, NLI 13,579, [53r–54r]. Cf. Rapallo A, NLI 13,578, [8r], page numbered 5, cited above, p. 84.

204 Rapallo B, NLI 13,579, [54r] and [2r].

205 Rapallo B, NLI 13,579, [60r], all cancelled, unnumbered page. Though not struck through, the word "by" in "understand by 'natural love'" goes with a cancelled formulation, substituted by "understand 'natural love' as," so it has been omitted in the transcription.

206 *PEP* 33.

207 The word after "V. de l Adam" is probably "context" or "contacts"—or possibly "extracts"—though none quite fits the outline of the letters; however, neither do readings like "Cambridge" or "Platonist"—this is WBY's handwriting at its most personal.

208 In *The Trembling of the Veil* (see n136), WBY noted that "Villiers de l'Isle Adam had shaped whatever in my *Rosa Alchemica* Pater had not shaped" (*Au* 320–21, *CW3* 247), and in the poem "The Phases of the Moon," he has Michael Robartes speak of how Mr. Yeats wrote "in that extravagant style / He had learned from Pater" (*CW13* 4 and 230–31 n7, *CW14* 42 and 341 n6); see also n182. Though it had appeared in fragmentary and serial form in periodicals from 1872 onwards, Auguste Villiers de l'Isle Adam's symbolist play *Axël* was not published in book form until the year after the author's death (Paris: Quantin, 1890); it had a great impact on WBY, who wrote a preface to H. P. R. Finberg's 1925 translation (*CW6* 156–58).

209 Corrina Salvadori's *Yeats and Castiglione, Poet and Courtier: A Study of Some Fundamental Concepts of the Philosophy and Poetic Creed of W. B. Yeats in the Light of Castiglione's "Il Libro Del Cortegiano"* (Dublin: A. Figgis, 1965) is still the principal study of the connection.

210 Maurice Maeterlinck's *Pelléas and Mélisande* (Brussels: Paul Lacomblez, 1892) premiered in 1893. Writing about it in 1905, Joseph Holloway recorded "Mr. Yeats said he never understood its meaning clearly until he saw Mrs. Patrick Campbell and Madame Bernhardt enact the roles of the lovers as if they were a pair of little children"; *CL3* 614 n1. In *Per Amica Silentia Lunae*, Mrs. Patrick Campbell was a point of reference for the opposition of her boisterous daily self to the roles she played of "those young queens imagined by Maeterlinck who have so little will, so little self, that they are like shadows sighing at the edge of the world" (*Myth* 327, *CW5* 5), though WBY was later contradicted in this supposition by GY's instructors; see George Mills Harper (general editor), *Yeats's "Vision" Papers*, 4 vols. (Iowa City: University of Iowa Press, 1992), vol. 1, 181; vol. 2, 17; vol. 3, 419. Michael McAteer draws parallels with Villiers de l'Isle Adam, Ibsen, and Maeterlinck in McAteer, *Yeats and European Drama* (Cambridge: Cambridge University Press, 2010), especially chapter one, where he outlines the influence of *Pelléas et Mélisande* on *The Countess Cathleen*, and also makes a connection with Andrew Lang's work on totemism (30–31); see also McAteer, "Music, Setting, Voice: Maeterlinck's *Pelléas et Mélisande* and Yeats's *The Countess Cathleen*," *IYS* 2, no. 1 (2017), article 2.

211 Guy Ducrey traces the phrase's use by writers including Balzac, Ibsen, Maeterlinck, and D'Annunzio in Ducrey, "'*Ne me touchez pas!*' Transgressions decadentes d'une parole biblique," *Nordlit* 28 (2011), 141–157. WBY may indeed be thinking of Christ's words to Mary Magdalene, "Touch me not: for I am not yet ascended to my Father" (John 20:17), usually given in Latin as "*Noli me tangere*"; this could in turn relate to *The Resurrection*, which was originally conceived ca. 1925 (*CL InteLex* 4725) and written in two versions of 1927 and 1932. This was drafted especially in Rapallo E, NLI 13,582, and the White Vellum Notebook (in private hands; see Chapman, "Yeats's White Vellum Notebook," *IYS* 2, no. 2 (2018), article 4); see Jared Curtis and Selina Guinness, *The Resurrection: Manuscript Materials* (Ithaca, NY: Cornell University Press, 2011). The question of the substance of the resurrected Christ fascinated WBY and was linked to psychic phenomena: the Greek's horror that "The heart of a phantom is beating" (*VPl* 931) draws on Sir William Crookes's experience when "he touched a materialised form and found the heart beating" (*VPl* 935).

212 See p. 87 above, on Rapallo A, NLI 13,578, [22r], page numbered 17.

213 Rapallo B, NLI 13,579, [68r–69r with insertion from 68v], pages numbered 15 and 16. Cf. Rapallo A, 13,578, [22r], page numbered 17, p. 86. In the phrase "called both a 'sequence,'" *both* appears to relate to the "kind of number" and the "work of art"; my thanks to Wayne Chapman for helping with this reading.

214 Rapallo B, NLI 13,579, [71r], page numbered 18. Following ". . . read him in astonishment," a cancelled sentence starts: "A phrase of Sir Thomas Brown comes into my mind," almost certainly alluding to Browne's opinion, "I do think that many mysteries ascribed to our own inventions have been the courteous revelations of Spirits. . . ."; see *Religio Medici* (London: J. M. Dent, 1896; *WBGYL* 297, *YL* 289), 46 (section 31). WBY used this quotation in "Swedenborg, Mediums, and the Desolate Places" (*Ex* 60, *CW5* 66), as well as in the drafts of the Robartes-Aherne dialogues, where it is rendered as "the courteous communication of spirits"; see *Yeats's "Vision" Papers*, vol. 4: *"The Discoveries of Michael Robartes," Version B ("The Great Wheel" and "The Twenty-Eight Embodiments")*, ed. George Mills Harper and Margaret Mills Harper, with Richard W. Stoops, Jr. (London: Palgrave, 2001), 45.

215 *PEP* 25; cf. *AVB* 18–19, *CW14* 14.

216 There is an unrelated paragraph tagged "A" on leaf [24], numbered 8, a cancelled section, itself intended for insertion "at page 6 (or rather at back of p. 5" (i.e., 2 or 3 pages earlier in the notebook).
217 Rapallo B, NLI 13,579, [76r], page numbered 1.
218 Rapallo B, NLI 13,579, [76r–77r], pages numbered 1 and 2.
219 Rapallo B, NLI 13,579, [83r–84r], pages numbered 4 and 5.
220 A passage from Rapallo A quoted above still speaks of "this 3 fold world" (Rapallo A, NLI 13,578, [21r], page numbered 16; see p. 86). For more detail on this topic, see Neil Mann, "The *Thirteenth Cone*," in *YVEC*, 159–93, and *ARGYV*, chapter ten.
221 Rapallo B, NLI 13,579, [87r], page numbered 7[bis].
222 Rapallo B, NLI 13,579, [88r], page numbered 8. The accurate quotation of Morris's version of the *Odyssey* (down to Morris's idiosyncratic spelling of "ancled" and, probably, also of "Here" rather than Hera—the letter is unclear) suggests that he had the book to hand; Morris, *The Collected Works of William Morris*, 24 vols. (London: Longman, Green, 1910–15; *WBGYL* 1401, *YL* 1389), 13:169.
223 Clark, "Cast-offs, Non-starters and Gnomic Illegibilities," 7–12.
224 Later termed *Meditation*, *Return*, *Shiftings*, *Beatitude*, *Purification*, and *Foreknowledge* (*AVB* 223–235, *CW14* 162–171), WBY's presentation of the nomenclature has proven confusing, with sub-stages placed in parallel with the main stages (*ARGYV* 253–54).
225 Rapallo B, NLI 13,579, [90r], page numbered 10, with insertion from [89v]. The reference to Blake is to the marginalia in *An Apology for the Bible* by R. Watson, Bishop of Llandaff (London: F. & C. Rivington, 1797); see D. V. Erdman, *The Complete Poetry and Prose of William Blake*, rev. edn. (New York: Anchor, 1988), 615. WBY had used the word "Shade" as a synonym for the *Passionate Body* in the notes to *The Dreaming of the Bones* (*VPl* 777–78, *CW2* 692–94), but the reading is uncertain.
226 *PEP* 11–33; later "Introduction to 'A Vision,'" *AVB* 8, *CW14* 7.
227 Rapallo B, NLI 13,579, [102r].
228 This cancelled sentence is replaced by a long insertion from the facing verso, which is largely the same as the closing section of the published section III.
229 Rapallo B, NLI 13,579, [91r–92r], pages numbered 1 and 2. Cf. *PEP* 12–14, and also *AVB* 8–10, *CW14* 7–8.
230 Richard Ellmann, *Yeats: The Man and the Masks*, 2nd edn. (1979; Harmondsworth: Penguin, 1987), xiv–xv; see Ann Saddlemyer, *Becoming George: The Life of Mrs W. B. Yeats* (Oxford: Oxford University Press, 2002), 102, and *ARGYV* 29–30.
231 See *VPl* 967–68, *CW2* 719–20, and *ARGYV* 32–34.
232 Rapallo B, NLI 13,579, [93r–94r], pages numbered 3 and 4; *AVB* 12–13, *CW14* 9–10.
233 Rapallo B, NLI 13,579, [96v], insertion to replace text on [97r] numbered 7. Cf. section IX (*AVB* 19, *CW14* 15). An earlier cancelled version on the same page has: "because my wife has a great distaste for spiritism in its common form, & hated being thought of as a medium, I introduced it by a piece of make believe, which could not & was not intended to deceive any body. The philosophy had been found in the Arabian desert by Michael Roberts the hero of an early story of mine. The spirits had wanted me to represent the system as my own creation but that I would not do."
234 Rapallo B, NLI 13,579, [100r–101r], pages numbered 10 and 11, insertion from [100v]. The passage contains much cancellation, but only one is transcribed to make sense of the structure.
235 *PEP* 28–29; cf. *AVB* 21–22, *CW14* 16–17.
236 See above, p. 117-18. The Cuala edition has almost exactly the same wording with "screen" and "lute-players" (*PEP* 29), while the transposed version in *A Vision* has "curtain" and

"flute-players" (*AVB* 215, *CW14* 158). Suzuki's version has a "brocade screen" and "flute-playing"; *Essays in Zen Buddhism*, 230.

237 Rapallo B, NLI 13,579, [102r], page numbered 12; this is the first draft of section XII in *PEP* 29–31; *AVB* 22–23, *CW14* 17.

238 Rapallo B, NLI 13,579, [102r–101v], page numbered 12 and facing verso; cf. *PEP* 29–30; *AVB* 22–23, *CW14* 17. In a slightly later draft WBY glosses "'the guides' those greater beings whose messengers are communicating spirits"; NLI 30,319(4), page numbered 20.

239 "He said also that when a spirit is given a special mission in 'state before birth' it is compensated by having a short life after," September 5, 1921, *Yeats's "Vision" Papers*, vol. 3, 97; see also Card File R1, vol. 3, 383.

240 Rapallo B, NLI 13,579, [102v]. Cancelled text included to clarify syntax.

241 See Catherine E. Paul, "W. B. Yeats and the Problem of Belief," *YA21* (2018), 297–311.

242 Rapallo B, NLI 13,579, [102v]. See Paul, "Problem of Belief," 298, whose readings differ in a few places; see also *ARGYV* 300.

243 In the early drafts for *A Vision*, the centaur seems to be associated with the unity or wisdom of Phase 4. Phase 18 is referred to as having "a wisdom as emotional as that of the Centaur Chiron was instinctive"; *Yeats's "Vision" Papers*, vol. 4, 200. Phase 18 is in the emotional quarter, standing opposite Phase 4 in the instinctive quarter, and there is a possible reading under Phase 4; *Yeats's "Vision" Papers*, vol. 4, 172. In the draft of his introduction to *Selections from the Poems of Dorothy Wellesley* (London: Macmillan, 1936), WBY writes of her poem "Matrix" as "the most moving philosophic poem of our time, and the most moving precisely because its wisdom bulked animal below the waist. In its abrupt lines, passion burst into thought without renouncing its dark quality" (September 8, [1935], *CL InteLex* 6335), and it seems that this combination of passion and wisdom suggests the centaur in his mind. In the typescript "Images" III, the fighting centaurs provide a contrast to Christ preaching his Sermon on the Mount (NLI 30,434); see Neil Mann, "Images: Unpublished Tableaux of Opposition," *YA8* (1992): 313–20. Elsewhere there are the "holy centaurs of the hills" (*VP* 344, *CW1* 146) in "Lines Written in Dejection" or the "Black Centaur by Edmund Dulac" stamping "my works . . . into the sultry mud" (*VP* 442, *CW1* 219), conveying a sense of wildness and freedom, as well as violence. See also Warwick Gould, "Afterword: The Centaur and the Daimon," *YA21* (2018): 312–13.

244 Rapallo B, NLI 13,579, [33v]; see above, p. 122.

245 Rapallo A, NLI 13,578, [22r], page numbered 17.

Appendix

Tabular Summaries

The following tables give a listing of the notebooks' leaves by:

1. **Leaf number**.
2. A **brief description**, indicating the corresponding work.
3. A summary of the **title** or the **section** number.
4. The **page number** as given by Yeats.
5. The first uncancelled line(s) of **text** (cancelled text is included where there is no uncancelled text).
6. **Notes** give points of physical description, including pages which are cancelled *in toto*, and indicate if the page includes a date.
7. The final column records where **published** transcriptions or final versions appear.

Please note:

- **Blank pages** are included, giving both recto and verso.
- Evidently **missing pages** are also included (with a single leaf number). Following restoration, most of these are now indicated by stubs of Japanese paper used to fix the counterparts on the other side of the stitching.
- Pages added at the beginning and end of the book during the rebinding process are indicated but not counted.

I am extremely grateful to Jack Quin for his help in checking the physical copy of the notebooks at the National Library of Ireland at a time when travel was impossible, and for helping to ensure the accuracy of this table and the details of the essay.

Tabular Summary 1: Rapallo Notebook A (NLI 13,578)

Note: in addition to the standard *IYS* abbreviations (see https://tigerprints.clemson.edu/iys/iys_abbreviations.html), the following abbreviations are used below: *PD1930* = *Pages from a Diary Written in Ninteen Hundred and Thirty* (Dublin: Cuala, 1944); *UP2* = *Uncollected Prose by W. B. Yeats*, ed. John P. Frayne and Colton Johnson, vol. 2 (New York: Columbia University Press, 1976); *WPQ* = Curtis Bradford, *W. B. Yeats: The Writing of "The Player Queen"* (DeKalb: Northern Illinois University Press, 1977).

Rapallo Notebook A (NLI 13,578)

<table>
<tr><th>Folio</th><th>Description</th><th>Title/ Content</th><th>WBY p. no.</th><th>First line of page (uncancelled)</th><th>Note</th><th>Pub.</th></tr>
<tr><td>Cover</td><td>Patterned</td><td>Marked "D"</td><td></td><td></td><td></td><td></td></tr>
<tr><td>Inside</td><td>Patterned</td><td></td><td></td><td></td><td></td><td></td></tr>
<tr><td>0</td><td>Flyleaf/ endpaper</td><td></td><td></td><td>papers added in restoration</td><td></td><td></td></tr>
<tr><td>0</td><td>Rebinding</td><td></td><td></td><td></td><td></td><td></td></tr>
<tr><td>1r</td><td>[Title]</td><td>Marked "A"</td><td>—</td><td>A</td><td></td><td></td></tr>
<tr><td>1v</td><td>Contents</td><td>Contents (notes on Plotinus)</td><td></td><td>Contents Great Year (final version) 20 pages</td><td></td><td></td></tr>
<tr><td>2r</td><td>Notes</td><td>[MacKenna Plotinus IV-Fifth Ennead]</td><td>—</td><td>Plot IV p 10 top of intellect symbolized by [circle] sensation by line</td><td></td><td></td></tr>
<tr><td>2v</td><td>[Blank]</td><td></td><td></td><td></td><td></td><td></td></tr>
<tr><td>3r</td><td>[Blank]</td><td></td><td></td><td></td><td></td><td></td></tr>
<tr><td>3v</td><td>[Blank]</td><td></td><td></td><td></td><td></td><td></td></tr>
<tr><td>4r</td><td>A Vision material</td><td>Great Year | I</td><td>1</td><td>The Great Year | I | To the time when Marius sat at home planning a sedition that began the . . .</td><td></td><td>cf. AVB 243–45, CW14 177–79</td></tr>
<tr><td>4v</td><td>[Blank]</td><td></td><td></td><td></td><td></td><td></td></tr>
<tr><td>5r</td><td>A Vision material</td><td>[§I cont.]</td><td>2</td><td>interpreting oracles had thought of anouncing in the Senate House that . . .</td><td></td><td>(cf. also notes to The Resurrection)</td></tr>
<tr><td>5v</td><td>Text to insert opposite</td><td></td><td></td><td>at some star, that marks the transition from the constellation . . .</td><td></td><td></td></tr>
<tr><td>6r</td><td>A Vision material</td><td>[§I cont.]</td><td>3</td><td>& Virgil goden [sic] age needed a longer gestation.</td><td></td><td></td></tr>
<tr><td>6v</td><td>[Blank]</td><td></td><td></td><td></td><td></td><td></td></tr>
<tr><td>7r</td><td>A Vision material</td><td>[~~H~~] II</td><td>4</td><td>II | It is upon Annus Platonicus that my instructors have founded their . . .</td><td></td><td></td></tr>
</table>

Rapallo Notebook A (NLI 13,578)

Folio	Description	Title/ Content	WBY p. no.	First line of page (uncancelled)	Note	Pub.
7v	[Blank]					cf. *AVB* 243–45, *CW14* 177–79 (cf. also notes to *The Resurrection*)
8r	*A Vision* material	[§II cont.] III	5	*In* [gap] *instance a writer of the time of Marcus Aurelius translated by . . .*		
8v	[Blank]					
9r	*A Vision* material	IV	6	*IV | The circle of twenty six thousand years is for one half the Great Wheel . . .*	Lower part (2 tables) all cancelled	
9v	[Blank]					
10r	*A Vision* material	[§IV cont.]	—	~~*Phase 15*~~ ~~*Phases 16.17.18*~~ ~~*Phases*~~	All cancelled (tables)	
10v	Calculations, cancelled			*Stet* [for cancelled para. opposite]		
11r	*A Vision* material	[§IV cont.]	7	*The months run as follows* *The first month coincides with phase 15 mid spring*		
11v	Cont. from previous recto & cancelled start to §V & text to insert opposite			*between phase 18 & phase 19 it will reach the climax of the next movement . . .*		
12r	*A Vision* material	V	8	*V | We have four symbols of change, the double cone, the wheel formed . . .*		
12v	[Blank]					
13r	*A Vision* material	[§V cont.]	9	*It is the contrary of the lunar & subjective Hourglass figure; expands . . .*		
13v	[Blank]					
14r	*A Vision* material	[§V cont.] VI	10	*The widest part is the Celestial Body or rather the whole cone is Celestial Body*		
14v	Text to insert opposite			*In the diamond there is only one gyre, because primary thought, needs . . .*		

RAPALLO NOTEBOOK A (NLI 13,578)

Folio	Description	Title/ Content	WBY p. no.	First line of page (uncancelled)	Note	Pub.
15r	*A Vision* material	[§VI cont.]	11	*At Phase 15 they coincide — Spirit & Husk at one end Celestial Body & . . .*		
15v	Substitute text, start §VII & text to insert opposite & stet for text opposite			~~*VII | But a civilization belong to its Husk (or Will) to its phase*~~ . . .	All cancelled	
16r	*A Vision* material	~~VII~~	—	~~*VII | If we take the halves of each symbol nearest Husk & Spirit*~~ . . .	All cancelled	
16v	Substitute text & text to insert opposite			*But each ~~civilization~~, or period of 2200 years, belongs to its phase to its Husk . . .*		
17r	*A Vision* material	[~~VII cont.~~] VII	12	~~*VIII*~~ *VII | So far I have considered the wheel of the Great Year as if its . . .*		
17v	Text to insert opposite			*drama renewed, the Heraclitean antythesis rediscovered, Hegel & Karl . . .*		
18r	*A Vision* material	[§VII cont.]	13	*can be drawn through all four faculties [diagram] I have shaded the cone, which . . .*		
18v	Diagram			*[intersecting triangles]*		
19r	*A Vision* material	[§VII cont.]	14	*When religious thought refuses to be Mask & Body of Fate when it insists . . .*		cf. *AVB* 256, *CW14* 187
19v	Text to insert opposite			*But even were it possible I would not follow beyond the range of concrete. . .*		
20r	*A Vision* material	[§VII cont.] VIII	15	*cones for period, where the Faculties of some larger cone fall, as I am told . . .*		
20v	[Blank]					
21r	*A Vision* material	IX	16	~~*VII*~~ *IX | The diagrams frequently make each of these months a half . . .*		
21v	[Blank]					
22r	*A Vision* material	X	17	*X | I reconstruct the wheel of the twenty eight incarnations till it . . .*		cf. *AVB* 202, 248, *CW14* 149, 181

RAPALLO NOTEBOOK A (NLI 13,578)

Folio	Description	Title/ Content	WBY p. no.	First line of page (uncancelled)	Note	Pub.
22v	Text to insert opposite			*a point that remains fixed like the ascend of the indiual horoscope*		cf. *AVB* 253n, *CW14* 184n
23r	*A Vision* material	[§X cont.] XI	18	*is now passing from phase 22 to phase 23, but a nation or individual or . . .*		
23v	[Blank]					
24r	*A Vision* material	XII	19	*XII | They tell me that the primary revelation comes soon after the . . .*		
24v	Text to insert opposite			*great nameless mountains, cattaracts falls through cloud into cloud an . . .*		
25r	*A Vision* material	[§XII cont.]	20	*When Christianity lost its first character when ecclesiastics became . . .*	Dated "Nov 1928"	
25v	[Blank]					
26r	? *A Vision* material	[?cont.]	—	~~*Plotinus in Samkara, but a Plotinus in Sankara its Plotinus*~~ . . .	All cancelled	
26v	[Blank]					
27r	[Blank]					
27v	[Blank]					
28r	[Blank]					
28v	[Blank]					
29r	[Blank]					
29v	[Blank]					
30r	[Blank]					
30v	Text to insert opposite			*Had Prof Trench made I would understand for he is as Ruskin said . . .*		cf. *CW10* 211–13; *UP2* 477–80
31r	Article	The Censorship & St Thomas Acquinas I, II	1	*The Censorship & St Thomas Acquinas. | I | "The Censorship of Publications Bill" declares in its preliminary section that "the word . . .*		
31v	Text to insert opposite			*Nobody can stray into that little Byzantine chappel at Palermo . . .*		
32r	Article	[§II cont.] III	—	*For centuries Byzantium, & Platonic Theology had dominated the thought . . .*		

Rapallo Notebook A (NLI 13,578)

Folio	Description	Title/ Content	WBY p. no.	First line of page (uncancelled)	Note	Pub.
32v	Text to insert opposite			*a corresponding change in tecnique [?evolved] here to [?imagine] her not . . .*		cf. *CW10* 211–13; *UP2* 477–80
33r	Article	[§III cont.] III [=IV]	2	*As if liberated from a conviction that only ideas were real, from the time of . . .*		
33v	[Blank]					
34r	[Blank]					
34v	[Blank]					
35r	[Blank]					
35v	[Blank]					
36r	[Blank]					
36v	[Blank]					
37r	[Blank]					
37v	Text to insert opposite			~~*In obedience to their will I remain a dramatist and if I define a thing*~~	All cancelled	
38	*Missing leaf*					
39r	*A Vision* material	[First Things] [§II cont.] III	2	*angry & said that each is perfect. I did not dare to ask why if each be perfect . . .*	ff. 39–44 were loose (see Harvard microfilm)	
39v	[Blank]					
40r	*A Vision* material	[§III cont.] IV	3	*and its desire is expressed by a vortex or gyre. Though the gyre always touches . . .*		
40v	Text to insert opposite			*that the Ought is unimpeded or unified emotion—Beauty—the Known thought . . .*		
41r	*A Vision* material	[§IV cont.]	4	*Time or subject [diagram cone] Space or object The mind only gathers it self up into it self by something that resists nor can . . .*		
41v	[Blank]					
42r	*A Vision* material	[§IV cont.] IV [bis]	5	*as they come war retires to the extreme boundary. . . . in proportion as it runs out a soft immortal stream of boundless . . .*		

RAPALLO NOTEBOOK A (NLI 13,578)

Folio	Description	Title/ Content	WBY p. no.	First line of page (uncancelled)	Note	Pub.
42v	[Blank]					
43r	*A Vision* material	[§IV bis cont.] V	6	*by fire when the expanding gyre of Love escapes in its turn, & its Vernal . . .*		
43v	[Blank]					
44r	*A Vision* material	[§V cont.]	7	*[diagram intersecting triangles] We have therefore four gyres AB . CD . . .*		
44v	Text to insert opposite			*~~If I did my instructors~~ ~~If he did~~*	All cancelled	
45r	*A Vision* material	[§V cont.]	8	*When Spirit has reached the narrow end of its cone, & Husk the broad end . . .*		
45v	Text to insert opposite			*It could not indeed be one did it not play that part, for it is action that . . .*		
46r	*A Vision* material	VI	9	*VI | The Husk emanates light that seen when we rub our eyes, that seen . . .*		cf. *AVB* 190–91, *CW14* 139–40
46v	Text to insert opposite			*I repeat familiar speculations to relate what many believe with a forgotten . . .*		
47r	*A Vision* material	[§VI cont.] VII VIII	10	*Because no tint & shade, no quality, can exist without a surface, though it . . .*		
47v	[Blank]					
48r	*A Vision* material	[§VIII cont.]	11	*and behind the picture only, behind fruit or tiger but behind all their . . .*		cf. *The Cat and the Moon*
48v	Text to insert opposite			*At midwinter Christ is born Christs Annunciation is in spring & . . .*	All cancelled	cf. *CW13* 133; *CW14* 156
49r	*A Vision* material	IX	12	*IX | When the Four Principles are one in the daimon there is no greater or . . .*		
49v	*A Vision* material	[Cont.] X		*~~X | At midwinter Christ is born, at midsummer St John,~~*	All cancelled	cf. *CW13* 133; *CW14* 156

Rapallo Notebook A (NLI 13,578)

Folio	Description	Title/ Content	WBY p. no.	First line of page (uncancelled)	Note	Pub.
50	[Page stub]					
51	[Page stub]					
52	[Page stub]					
53	[Page stub]					
54	[Page stub]					
55	[Page stub]					
56	[Page stub]					
57	[Page stub]					
58r	Play	*Player Queen*	1	*Player Queen* | *corrections for sake of dancers* | *Page 403*	Page nos. are those of US *Plays in Prose and Verse* (1924)	*WPQ* "Draft 32" 447–51 Transcribed (without cancelled text) *WPQ* 447–48
58v	Text to insert opposite			*1 P* | *It is of me that they are*		*WPQ* 448
59r	Play	[Cont.] Page 407	2	~~*but no no step I will*~~... *Yet what do I care who it is*		*WPQ* 448
59v	[Blank]					
60r	Play	[Cont.]	3	~~*in the old Play the Burning of Troy*~~	All cancelled	
60v	[Blank]					
61r	Play	[Cont.] page 409 & 410	4	*page 409* | *"delete cloak of Noah*		*WPQ* 449
61v	Play	[Cont.]		*cast him beyond the border*		*WPQ* 449
62r	Play	[Cont.]	5	*Player Queen* | ~~*Yes let all be banished*~~		
62v	Text to insert opposite			*P.Q.* | *Let them well rewarded*		*WPQ* 449–50
63r	Play	[Cont.]	6	~~*Look It fits me as if*~~.... *I am told she was such a woman*		*WPQ* 450
63v	Substitute text & text to insert opposite			*Milles & Maestrovic the famous Servian sculptor & medalist*		
64r	Article	Editorial [Essay on coinage]	1	*Editorial* | *What advice should we give the government*...		cf. *CW6* 166–71
64v	Substitute text & text to insert opposite			*for Charles Ricketts had recommended Carline, we selected on the*...		

Rapallo Notebook A (NLI 13,578)

Folio	Description	Title/ Content	WBY p. no.	First line of page (uncancelled)	Note	Pub.
65r	Article	[§I cont.] II	2	*but after some hesitation for Charles Ricketts, & the secretary of the school . . .*		cf. *CW6* 166–71
65v	Insert			*quote Blake*		
66r	Article	[§II cont.]	3	*as the deputy master of the mint has commended, a precaution which . . .*		
66v	Text to substitute opposite			*The other night I woke with a sense of well being of recovered health & vigour.*		cf. *CW10* 214–18; *UP2* 480–85
67r	Article	"The Irish Censorship" I	1	*The Irish Censorship | I*	All cancelled	
67v	Text to insert opposite			*some of these ecclesiastics are of an incredible ignorance*		
68r	Article	[§I cont.] II	2	*upon them . . . by ecclesiastics who shy at the modern world as horses in my . . .*		
68v	Text to insert opposite			*& under this section "The Spectator" "The Nation" "The New Statesman" . . .*		
69r	Article	[§II cont.] ~~III~~ IV	3	*subject for judgment book or periodical. These five persons must then say . . .*		
69v	Text to insert opposite			*Though it was almost inevitable that the one remaining Catholic [?county] . . .*		
70r	Article	[§IV cont.]	4	*are right who say that in a hundred years the population will overtake . . .*		
70v	Substitute text & text to insert opposite			*permits him to exclude such works as the Origin of Species, Mr Marxs . . .*		
71r	Article	III	6	*III | This bill, if it becomes law will give one man, the Minister of Justice . . .*		
71v	Substitute text & text to insert opposite			*Neither the government, nor the comission on which the bill based, nor . . .*		

Rapallo Notebook A (NLI 13,578)

Folio	Description	Title/ Content	WBY p. no.	First line of page (uncancelled)	Note	Pub.
72r	Article	[§III cont.]	7	*But in legislation intentions are nothing & the letter of the law is everything.*		cf. *CW10* 214–18; *UP2* 480–85
72v	Substitute text & text to insert opposite			*an educated press, & a [?better] understanding among creative writers . . .*		
73r	Article	V	8	*V | The fanatics, who hold trains are no doubt influenced in some sense . . .*		
73v	[Blank]					
74r	Notes	VI [1 line cancelled] [notes on kalpas]	—	~~*VI | Yet I am not such that*~~ *I would have them | Indian ages of world*	Loose leaf; at end of vol. in Harvard microfilm	
74v	[Notes on kalpas etc.]			*A manvantara of which 14 = Kalpa*		
75r	Article	[§V cont.] VI	9	*There is no remedy but better education, & taste for reading, & enough mature . . .*		cf. *CW10* 217–18; *UP2* 484–85
75v	[Blank]					
76r	Article	[§VI cont.]	10	*The power to create great character, or possess cannot long survive the certainty . . .*	Signed "W B Yeats"	
76v	[Blank]					
77r	[Draft letter]	[Letter in reply to Miss H (on Wagner)]	—	*Dear Sr | Miss Horniman is quite right to say that Wagner got part of the . . .*		cf. *CLInteLex* 5176; *UP2* 485–86
77v	[Blank]					
78r	Note for article	[Note from essay on coinage]	—	*Mestrovic was in Checko-Slovakia & one letter went astray. He made one . . .*		cf. *CW6* 297n10
78v	[Blank]					
79r	Diary	Diary (Oct 20 continued)	—	*Diary (Oct 20 continued) | . . . Dogmatic protestantism. Much of the emotional energy in our civil war . . .*	Diary of 1930	*PD1930* 56–57; *Ex* 338-39

Rapallo Notebook A (NLI 13,578)

Folio	Description	Title/ Content	WBY p. no.	First line of page (uncancelled)	Note	Pub.
79v	[Blank]					
80r	[Blank]					
80v	[Blank]					
81r	[Blank]					
81v	[Blank]					
82r	[Blank]					
82v	[Blank]					
83r	[Blank]					
83v	[Blank]					
84r	[Blank]					
84v	[Blank]					
85r	[Blank]					
85v	[Blank]					
86r	[Blank]					
86v	[Blank]					
87r	[Blank]					
87v	[Blank]					
88r	[Blank]					
88v	[Blank]					
89r	[Blank]					
89v	[Blank]					
90r	[Blank]					
90v	[Blank]					
91r	[Blank]					
91v	[Blank]					
92r	[Blank]					
92v	[Blank]					
93r	[Blank]					
93v	[Blank]					
94r	[Blank]					
94v	[Blank]					
95r	[Blank]					
95v	[Blank]					
0	Binding					
0	Flyleaf/ endpaper					
Inside	Patterned	[Conservation summary]				
Cover	Patterned					

Tabular Summary: Rapallo Notebook B (NLI 13,579)

Note: in addition to the standard *IYS* abbreviations (see https://tigerprints.clemson.edu/iys/iys_abbreviations.html), the following abbreviation is used below: *PEP* = *A Packet for Ezra Pound* (Dublin: Cuala, 1929).

RAPALLO NOTEBOOK B (NLI 13,579)

Folio	Description	Title/ section	WBY p. no.	First line of page (uncancelled)	Note	Pub.
Cover	Patterned			Finished, Oct 9, | 1928		
Inside	Patterned					
0	Flyleaf/ endpaper			Papers added in restoration		
0	Rebinding					
1r			—	*B | Prose | ?Siris*		
1v	Contents		—	*Contents* *~~Notes on Rapallo~~* *Rapallo in Spring 9 pages* *First 4 to be used*		
2r	Rapallo in Spring/*PEP*	I	1	*~~Siris~~ Rapallo in Spring*		cf. *PEP* 1–5, *AVB* 3–6, *CW14* 3–6
2v	Revisions for insertion on opposite page	II		*Foot note –* *Mr Wyndham Lewis*		
3r	Rapallo in Spring/*PEP*		2	*I shall not lack conversation, for ~~Ezra Pound~~ a man with whom I should quarell more than with anybody . . .*		
3v	Text to insert opposite			*To explain, a structure that is musical or perhaps one should say . . .*		
4r	Rapallo in Spring/*PEP*	[§II cont.] III	3	*ABCDJ then JKLM & then each set of letters reflected, & then ABCD . . .*		
4v	Text to insert opposite			*He ~~no knows their~~ all their histories. That fat grey cat is the an hotel . . .*		
5r	Rapallo in Spring/*PEP*	[§III cont.] IV	4	*seeking expression without ornament or emphasis not inherent in the . . .*		
5v	Text to insert opposite			*I was accustomed to compare such poetry with that painting . . .*		
6r	Rapallo in Spring/*PEP*	[§IV cont.] ~~V~~	5	*~~confounding all together in his powerful invented symbols & metaphor~~*	All cancelled	
6v	[Blank]					

Rapallo Notebook B (NLI 13,579)

Folio	Description	Title/ section	WBY p. no.	First line of page (uncancelled)	Note	Pub.
7r	Rapallo in Spring/*PEP*	[§IV cont.]	6	*A friend tells me that Cezanne deduced his art from certain passages in Balzac Chef D'oevre Inconnu*		
7v	[Blank]					
8r	Rapallo in Spring/*PEP*	V	7	*In the sixteen[th] & seven[teen]th centuries imagination recovered its autonomy*		
8v	[Blank]					
9r	Rapallo in Spring/*PEP*	[§V cont.]	8	*As we talked ~~dreams~~ of my youth return to me, & I remembered . . .*		
9v	[Blank]					
10r	Rapallo in Spring/*PEP*		9	*all promising rest from the self creating all creating soul . . .*		
10v	Text to insert opposite	I		*I | This book would be different if it had not come from those, who claim to have died many times . . .*		
11r	*A Vision* material	I	1	*First things* *II* *I begin with the daimon & of the daimon I know little, but content . . .*		
11v	Text to insert opposite			*At first the daimon knows all other daimons within itself as separate . . .*	All or most cancelled	
12	Page removed					
13	Stub			*a | one | exis | to. . . .*		
14	Page removed					
15r	*A Vision* material	III	2	*III* *A line is movemt without extension . . .*		
15v	Text to insert opposite			*But the mind has two movements one into an imagined space within it self*	Cancelled but "stet"	
16r	*A Vision* material	[§III cont.]	3	*perpetually gives way a mere limit, but creates itself through continual conflict or finds its object through . . .*		

RAPALLO NOTEBOOK B (NLI 13,579)

Folio	Description	Title/ section	WBY p. no.	First line of page (uncancelled)	Note	Pub.
16v	*A Vision* material	~~III~~ IV	4	*IV At roots of all most all that I have to say is pchologial truth which I cannot prove by abstract exposition . . .*		
17r	*A Vision* material	[?I~~V~~]	6	*~~to first devide it into Four Principles, which elaborate & are the creation of natural things.~~ |~~V~~| ~~The devide into War & Love is too simple . . .~~*	All cancelled	
17v	Text to insert on previous page		5	*insert at top of previous page In the shaded cone, which are called Spirit & Celestial Body . . .*		
18r	*A Vision* material		7	*~~with substance, cause & effect,~~*	All cancelled	
18v	Text to insert opposite		~~8~~ 9	*When Spirit & Celestial Body are united in contemplation . . .*		
19r	*A Vision* material	VII	10	*When we are in Spirit & Celestial Body whether in meditation or the in the purification state . . .*		
19v	Notes for opposite			**1 The Double vortex is the year . . .*		
20r	*A Vision* material	VIII	11	*define Fate as all things determined from without & describe it as Daimon*		
20v	Text to insert opposite (i.e., 22r)			*Nature, where the subjective experience of the diamon— mirror of all daimons— are reflected as all animate & incarnate bodies*	Arrows connect 20v to 22r, so postdate removal of leaf 21	
21	Page removed					
22r	*A Vision* material	V	6	*V In the gyre or cone of Husk & Passionate Body is light phisical light*		
22v	Text to insert opposite		6.a	*the source of the light, which reveals that being as in a mirror . . .*		
23r	*A Vision* material	VI	7	*VI It is comestary [sic] to deny or affirm a substratum behind sensation . . .*	Much cancelled	

Rapallo Notebook B (NLI 13,579)

Folio	Description	Title/ section	WBY p. no.	First line of page (uncancelled)	Note	Pub.
23v	Text to insert?			~~*Therefore Husk too it had separate shape . . .*~~	Cancelled	
24r	*A Vision* material	[§VI cont.]	~~6~~ 8	*Passionate Body and Celestial Body exceeds human emotion & human intellect alike. . . .* *(for 9, 10 Etc see some pages back)*		
24v	Text to insert opposite			*No moment of the light is the same as any other, & the Spirit seeks to . . .*		
25r	*A Vision* material	~~VIII~~ ~~IX~~	12	~~*The Principles show what ever? is its own evidence, [?all this] is born . . .*~~	All cancelled	
25v	Text to insert			*Husk from birth to death, living events in the order of time, finds . . .*		
26r	*A Vision* material	IX	9	*The Principles show what is visable to sense necessary of thought, all . . .*	Much cancelled	
26v	?Text to insert	at head of Chap III		*at head of Chap III* *Between this symbol & the next given by my instructors, the double vortex. . . .*		
27r	*A Vision* material		—	~~*when we substitute discursive mind argument & silogism, classification. . .*~~	All cancelled	
27v	Sentences to insert opposite			*Principles alone cannot distinguish between fact & hallucination . . .*		
28r	*A Vision* material		10	*Husk gives way to Will, in all that is done to prolong our existence . . .*		
28v	Text to insert opposite	[X]		*[?Morality] is the submission of our Will & Creative Mind to the body of . . .*		
29r	*A Vision* material		—	*Spirit & Celestial are alive, intellect masculine, Husk & Passionate . . .*	Upper part all cancelled	
29v	Diagram to insert			[3 diagrams of double cones (all but central one cancelled)]		
30r	*A Vision* material	X	11	*The Four Principles include in the the* [sic] *Double Vortex the figure . . .*		

Rapallo Notebook B (NLI 13,579)

Folio	Description	Title/ section	WBY p. no.	First line of page (uncancelled)	Note	Pub.
30v	Sentence to insert			*after each complete year or month of the faculties, there is the change . . .*		
31r	*A Vision* material	[§X cont.] XI	12	*are human life alone when united to Husk & Passionate Body, are & . . .*		
31v	Text to insert			*We can represent man & woman so opposed as part of the same vortex . . .*		
32r	*A Vision* material	[§XI cont.]	13	*Each however is antithetical to itself, & sees the other as its object & . . .*		
32v	Text to insert			*The God, "boundless love" the universal self is always . . .*		
33r	*A Vision* material	[§XI cont.] XII	14	*Coventry Patmore called St John "natural love" & . . .*		
33v	Text to insert			*At first we are subject to Destiny, or Passionate Body, to Fate or . . .*		
34r	*A Vision* material	[§XII cont.] XIII	15	*an ideal history, determined by the nature of the mind alone, and I . . .*	Dated "March 1928"	
34v	Text to add			*I am a dramatist & symbolist, & often content with such definition. . . .*		
35r	*A Vision* material			*~~Religio Poetae~~ | ~~Book II~~ | ~~1. The Great Wheel~~ | ~~The double vortex of Heraclitus was too simple, we . . .~~*	All cancelled	
35v	[Blank]					
36r	*A Vision* material		1	*~~Siris~~ | ~~a Foundation~~ | Book II | I. The Great Wheel | When my instructors began, I was taught to . . .*		
36v	[Blank]					
37r	*A Vision* material		2	*~~A Foundation~~ | ~~I~~ | ~~This book would be different~~ | & PB, Will & Mask moves from left to right & Spirit . . .*		
37v	[Blank]					
38r	*A Vision* material			*~~When for many weeks, after~~ | ~~when my instructors first taught me, they~~*	All cancelled	
38v	Text to substitute			*(I) Introduction. I have used hitherto the double cone & four gyres . . .*		

Rapallo Notebook B (NLI 13,579)

Folio	Description	Title/ section	WBY p. no.	First line of page (uncancelled)	Note	Pub.
39r	*A Vision* material		3	*I. Introduction | The Great Wheel is a circle of 28 lunar phases or of 27 phases and a moonless night . . .*		
39v	Text to substitute			*the cone of objective life & it lives in the same degree for Creative Mind*		
40r	*A Vision* material		4	*When I wrote my second Book as it was for the first edition of this book . . .*		
40v	[Blank]					
41r	*A Vision* material		5	*I wrote this book in my first excitement when it seemed that I . . .*		
41v	[Blank]					
42r	*A Vision* material		6	*So far as this second book is concerned the Great Wheel is the 28 types of incarnation, that are one . . .*	Cancelled text contains date: May 1928	
42v	[Blank]					
43r	*A Vision* material		7	*& the moment of this possible attainment "could in found . . .*	May 1928	
43v	Notes, referring to *AVA*			[diagram of cones] *Page 12 | line 6 | put "picturesque" before "method". full stop after . . .*		
44r	Notes, referring to *AVA*		7	*Page 14 | line 3 | after subjective read I understand by the word . . .*		
44v	[Blank]					
45	Page removed?					
46	Page removed?					
47	Page removed?					
48r	*Vision* material	II	~~8~~	~~*II. In the Great Wheel there are alternate of Primary & Antithetical*~~	All cancelled	
48v	[Almost blank]			[triangle]		
49r	*A Vision* material			~~*the religious life contracts into a point, & begins to expand once more*~~	All cancelled	
49v	[Blank]					
50r	*A Vision* material			~~*such a symbol would show at the birth of Christ the greatest . . .*~~	All cancelled	
50v	[Blank]					

Rapallo Notebook B (NLI 13,579)

Folio	Description	Title/ section	WBY p. no.	First line of page (uncancelled)	Note	Pub.
51r	*A Vision* material			~~*(II.)"By common custom" Cicero wrote in the Dream of Scipio "men . . .*~~	All cancelled	
51v	Text to insert opposite			*and foretold the future of civilization believing their mind made & not . . .*		
52r	*A Vision* material		1	*II. I do not know all that was in my instructors mind when they decided . . .*		
52v	Text to insert opposite			*an abstract ideal is e* **I do not know when the map was . . .*		
53r	*A Vision* material		2	*Their Great Year starts where the Fishes of the star map touch the . . .*		
53v	[Blank]					
54r	*A Vision* material	~~III~~ III	3	*An ideal separated from its opposite is lyrical & its phantastic imobility . . .*		
54v	Text to insert opposite			*Phase 1, mid autumn, Solar West* *[Libra] begins at central point*		
55r	*A Vision* material		4	*The following is the table of the months, & of the solar signs—I leave . . .*		
55v	Text to insert opposite			*The Faculties have overpowered ~~the Principles as all are out of phase~~*	All cancelled	
56r	*A Vision* material		5	*Phases 23.24.25* *[Leo] " " "* *Phases 26.27.28* *[Virgo] " " "*	Cancelled after first two lines	
56v	Text to insert opposite			*It is as it were the astrological horoscope of a spiritual . . .*		
57r	*A Vision* material		6	*The Great Year began with <u>Husk</u> in the middle of phase Fifteen and . . .*		
57v	Text to insert opposite			~~*Our civilizations must move through the moment of greatest intectual*~~ *. . .*	All cancelled	
58r	*A Vision* material		7	*the world was therefore at phase 15, or rather between phases 14 & 16 . . .*		

Rapallo Notebook B (NLI 13,579)

Folio	Description	Title/ section	WBY p. no.	First line of page (uncancelled)	Note	Pub.
58v	Text to insert opposite			*The early Christians had some similar thought when they alloted . . .*	All cancelled	
59r	*A Vision* material		8	~~*Early Christian They face one another again as early Christian*~~ . . .	All cancelled	
59v	[Blank]					
60r	*A Vision* material		—	*I am puzzled by a symbolism which Patmore must have though that of . . .*	All cancelled	
60v	Text to insert opposite			*We are now all but through one twelvth part and as the signs and . . .*	All cancelled	
61r	*A Vision* material		8	*Hitherto we have had three symbols of change that of the double cone . . .*		
61v	Text to insert opposite			[diagrams] *The antithetical life passes [?away] into its object, & is [?loss from] it . . .*		
62r	*A Vision* material		9	*The other is in a diamond shaped figure which passess through the . . .*		
62v	Text to insert opposite			*We can can consider half cone as containing [?our one] gyre that of . . .*		
63r	*A Vision* material		10	*Sometimes the documents from which this book is made represent the . . .*		
63v	Text to insert opposite			*Will & CM now make their cone constitute secular or political . . .*		
64r	*A Vision* material		11	*the cones drawn between Husk and Body of Fate & contain both the . . .*		
64v	[Blank]					
65r	*A Vision* material		12	*of this shaded cone. As antithetical life, Particular & Universal Self . . .*		
65v	Text to insert opposite			*It was a long time before I understood the line with the four . . .*		
66r	*A Vision* material		13	*tenth century or greatest expansion, while the gyre of civilization had . . .*		

Rapallo Notebook B (NLI 13,579)

Folio	Description	Title/ section	WBY p. no.	First line of page (uncancelled)	Note	Pub.
66v	Notes (for a talk/lecture?)			*? Materlinck do not touch me ?what about Lang, Etc.*		
67r	*A Vision* material		14	*the date upon the line fell into the places of its Four Faculties*		
67v	[Almost blank]			*~~[when] [would return]~~*		
68r	*A Vision* material	III	15	*I reconstruct the wheel of incarnations but it . . .*		
68v	Text to insert opposite			*In pure "sequence["] there is no "allusion" all is from the whole & . . .*		
69r	*A Vision* material		16	*of number to a work of art, because in the work of art each separate . . .*		
69v	[Blank]					
70r	*A Vision* material		17	*I do not know when the wheel which has Christian history for the first . . .*		
70v	[Blank]					
71r	*A Vision* material		18	*I have left what follows, except for the change of Fountain into . . .*		
71v	Line to insert			*360 days of a hundred years apiece*		
72r	*A Vision* material		19	*insert at A What Great Year was coming to an end. An Etruscan cycle of some . . .*		
72v	[Blank]					
73r	*A Vision* material		20	*writers usually attributed to the first & second centuries, & [?one knows] . . .*		
73v	[Blank]					
74r	*A Vision* material		21	*not [?be] spoken from exact knowledge, or any other knowledge . . .*		
74v	[Blank]					
75r	[Blank]					
75v	[Blank]					
76r	*A Vision* material	I	1	*Soul in Judgement | ~~Life after Death~~ | I | Coventry Patmore thought Da Vinci had a philosophical intention . . .*		
76v	[Blank]					

RAPALLO NOTEBOOK B (NLI 13,579)

Folio	Description	Title/ section	WBY p. no.	First line of page (uncancelled)	Note	Pub.
77r	*A Vision* material		2	*when in the middle moment between Life and Death it is called back . . .*		
77v	[Blank]					
78r	*A Vision* material		3	~~*before I must once more consider the symbolism of life before passing to . . .*~~	All cancelled	
78v	Text to substitute			*Phase 15 & phase 1 are now called Critical Moments & phases or gyres . . .*		
79r	*A Vision* material			~~*the man. In the first moment & before the woman in the second is . . .*~~	All cancelled	
79v	[Blank]					
80r	*A Vision* material			~~*If I place it upon the great wheel itslef a gyre in a greater cone, & . . .*~~	All cancelled	
80v	[Blank]					
81r	*A Vision* material			~~*At this moment the soul, which might be dragged from historic phase*~~	All cancelled	
81v	[Blank]					
82r	*A Vision* material	II	3	*The Wheel of the Incarnations, has the same geometric structure as . . .*		
82v	[Blank]					
83r	*A Vision* material		4	*and we consider the movements of the Faculties round the circle as . . .*		
83v	[Blank]					
84r	*A Vision* material		5	*fortnight to the dark; . . . The 13th sphere is the present dwelling place . . .*		
84v	Cancelled note			~~*Each equinox or equinoctial sign has [?at the] first has the side of . . .*~~	All cancelled	
85r	*A Vision* material		6	*When the gyre of Spirit moving from right to left is at [Libra] of shaded . . .*		
85v	[Blank]					
86r	*A Vision* material	III	7	~~*[?arrow] that Anne cone is at phase 16 of Creative Mind & Michael . . .*~~	All cancelled	
86v	[Blank]					

Rapallo Notebook B (NLI 13,579)

Folio	Description	Title/ section	WBY p. no.	First line of page (uncancelled)	Note	Pub.
87r	*A Vision* material		7	*That the Principles contain in their complete movement life as the . . .*		
87v	[Blank]					
88r	*A Vision* material	IV	8	*St John of Cross had the same thought when he said . . .*		
88v	[Blank]					
89r	*A Vision* material		9	*haunting the place where they had lived that fill the poetry & prose . . .*		
89v	Text to insert			*Even while we live, the more our state aproximates to phase 15 . . .*		
90r	*A Vision* material		10	*at "the opening of the Tinctures" it seeks a reverse past experience . . .*		
90v	[Blank]					
91r	*PEP/A Vision* material		1	*Introduction | I | The other day Lady Gregory said to me "you are a much better educated man than . . .*		cf. *PEP* 11–25, *AVB* 8–19, *CW14* 7–14
91v	Text to insert			*as a little later almost all communication took place in that . . .*		
92r	*PEP/A Vision* material		2	*My wife bored & fatigued by the almost daily task I think & talking . . .*		
92v	[Blank]					
93r	*PEP/A Vision* material		3	*upon the interaction of two cones, & . . . Just when I was interested in . . .*		
93v	Text to insert			*was never adequately explained, for the explanation in Book IV leaves . . .*		
94r	*PEP/A Vision* material		4	*two or three of the principal Platonic dialogues I know no philosophy . . .*		
94v	Text to insert			*was he was constrained by a drama which was part of the conditions . . .*		
95r	*PEP/A Vision* material	IV	5	*Whether my question has to be asked before his own mind cleared or if he . . .*		
95v	Text to insert			*I noticed that their sweet smells came more often when we were passing . . .*		

Rapallo Notebook B (NLI 13,579)

Folio	Description	Title/ section	WBY p. no.	First line of page (uncancelled)	Note	Pub.
96r	*PEP/A Vision* material		6	*was sometimes shown approval for something said or thought as when . . .*		cf. *PEP* 11–25, *AVB* 8–19, *CW14* 7–14
96v	Text to insert	V		*V | When I prepared for publication the first confused incomplete . . .*		
97r	*PEP/A Vision* material	[V] VI	7	*though I had mastered nothing but the 28 phases, & the general ideas . . .*		
97v	[Blank]					
98r	*PEP/A Vision* material		8	*soldier, who had a little later to turn his own house in fort told me that . . .*		
98v	[Blank]					
99r	*PEP/A Vision* material	VII	9	*I might have read for two or three more years but for something that . . .*		
99v	[Blank]					
100r	*PEP/A Vision* material		10	*& then having locked the door of bedroom lay down upon the edge of . . .*		
100v	Text to insert			*It was obvious that though he tolerated my philosophical studies . . .*		
101r	*PEP/A Vision* material		11	*as my embarrassment was increased by his irritability —from Plato & . . .*		
101v	Text to insert opposite			*without acquiring meaning, —sometimes she spoke with her own . . .*		
102r	*PEP/A Vision* material	VIII	12	~~*Beginning for account of origin of system | I | A friend sad the other . . .*~~ *After a fortnight of communication made possible they explained . . .*		
102v	*PEP/A Vision* material	IX		*given in this book, or rather touched & skimmed for I find I understand . . .*		
0	*Binding page*					
0	*Binding page*					
Inside	Patterned					
Cover	Patterned					

A Review of *The Poems of W.B. Yeats Volume One: 1882-1889* and *The Poems of W.B. Yeats Volume Two: 1890-1898*, Edited by Peter McDonald

Peter McDonald, ed. *The Poems of W. B. Yeats Volume One: 1882–1889*, Routledge, 2020, ISBN 9780367495602. VitalBook file.
Peter McDonald, ed. *The Poems of W. B. Yeats Volume Two: 1890–1898*, Routledge, 2020, ISBN 9780367497620. VitalBook file.

Reviewed by Ragini Mohite

The first two volumes of *The Poems of W. B. Yeats* inaugurate the new critical edition by the poet and critic Peter McDonald, whose editorial detail is matched by his prosodic sensitivity to Yeats's early works. These volumes are part of the Longman Annotated English Poets series, and McDonald is attentive to Yeats as an Irish poet and to the specific cultural context of his writings—an important caveat in order to situate him within this series. The general editors' note restates the original intention for the series to provide students, teachers, and general readers with "fully annotated editions of the major English poets;" to be concerned "primarily with the *meaning* of the extant texts in their various contexts;" and to combine the editor's own research with ongoing criticism in Yeats studies (Vol. 1, xi). McDonald seems to me just such a student and teacher. His editorial work is self-consciously indebted to Yeats's previous critical editors, particularly George Bornstein (whose impact is visible throughout the texts) and, among others, Jon Stallworthy and John Kelly (to whom the first two editions are dedicated). Undertaken by a single editor, the two initial volumes are remarkably cohesive. But unlike the Cornell Yeats series, which is bound in blue and bears the author's signature on the cover, this series places different artistic renditions of the young Yeats on a green cover, indicating the evolution of Yeats's own poetic prowess and public image over the years. Volume one covers the years 1882–1889 and volume two, 1890–1898. Each volume contains a chronology Yeats's life and publications for the years to which it is dedicated.

The volumes chronologically organize published poems, verse dramas, unpublished poems, and fragments that "possess inherent interest for critical reading" and point to the poet's creative developments have been included by the editor (Vol. 1, xx). This organization is, for me, the most striking element of the series. It is a useful departure from the practice of organizing by collections as the *Variorum Edition of the Poems of W. B. Yeats*, collected editions, and the Cornell series of his manuscripts follow. In this regard it flouts the primacy of authorial intention which has historically been upheld by such critical editions. Those looking to study closely Yeats's revisions, editing, and sequencing of poems into individual "design[ed]" collections can look to other critical editions (Vol. 1, xx). This series is more invested in examining the evolving linguistic codes of the poems themselves as Yeats developed organically as a poet. In charting the changing face of Yeats's poetry beyond collections, McDonald highlights the processes that underlie what Daniel Albright has called the poet's "authority to unwrite his poems as well as to write them."[1] The organization enables a simultaneous bird's eye view on Yeats's developing thematic interests, his reading and literary influences, and his attempts at developing formal proficiency during "the years of his poetic apprenticeship" (Vol. 1, xxi). "The Song of the Happy Shepherd," for instance, appears early in *The Wanderings of Oisin and Other Poems* (1899) and inaugurates *Crossways*, but according to McDonald, is one that, chronologically speaking, publicly signals the end of a creative phase (Vol. 1, 372). The appendixes for volume one list the contents of *The Wanderings of Oisin and Other Poems* and the initial prose draft of *The Island of Statues*. The appendixes for Volume Two provide the content lists for Yeats's poetry volumes of the years 1892–1899 and the late 1890s draft "Subject for Lyric." The first appendixes for each volume recognize sequencing as a compositional act, albeit one that is not the primary subject of examination here.

McDonald judiciously considers the inclusion of verse dramas; these are particularly important components of Yeats's early works. He excludes verse dramas that were intended for the stage but includes lyrics from these dramas that were printed separately. Here, he brings together verse that Yeats—persuaded by Harold Macmillan to keep the popular market and reader in mind—separated as lyric or narrative and dramatic.[2] Early verse dramas which were not intended for the stage and were later published as poems—being particularly indebted to nineteenth-century traditions—such as *Vivien and Time and Love and Death* are included. The inclusion of the prose draft of *The Island of Statues* indicates the importance of the line endings of the notebook text as Yeats revised the work. Appendix two of volume one provides a comparative context for the play in its prose and verse versions. The earlier *Variorum Edition of the Plays of W. B. Yeats* places prose and verse versions and versions of significantly revised texts like *The Countess Cathleen* on adjacent verso and recto pages to facilitate direct comparison; it includes *The Island of Statues* only in verse. Though not mirroring the arrangement of the *Variorum* edition of the plays, this Appendix pays homage to the work of Russell

K. Alspach and Catharine C. Alspach by acknowledging the comparative potential of this play. The second volume includes *The Shadowy Waters*, whose generic shifts and compositional history compel some meditation. McDonald marks the 1896 transcript version as most resolutely a dramatic poem. In the introductory notes to this poem, he identifies the unfruitful plan to include illustrations by Aubrey Beardsley indicating, at the early stages of this series, Yeats's own attention to the bibliographical codes of his published works (Vol. 1, 474–76). It remains to be seen how the contents of future appendixes in subsequent volumes address these bibliographical codes, including the cover art for important texts such as *The Tower*.

For most of the poems, McDonald uses the two-volume 1949 collection of poems made by George Yeats and Thomas Mark (copyeditor at Macmillan). The editor is attuned to the role of the trusted reader and editor. The use of this edition acknowledges Mark's input on Yeats's otherwise disordered spelling and punctuation. McDonald supposes, as Albright did, that this results from Yeats's ignorance of punctuation rather than a deliberate choice to punctuate rhetorically. Important textual variants are recorded in the notes, as are the changes in titles. The editor makes smaller changes in spelling and punctuation to poems that exist only in manuscript form in the cases where his reading differs from that of previous editors—the task of deciphering Yeats's hand is admittedly an odious one. He acknowledges Yeats's inconsistent use of Irish proper names and uses the first-written versions. While the Cornell series is the most comprehensive account of the manuscript materials and prioritizes the fidelity of the transcriptions, the *Variorum* editions provide the fullest record of the printed variants. McDonald here presents the significant textual variants in relationship to their context and criticism, demystifying the editorial detail of the previous editors' efforts. While unable to reproduce the materiality of the manuscripts in the same way as the Cornell series, the editor recounts the key bibliographical codes of the manuscripts and notebooks, making notes of ink and pencil revisions, additional hands, the adjacent placements of key poems in these papers, the unavailability of certain drafts, and the locations of others in archives across the globe.

First, the dates of composition are included when available. Where manuscripts are undated, the editor approximates these based on Yeats's correspondence, style, and the bibliographical codes in the manuscript pages. Among the critical apparatus, McDonald introduces each work with important contextual and critical information: mythological, artistic, and historical sources and Yeats's knowledge of these (which was not always accurate), stylistic influences, and the details of its publication history. For instance, the notes to "King Goll: An Irish Legend" discuss the likely misdating of the first title by George Yeats at 1884. McDonald suggests that the stylistic refinement of this poem is incongruent with his other works of 1884 and that it is better dated as a composition of 1887 (Vol. 1, 460). While reference to ongoing criticism is not comprehensive—nor can it be, in an undertaking such as this—an overview of texts' interpretation and criticism is provided through the "major critical contributions" (Vol. 1, xxiv). The works of criticism invoked here are foundational for students of Yeats's poetry, from Forrest Reid's 1915 critical study to more contemporary works by Helen Vendler, Ronald Schuchard, Matthew Campbell, and others—scholars who themselves recognize the importance of editorial practice. McDonald also refers to Yeats's other writings, correspondence, the various edited collections of his poetry and, importantly in the Modernist context, the periodicals in which poems were published.

The notes also indicate where the author alludes to the works of other poets, follows particular poetic conventions, or where there exists an unintended "convergence with another poetic text" (Vol. 1, xxiv). This feature of the editorial work is an asset for comparatists and includes sparing reference to later work influenced by Yeats and the poet's own subsequent works. This is particularly striking, and McDonald's intention is to understand "the degree to which his poetry is self-feeding and self-perpetuating" (Vol. 1, xxiv). For instance, "deep heart's core," the final phrase of the most famous of Yeats's early poems, is heavily annotated for its comparative possibilities. In the notes, McDonald invokes Shakespeare's *Hamlet*, Swinburne's "John Jones's Wife," *The Heptalogia*, Edward Dowden's "Love Tokens," and an *Irish Monthly* review of Sir Samuel Ferguson's poetry. McDonald also references Matthew Campbell's critique of the triple-stressed "foot" inspired by Ferguson and comments on a similar metrical effect in Keats's "La Belle Dame Sans Merci" (Vol. 1, 677–78). Most significantly to Yeats's own compositional journey, he invokes early renditions of the phrase in Act 1, scene 4, ll.14-5 of *Vivien and Time* (Vol. 1, 59), and even earlier in line 1 of "A Flower Has Blossomed"—the poem that opens the first volume and that was composed as early as 1881–82 (Vol. 1, 3). These are a clear indication of Yeats's tendency to metrically refine his verse while also revising it macroscopically.

These comparative notes will likely prove an arduous task in the later volumes, as Yeats's work matured, was revised, and his influence was taken up by later writers. To this end, the editor also makes the diplomatic choice to "freeze" (Vol.1, xxvi) poems in time in cases where they were taken up for revision across many years and changed materially. This act of freezing situates each version of a revised poem into the stylistic period of Yeats's craft to which it was true and avoids muddying the chronological ordering. It also enables extended commentary on sources and contexts for poems and their compositions, overviews of their early reception and reviews, and later criticism and interpretation. The first volume contains "The Wanderings of Oisin and

How a Demon Trapped Him" (522–624), which is preceded by extensive critical apparatus on its background, textual history, and mythological sources and provides comparative insight into its literary sources. It also includes notes on the poem's early reception and reviews including an unsigned one by Oscar Wilde, which was of some importance to Yeats. Meanwhile the editorial notes to "The Wanderings of Oisin" (270–359) in the second volume focus prominently on its contexts of formal and stylistic revision and inclusion in various collections over the years. It also includes a repeated discussion of the key sources for those coming to the volume individually, and critical material on the revised poem.

In making room for early reviews, McDonald highlights Yeats's own attentiveness to the intent and reception of his works. Among other editorial inclusions, he acknowledges the author's critical view of poems such as the hastily written elegy for Parnell, "Mourn—And then Onward" (Vol. 2, 56–58), the deliberate exclusion of certain poems from later collections, an awareness of his audiences (as both author and editor), public dialogues and controversies regarding some poems ("The Ballad of Father Gilligan," Vol. 2, 6–12), and the uncertain journeys to publication made by others ("To - (Remembrance)," (Vol. 1, 429–32). Additionally, by including lyrics that were published independently while also being part of dramatic or prose texts, McDonald—like Yeats—remains cognizant of the overlapping audiences of these works and the generic interactions in key writings by the Modernist author. This is particularly evident in the lyrics from *The Countess Kathleen*. For instance, "Who goes with Fergus" (Vol. 1, 698–702) is introduced with the recognition of its impact on James Joyce (who heard it chanted by Florence Farr). The other significant inclusion is "I Never Have Seen Maid Quiet" (Vol. 2, 166–67), which had multiple revisions and was a part of Yeats's story "The Twisting of the Rope" (1892). Key poems in volume two contain notes after the copy-text that provide other important versions and accompanying notes by the author, such as his commentary on "The Secret Rose" from the 1899 *The Wind Among the Reeds* (Vol. 2, 457–58).

The first two volumes reveal Yeats's developmental work on key subjects in addition to form and style. This includes a movement towards political subject matter and his later editorial work with translation. "The Two Titans" (Vol. 1, 387–94) arrives as the author's self-described political poem. "Hushed in the Vale of Dajestan" (Vol. 1, 347–49) is his translation of the Russian poem "The Dream" by Mikhail Lermontov, and "How Ferencz Renyi Kept Silent" is a poem on Hungarian nationalist themes (Vol. 1, 480–94). Yeats is inclined to preserve the lyric form and rhyme scheme of the former's source text. Both for these poems and for "When You are Old" (in Vol. 2, 59–62, a version of a French sonnet by Pierre de Ronsard), the editor provides originals and/or prose transcriptions of the source poems and extracts from sources from which Yeats drew. I am not surprised to find a young poet using translation to strengthen his poetic foundations, and it clearly indicates—as *Mosada* (Vol. 1, 218–50) does—Yeats's early predilection for international and oriental influences that developed in nuance alongside his formal mastery.

Close attention reveals that the formal nuances of Yeats's later years were also being developed early. The broken line in the sestet of "Leda and the Swan" is foreshadowed by the broken final line of the octave in the unprinted 1883 "As Me Upon My Way The Tram-Car Whirled," a sonnet which McDonald calls "an exercise in verse form" (Vol. 1, 76). This is one way in which the first volume acts as a critical and editorial companion piece to the 1994 volume of the Cornell edition edited by Bornstein: *The Early Poetry, Volume II, The Wanderings of Oisin and Other Early Poems to 1895: Manuscript Materials by W. B. Yeats.*[3] Reviewing four volumes of the Cornell series, Robin Gail Schulze recognizes Bornstein's attention to pictorial and bibliographical codes, noting that a doodle of a "winding vortex, a tornado-like swirl" resembling the later gyres on the manuscript pages of "Pan" "speaks to the first flush of his symbolical imagination and to his early sense of the pyrning phases of history."[4] While McDonald's edition certainly prioritizes the linguistic codes, its layered use of editorial and critical practice also illustrates Yeats's increasing formal and stylistic arsenal. It builds on Bornstein's arguments for the textual process rather than "finished" products. Indeed, McDonald reiterates that Yeats's acts of revision were deliberate, compositional, and creative in nature. Future volumes will likely help the reader infer that they not so much culminated in a final text as were interrupted by the author's death. The reader also sees the timely presence of key players in Yeats's oeuvre, whether it is literary influences like Shelley, Keats, Tennyson, Browning, Aubrey De Vere, and others; political figures like Charles Stewart Parnell, or personal interlocutors like Laura Armstrong, Katharine Tynan, Maud Gonne, and Olivia Shakespear.

McDonald provides annotations for Irish names, local places, and legends referenced in Yeats's work; this is particularly useful for general readers and international students unfamiliar with Irish legends and geography. However, several other aspects of Yeats's writing also require attention, as is evident in notes to poems like "The Cap and Bells" (Vol. 2, 183–96) and "The Moods" (Vol. 2, 197–202). "The Two Trees" (Vol. 2, 102–13) compels the editor to contextualize Yeats's hand in Maud Gonne's initiation into the Order of the Golden Dawn, his work on Blake, and Sephiroth imagery. The rose poems require significant explication on the complex, multi-layered symbolism at play. These are introduced with discussions of the mystical and magical connotations of the rose, its romantic significance, the rose of Irish nationalism (and connectedly, the genre of emigrant poems). McDonald clarifies that the rose symbolism "possesses both public and more private aspects for WBY"

(Vol. 2, 114), and its deliberate foregrounding contextualizes the "symbol-led aesthetic" of his 1890s poetry, blurring the lines between "religion, eroticism, and nationalism" (Vol. 2, 118). This explication usefully indicates the editorial and critical work to come in the volumes on Yeats's later poetry; given the long-term development of Yeats's symbols, the later volumes of this edition will inevitably need to sustain a referential relationship to these initial volumes.

Texts of this nature require comments on their materiality in addition to that which they interrogate. This series has been published both in hardcover and eBook formats. The latter, however, presents unique possibilities and challenges for a text of this nature. The VitalSource software—designed to disseminate educational reading materials—on which the eBooks are made available by Routledge provides useful academic functionality, allowing readers to highlight and to make notes and flashcards. Though it is one of several such software programs and may not be as widely used internationally across institutions (based on affordability and digital access constraints), it supports the series' editorial intention to design texts for university scholars alongside general readers. However, the fixed formatting of these e-volumes prevents alterations and imposes onto the eBook the restrictions of the printed page, limiting the search option's abilities and rendering the text enlargement and highlighting options futile. This poses a challenge on devices with smaller screen sizes. Each volume provides an index of poem titles and their first lines. However, given the range of contextual and critical material in the volumes, a reflowable format and enhanced search option would enable better navigation and supplement the indexes well. With greater demand for digital texts in libraries as universities move to online or hybrid learning, such technological support for the editorial process would rejuvenate what Bornstein describes as "forms of display that represent a dynamic development" of textual processes and would therefore add a further layer of bibliographical code in the digital format.[5]

NOTES

1 *W. B. Yeats: The Poems*, ed. Daniel Albright (London: Everyman's Library, 1992), li.

2 *W. B. Yeats: The Poems*, l.

3 W. B. Yeats, *The Early Poetry, Volume II: "The Wanderings of Oisin" and Other Early Poems to 1895*, ed. George Bornstein (Ithaca and London: Cornell University Press, 1994).

4 Robin Gail Schulze, "The One and the Many: Reading the Cornell Yeats," *Text* 10 (1997), 334–35.

5 George Bornstein, "Teaching Editorial Theory to Non-Editors: What? Why? How?" *Text* 9 (1996), 150.

A Review of *Yeats Now: Echoing into Life*, by Joseph M. Hassett

Joseph M. Hassett, *Yeats Now: Echoing into Life* (Dublin: The Lilliput Press Ltd, 2020), pp.188, ISBN: 9781843517788.

Reviewed by Edward Clarke

Yeats Now: Echoing into Life reads like an annotated edition of Joseph M. Hassett's commonplace-books. The author has been kind enough to arrange under different headings lines he has noted, mostly from Yeats's poetry, and to provide his musings on them, reflections that are usually full of quotations from other writers. The headings include such themes as "Making Your Soul," "Loving," "Marrying," "Growing Old," and "Facing Death," and so this book allows Yeats's *Collected Poems* to function as a guide to life. This personal, and not academic, engagement with the poet is enhanced by interspersed photographs of book covers, portraits, a poets' house, and two graves, some of them taken, I believe, by Hassett himself.

It has been a refreshing pleasure to encounter Yeats in such a setting. Leafing through these pages often I found myself surprised by lines that I had long overlooked or daydreaming through the windows of some of the more famous places in his poetry. I began to enjoy him again, just as I used to before I ever studied the distinguished poet in earnest. I perceived the lyrics to glimmer as they began to fulfil both Yeats's and Hassett's hope that they "'take on a second beauty, passing as it were out of literature and becoming life'" (inside front cover).

In the section called "Loving" we are directed to one of Yeats's "signature sound bites": "*I have spread my dreams under your feet; | Tread softly because you tread on my dreams*" (57),[1] and I believe that this book heeds the speaker's request here as it treads through the *Collected Poems*. After briefly referencing Patti Smith, Hassett is careful to explain how these lines are designed "to be read in a very specific way" and thus "embody an immensely powerful dramatic trick:" they are part of "a series of statements and invocations that require the reader to pause dramatically at the end of each line" (58). In the section called "Hospitable Places," Hassett quotes from the poem "To be Carved on a Stone at Thoor Ballylee": "*And may these characters remain / When all is ruin once again*," to demonstrate how "In our world of evanescent electronic communication, Yeats's poem gives permanence to the idea that carefully crafted writing continues to exert influence long after its author's death" (72).

Each time Hassett ruminates on the lines he has extracted from the *Collected Poems* and elsewhere, he draws on an array of later writers, from Paul Ricoeur to Ben Lerner. The more I encountered such later writers the more I began to wonder about Yeats's possible reaction to this arsenal of reference. Would he have appreciated his work being so smothered in Seamus Heaney's benign appraisals as it is throughout *Yeats Now*? The cantankerous old poet was careful enough to make his poems speak from the traditional place of wisdom, which must always break out of the now, and so his lines make any later writer quoted by Hassett who does not speak so carefully from that place, already seem somewhat dated. Matthew Arnold would have described as "touchstones" the Yeats lines quoted by Hassett,[2] and I wonder about the metal of some of the authors scraped against them in this book.

Unlike contemporary sound bites or tweets, Yeats's conceptions have been packed into the ice or salt of poetic form for their long journey to the future; his thoughts are not commonplace because they have been transformed into something stranger during this process of preparation. In this way they already speak from their destination, which may not necessarily be gained today, and sometimes they seem to be slightly out of reach of Hassett's attempts to read them in terms of such contemporary authors as Patti Smith or Zadie Smith.

Although this book has the feeling of a non-discursive commonplace-book it is quite carefully put together. I note that at its very center, for example, Hassett quotes what might be perceived as the preeminent line of Yeats for our age: "*Things fall apart; the centre cannot hold*", which is also "frequently quoted by politicians and journalists" and often tweeted in response to the news today. It is good to be reminded that as much as this line describes the ever-spiralling chaos of contemporary life, the reason for its popularity is its "enormous power of 'poetic concentration'" (93). The ending of *Yeats Now* is also quite eschatological as it moves from "Growing Old" to "Facing Death" and "Last Words." Here Heaney presides and the arrangement of quotations and commentary seems like a kind of elegy for the later poet.

One of the strengths of this book is its interplay of texts and images. I loved the way we are first introduced to Althea Gyles through a photograph of her in 1893; then we are shown her beautiful cover for *The Wind among the Reeds* before she is finally mentioned in the body of Hassett's text itself, six or seven pages later, when two more of her rich covers are reproduced. Gyles was keen to make Yeats's 1897 volume *The Secret Rose* "look like a textbook of magic called a grimoire" (20). Hassett does not quite make Yeats's *Collected Poems* into a magician's manual, although I do feel that Gyles could preside as an anthologizing spirit over his book: as Hassett notes, Yeats commented that "'she collects the necessities of life from her friends and spends her money on flowers'" (21).

Yeats Now is full of many beautiful flowers of verse, but I think its author has also collected the necessities of life from Yeats's writings. Its cover is not inspired by Gyles's designs but by that other great maker of Yeats's covers, Thomas Sturge Moore. Underneath Hassett's juxtaposition of our "evanescent electronic communication" (72) with the well-crafted permanence of Yeats's poetry, you will find a photograph of the winding stair in Thoor Ballylee, side by side with Sturge Moore's cover design for *The Winding Stair*. It seems fitting to have this image replicated on the cover of *Yeats Now* since the book would wind its way through the heart of the *Collected Poems*. As it treads its winding course there it expresses "the energy and strength that can be tapped by maintaining a psychological link with our ancestors" (73) even as confusion falls upon our thought today.

NOTES

1 Throughout this review I have retained the italics used by Hassett for the Yeats quotations that form the titles to sections of his book.

2 See Matthew Arnold, "The Study of Poetry," *Culture and Anarchy and Other Selected Prose*, ed. P. J. Keating (London: Penguin, 2015), 334.

A Review of *Kipling and Yeats at 150: Retrospectives / Perspectives*

Promodini Varma and Anubhav Pradhan, eds., *Kipling and Yeats at 150: Retrospectives / Perspectives* (London and New York: Routledge, 2019), pp. 286, ISBN: 9780367728328

Reviewed by Kaori Nagai

Rudyard Kipling was born on December 30, 1865; in his memoir, *Something of Myself*, he congratulates his first daughter on "her sense of the fitness of things" in joining him in the end-of-year club by being born on the twenty-ninth of the same month, especially as his wife's birthday falls on New Year Eve.[1] This made his birthday very personal and special for him, besides being an occasion on which he could look back over the entire year.

I begin this review by congratulating Kipling on his "sense of the fitness of things" in having been born in the same year as William Butler Yeats (born June 13, 1865). *Kipling and Yeats at 150: Retrospectives / Perspectives* originated in a series of conferences in Delhi, Rajkot, and Shimla, India held in 2015 to commemorate the 150th anniversary of their births (6). By bringing together recent scholarship on Kipling and Yeats, the book establishes "family" connections between the two through their shared contemporaneity, cultural heritage, and literary tradition, while critically assessing their many differences, both politically and aesthetically. If Kipling had arrived a few days later to join the 1866 birth club, this anniversary volume would not have been possible.

Kipling and Yeats at 150 contains seventeen essays (excluding the introduction), and is divided into four parts: "Influences and Legacies" (Part I), "Self and Society" (Part II), "Craft, Medium, Politics" (Part III), and "Masculinity and/as Empire" (Part IV). Each section is headed by an essay comparing Kipling and Yeats. R. W. Desai's, which opens Part I, usefully establishes "parallels, divergences, and convergences" between the careers and works of the two authors, to set the tone for the section as well as for the whole volume. Part II is introduced by Malabika Sarkar's "Yeats, Kipling, and the Haven-Finding Art," which identifies voyaging to find a sanctuary as a common trope running through the two authors' works, reflecting their journeys of self-discovery through their interactions with the wider world. In Part III, Robert S. White's brilliant essay "The Chameleon and the Peacock:

Kipling and Yeats as Creative Readers of Shakespeare" challenges the common perception of Kipling as a bullish, egotistical imperialist by characterizing him as a Keatsian "chameleon": "driven by open-minded curiosities" (138). Kipling, like Shakespeare before him, fluidly takes on the many different identities of the characters he invents. In contrast, Yeats is a "peacock," or a Wordsworthian poet of the "egoistical sublime," who creatively appropriates Shakespeare to enhance his self-expression. In Part IV, Alexander Bubb's opening essay compares both authors' aesthetics of violence and heroism to launch the section's theme. Bubb is the author of *Meeting Without Knowing It: Kipling and Yeats at the Fin de Siècle*,[2] an innovative and pioneering comparative study which has helped to shape the terms of discussion in this book (15). Bubb's essay adds to our sense of the volume's aims and scope, as it gives an account of his experience of studying the two authors together, and of the rewards and challenges of this endeavor. Part IV ends with another comparative essay by Anubhav Pradhan, which also serves as the concluding piece of the volume. Intriguingly titled "Chaps," the essay argues that Kipling's and Yeats's celebrations of masculinity and heroism make apparent the internal fracturing of imperialism as an empire of men; Pradhan does this by drawing on the double meaning of the word "chap," at once "a man or boy" and "a crack or sore patch on the skin" (256).

Kipling and Yeats at 150 opens with the editors' statement that "At first sight it does seem that Kipling and Yeats have been by violence yoked together in this volume" (1). One of the book's suppositions is that Kipling and Yeats, despite their contemporaneity and many similarities, are two very different writers: to quote Bubb, comparing the two has often been described as "pairing chalk and cheese" (213). For me, however, the sense of forced comparison comes more from the fact that twelve out of the seventeen essays in the volume discuss only one author, Kipling or Yeats, without making any reference to the other. This is a missed opportunity, as the main strength lies in its intriguing juxtaposition of Kipling and Yeats scholarship. Some cross-referencing between the Kipling and Yeats chapters would have greatly added to the book's commitment to cultivating fresh comparative perspectives in which to bring these two seemingly dissimilar authors together.

One thing Kipling and Yeats had in common was their deep interest in, and engagement with, India: "Kipling in more obvious ways but also Yeats, as his advocacy of Mohini Chatterjee, Purohit Swami, and Rabindranath Tagore attests" (1). Interestingly, this collection, in the making of which Indian scholars played a leading role, does not include any essays which compare Kipling's and Yeats's attitudes toward India. Instead, several essays offer fascinating interpretations of Kipling's or Yeats's texts in light of ancient Indian literature and philosophy. For instance, Amiya Bhushan Sharma, in her essay on Yeats's poem "Ego Dominus Tuus," draws on the Sanskrit concept of *karayitri pratibha* (creative talent) to guide his discussion. I especially enjoyed reading Mythil Kaul's essay, which discusses the similarities between Kipling's *Jungle Books* and the *Panchatantra*, and insightfully relates Kipling's "Law of the Jungle" to "niti": "the wise conduct of life" which Indian fables like the *Panchatantra* teach (41). Similarly, Ruth Vanita offers an Upanishadic reading of Yeats's "A Prayer for My Daughter," through which she critiques the unidimensional ways in which European scholars have approached the poem. Nanditha Rajaram Shastry even goes so far as to suggest that Kipling's famous poem "If" is hardly original but an appropriation of the teachings in *Bhagavad Gita*. I found these readings refreshing and important, as they reverse not only Kipling's and Yeats's practices of appropriating oriental texts, but also the Eurocentric critical practices which we are so accustomed to, in which non-Western texts can never be the authoritative frame of reference.

It may be noted that the collection's emphasis falls more on Kipling than Yeats: eight out of the twelve non-comparative essays are about him. In addition to the two Kipling essays mentioned above, the book collects essays on: Kipling and cultural hybridity (Grover); Kipling as an educator (Krishna); Kipling as a journalist (Lee); Kipling's Indian short stories (Gupta); Kim and Imperial boyhood (Mudiganti); and Kipling as a global writer (Davies), whose imagination is wired into the expanding network of technologies, such as trains, ships, and even the deep sea cables connecting the world by telegraph. The four Yeats essays include those by Vanita and Sharma discussed above. The remaining two both center on the figure of Yeats as a nationalist writer. Prashant K. Sinha explores Yeats's political visions through select plays such as T*he Countess Cathleen, Cathleen ni Houlihan, The Dreaming of the Bones*, and *Purgatory*, and a selection of his nationalist poems. In his "Songs of the Wandering Aengus," Peter Schulman considers Yeats's political and literary legacies in his reading of Dorothy Salisbury Davis's novel *The Habit of Fear* (1987), which traces the protagonist's journey to conflict-riven Ireland in search of her father, a Yeats-like poet and political activist.

Overall, the collection is a rich record of international collaborations, which offers fresh perspectives not only on both authors, but also on the field of comparative literary study. Now that the celebration of a joint birth anniversary has joined Kipling and Yeats scholars together in an extended family, I hope many future reunions will follow.

Notes

1 Rudyard Kipling, *Something of Myself*, ed. Robert Hampson, with an introduction by Richard Holmes (Harmondsworth: Penguin Books, 1988), 101.

2 Alexander Bubb, *Meeting Without Knowing It: Kipling and Yeats at the Fin de Siècle* (Oxford: Oxford University Press, 2016).

Irish and Protestant: Commitment and Acceptance in the Twentieth Century, a Review of *Protestant Nationalists in Ireland, 1900-1923*, by Conor Morrissey, and *Protestant* and *Irish: The Minority's Search for Place in Independent Ireland*, Edited by Ian d'Alton and Ida Milne

Conor Morrissey, *Protestant Nationalists in Ireland, 1900–1923* (Cambridge: Cambridge University Press, 2019), pp. 249. ISBN: 978-1-108-47386-6.
Ian d'Alton and Ida Milne eds., *Protestant and Irish: The Minority's Search for Place in Independent Ireland* (Cork: Cork University Press, 2019), pp. 371. ISBN: 978-1-78205-298-2.

Reviewed by Feargal Whelan

In his survey of the impulses which drove the cultural revolution in Ireland at the end of the nineteenth century, Vivian Mercier makes a novel, somewhat outlandish claim that while:

> it would be outrageous to suggest that the true purpose of the Irish Literary Revival was to provide alternative employment for the sons of clergymen after Disestablishment had reduced the number of livings provided by the Church of Ireland. Nevertheless, the Revival [. . .] did have this unintended side-effect.[1]

It is from a similar starting point that Conor Morrissey begins his hugely detailed, indispensable, and extremely readable survey of the role played by Irish Protestants in the development of Irish cultural and political life in its most formative period, from the beginning of the twentieth century to the foundation of the Free State, and slightly beyond. His monograph, *Protestant Nationalists in Ireland, 1900–1923*, details the engagement by Protestants of all hues in the broad movement of Irish nationalism as it developed to its endpoint of political independence in 1923.

Morrissey meticulously harvests data from the multifarious clubs and organizations associated with the broader movement at the time to map connections of networks. The sheer number of clubs, committees, and guilds, all with defined structures and governance, is difficult to fathom in a contemporary context, particularly when their primary concern was debating in public and private meetings or social gatherings. What is revealed is a picture of a populace spending most of its leisure time in many rooms of varying sizes listening to similar discourses from a small number of voices. Given that the Protestant population was a minority and further, that a small minority of that group was actively involved in the movement, the picture of a tight core of individuals with an even smaller number of principal actors emerges, so that the dissemination of ideas becomes an obvious, organic process. Morrissey promotes viewing a nationalist Protestant grouping as a separate "counterculture," distinct from their co-religionists and the majority view, while also carefully distinguishing between "advanced nationalism" (active involvement in the independence movement) and displays of cultural affinity with a Gaelic Ireland (2). In the process, he emphasizes the importance of the Gaelic League as an organization whose significance hugely outweighed its original ideal of promotion of the Irish language and Irish culture. Given its size and the diversity within its membership it becomes apparent that an inclusivity developed, affording a space for the development and encouragement of nationalism within the Protestant community. Morrissey details the movement of prominent Protestant individuals within the League and also draws attention to their disproportionate numbers holding senior positions, from time to time, in the Irish Volunteers and the Irish Citizen Army, as well as sketching in detail lesser-known wholly Protestant nationalist organizations such as the Irish Guild of the Church and the Independent Orange Order.

The common thread of the cross-pollination of ideas through exposure in debating clubs is encapsulated in the person of Bulmer Hobson, who is described here as "an inveterate joiner" (50). Indeed, Hobson personifies so many of the superficial contradictions of the age that he is a worthy choice of persona to follow as a key to it all. A Belfast Protestant and a republican nationalist who was hugely influenced by the 1798 Rising, as well as by the promotion of Irish separatism through public discourse in local debating circles, Hobson joined the Gaelic Athletic Association and the Irish Republican Brotherhood before moving to Dublin and continuing his influence on the revolution at a very high level (50). Yet, he was also central to the development of the Ulster Literary Theatre, modelled on Yeats and Lady Gregory's counterpart in Dublin. Morrissey manages to amplify the resonances of Hobson not by focusing primarily on his political work but by providing a detailed biography, exposing the anomalies and contradictions in the subject's biography, allowing for a fuller appreciation of the milieu. Morrissey's attention to the individual participants is an enormous strength of the book, as he affords many the same space and detail as Hobson. Leading figures such as Erskine Childers, Constance Markievicz, Robert Barton, Kathleen Lynn, and Ernest Blythe naturally figure frequently, but proper space is given to Albinia Brodrick, Mabel Fitzgerald, Robert Lindsay Crawford, and Alice Milligan among many other frequently ignored individuals, providing a particularly detailed and complex portrait of the community. In particular, there is a welcome emphasis on the crucial role played by Protestant women throughout the period, and to the particular intensity many of them displayed in their beliefs as witnessed by their frequent refusal to accept the Treaty and their enduring active republicanism.

The one frustration I felt with the book is its abrupt halt at the foundation of the Irish Free State, though this is mainly because I was hungry for more of Morrissey's excellent analysis. While some detail is given on the "afterlife," as it were, of individuals such as Hobson, Blythe, and the Gilmore Brothers (218–20), the complex engagements by Protestant nationalists in the initial years of the Free State, certainly until 1932, is ignored because of the study's scope. We are therefore robbed of any meditation on Jack Yeats's enduring republicanism and its effect on his aesthetic (brilliantly argued by David Lloyd in *Beckett's Thing)*[2] or the depiction of the withdrawal of republican Protestants from society, detailed in Mary Manning's novel *Mount Venus*[3] as they waited in a sulk until rescued by commitment to the Spanish Civil War. Equally, we miss out on the Protestant counterbalance of their vision of a new Ireland as viewed at the Gate Theatre in those years through MacLiammóir, Edwards, and Longford's representations of Ireland, seen most startlingly in Denis Johnston's *The Old Lady Says No!*[4] These examples from that formative period should have been fundamental, I would have thought, to Ian d'Alton and Ida Milne's collection *Protestant* and *Irish: The Minority's Search for Place in Independent Ireland*, and yet they are wholly absent, a flaw perhaps of heightened expectations following Morrissey's bravura performance.

In *Protestant* and *Irish*, maybe because of its form as a collection of essays, the focus is much more on the impact of the newly independent Ireland on individuals or specific groups within the community, and their reaction to it. For this reason, it is less a question of analyzing *commitment* and more an exercise in detailing *accommodation* or *acceptance*, to use d'Alton's coinage (20). Although many individual politicians are alluded to separately, I would have liked a more comprehensive analysis of the role of those Protestants who committed to national and local party politics throughout the development of the state, both in Fianna Fáil and Fine Gael, which might have provided a sketch of a continuation of the long historical thread of commitment.

The sense of a "state within a state" described by d'Alton (30), in which the Protestant community could continue almost as if nothing had changed bar the color of the post boxes—at least until 1948, when the Republic was declared and the state left the Commonwealth—describes a mixture of insouciance and paranoia which is highlighted at various stages throughout the book's contributions. It is captured perfectly in Caleb Richardson's study of the humorist Patrick Campbell, grandson of and eventual heir to the hereditary title of Lord Glenavy. Campbell's grandfather became the first Cathaoirleach of the Seanad, while his father was departmental secretary, the highest ranking civil servant in the Department of Industry and Commerce, and a director of the Bank of Ireland. Despite this, the family was burned out of their house by republican forces on Christmas Eve, 1922. Outwardly committed to and successful in the fledgling state, we are told that Glanavy told his grandson that "Two little boys outside Doyle's cottage" (282) in Terenure would throw mud at his car because they had it in for him, demonstrating a combination of both his comfortable bravura and his lingering sense of siege in his environment. In various essays, reference is made to the siege mentality of the community and by reference to the *Ne Temere* decree of the Catholic Church, in which it was demanded that written consent must be given before marriage that all children of mixed unions would be brought up Catholic. The 1950 Tilson case saw the Supreme Court uphold the validity of the written undertakings, in effect enshrining the practice in law for all followers of both churches. The adoption of this decree as a simplistic bogeyman by the community is obvious, yet its status as such is queried in Catherine O'Connor's chapter on the infamous boycott of Protestant businesses in the town of Fethard-on-Sea in 1957, as she uses oral testimonies of local Protestant women to query the severity of the actions at the time, arguing that the event became more emblematic outside of its original location.

Oral histories are among rich and novel sources mined to good effect throughout the collection. Deirdre Nutall's contribution focuses on the marginalization of working-class and poor Protestants, viewing their erasure as an intimate loss. Recounting their gathered oral testimonies she depicts a strong sense of ill-comprehended dislocation, as individuals found themselves "suddenly vulnerable and lost, even when nothing happened and nobody even looked at them; they were not necessarily resented, but simply irrelevant" (87). It is a deeply affecting story of those disregarded within an already marginalized community, which also skewers the frequently mentioned misconception among the Catholic population that their Protestant counterparts were always wealthy. Another novel source for study is Brian Hughes's trawl of the Irish Grants Committee, set up by the British Government to compensate for losses to "loyalist" subjects during the latter part of the war of independence and the whole of the Civil War, which led to the direct confrontation of modes of commitment and loyalty for all those who made claims.

Counterbalancing studies of forgotten individuals and monolithic institutions yield insights of varying importance. While the biographical sketches of Bolton C. Waller by Conor Morrisey and Edward Richards-Orpen by Philip Bull manage to describe a traceable impact on their own and their wider community, Miriam Moffit's study of the great national debate in the Church of Ireland over the Prayers of Allegiance, and Tomás Irish's portrait of Trinity College Dublin's engagement with the state in its infancy, tell us little about the impact outside of the individual institutions. This is not a criticism of the authors or their excellent work but is probably a reflection of the unease within monumental organizations. Richards-Orpen became an influential individual in Fine Gael and a central, though now forgotten, figure within industrial and agricultural discourse, as well as being crucial to general rural development through his work with the rural organization Muinitir na Tíre. In much the way that Morrissey allows Bulmer Hobson to carry his narrative in his monograph, Bull deftly allows Richards-Orpen the opportunity to offer a commentary on wider national development and its impact on all communities within it.

It is no coincidence that Yeats's contribution to the 1925 Seanad debate, in which he grandiloquently referred to his Protestant counterparts as "no petty people" (268), should be referred to on more than one occasion in this collection, and also in Morrissey's book. Indeed, it is possible that rather than articulate the voice of his people in the hope of making a space for its continued appearance, the actual effect of Yeats's phrase was to silence that voice, resulting in years of virtual invisibility. The aim of d'Alton and Milne's collection, as articulated in their introduction, is to "uncover a southern Irish Protestant story more nuanced and complex than a Dostoyevskian dystopia of unhappiness and alienation" (1), and it certainly succeeds in providing a much more complete depiction of its subject, although it is difficult to make out to whom they attribute the assumption of a grim, poorly functioning group. Is the dystopian grimness a truism for an ill-informed Catholic nation, or is it the shared imagining of a Protestant community under siege? The use of the grating term "southern" to denote independent Ireland here and later in d'Alton's solo contribution injects an unnecessary sense of condescension, albeit one which is gaining currency as witnessed by the title of Robin Bury's *Buried Lives: The Protestants of Southern Ireland*[5] as it (unintentionally?) implies a trivialization of Irish political legitimacy by merely naming the state as a geographical entity rather than as a sovereign country. Nonetheless, the collection will add to the thankfully growing list of works belatedly addressing the role of the Protestant experience in the bringing into being and the shaping of the nation, which includes Bury's volume, Heather Crawford's *Outside the Glow*[6], Brian Walker's *A Political History of the Two Irelands*[7] and Kurt Bowen's earlier *Protestants in a Catholic State*.[8] As a result, both Morrissey's and d'Alton and Mills's contributions should help to provide a richer and more positive engagement with Protestant Irish history. As Morrissey notes, the "Protestant nationalists did not achieve their aims. However, [. . .] they reward our scrutiny and prompt us to reconsider the era from which they came" (222).

Notes

1 Vivian Mercier, "Evangelical Revival in the Church of Ireland, 1800–69," *Modern Irish Literature: Sources and Founders* (Oxford: Clarendon Press, 1994), 64.
2 David Lloyd, *Beckett's Thing: Painting and Theatre*, (Edinburgh: Edinburgh University Press, 2016).
3 Mary Manning, *Mount Venus*, (Boston: Houghton Mifflin,1938).
4 Denis Johnston, *The Old Lady Says No!* (1929), (Washington D.C.: Catholic University of America Press, 1992).
5 Robin Bury, *Buried Lives: The Protestants of Southern Ireland*, (Dublin: The History Press of Ireland, 2017).
6 Heather Crawford, *Outside the Glow: Protestants and Irishness in Independent Ireland*, (Dublin: UCD Press, 2010).
7 Brian Walker, *A Political History of the Two Irelands: From Partition to Peace*, (London: Palgrave, 2021).
8 Kurt Bowen, *Protestants in a Catholic State: Ireland's Privileged Minority*, (Montreal: McGill—Queen's University Press, 1983).

A Review of *Thomas MacGreevy and the Rise of the Irish Avant-Garde*, by Francis Hutton-Williams

Francis Hutton-Williams, *Thomas MacGreevy and the Rise of the Irish Avant-Garde* (Cork: Cork University Press, 2019), hardback, pp. 160, ISBN 978-1-78205-356-9.

Reviewed by Benjamin Keatinge

This new study of the important Irish poet, art historian, and museum curator Thomas MacGreevy (1893–1967) seeks to recalibrate our understanding of post-Independence Irish culture by arguing that MacGreevy's multifarious contributions amounted to a campaign for "a new edifice of the mind" (15) and that his poetry and cultural criticism enable us to "rewrite the map" (25) of a period traditionally seen as one of "censorship, national conservatism and cultural homogeneity," as the back cover of this elegant volume argues. MacGreevy's close friend, Samuel Beckett, memorably summed up the cultural situation of 1930s Ireland in his novel *Murphy* (1938), where the pundit Ramaswami Krishnaswami Narayanaswami Suk, reader of Murphy's horoscope, is described as "*Famous throughout the Civilised World and Irish Free State*".[1] The incivilities of Irish society in the post-Revolutionary period are widely attested to, notably by John Banville, who characterizes post-Independence Ireland as being governed by "monolithic, impregnable, eternal" forces "before which the individual must bend, or break".[2] No less trenchantly, Seán Ó Faoláin alludes to the overbearing dominance of "a completely obscurantist, repressive, regressive and uncultivated Church" in his contribution to the well-known documentary film, *Rocky Road to Dublin*, directed by Peter Lennon (1967). A devout Catholic, MacGreevy found an accommodation with the new order and Hutton-Williams's study carefully delineates the many ways in which MacGreevy's brand of Catholic nationalism challenged the monolith described by Banville. Indeed, the book's central contention is that the evolution of MacGreevy's interests, from private poet to public intellectual (he was Director of the National Gallery of Ireland from 1950–1963) enabled "contemporary art [. . .] to re-enter the Irish mainstream" and to be "within the reach of all" (104).

In this evolution, MacGreevy's disagreement with his close friend Samuel Beckett about the status of Jack B. Yeats as "national painter" (76) takes on particular importance and is the focus of Chapter 4 of Hutton-Williams's study. Reviewing MacGreevy's monograph, *Jack B. Yeats: An Appreciation and an Interpretation* (1945) in the Irish Times, Beckett publicly challenged MacGreevy's advocacy of Yeats as "The first genuine artist [. . .] who so identified himself with the people of Ireland as to be able to give true and good and beautiful artistic expression to the life they lived, and to that sense of themselves as the Irish nation".[3] Beckett argues instead for an existential Yeats who looks inward rather than outward and thus illuminates, according to Beckett, "the issueless predicament of existence".[4] Leading Beckett scholar Seán Kennedy notes in his essay "MacGreevy, Beckett and the Catholic Irish Nation" that "Beckett's writings of the period place him at profound odds with the entire thrust of MacGreevy's decolonizing project,"[5] and the intimacy they had maintained during the 1930s foundered upon MacGreevy's valorization of Yeats's national imaginary.

The spectrum of interests that MacGreevy's career embodies makes him a potentially unwieldy subject for a monograph study. Hutton-Williams has done much in just over one hundred pages to encompass MacGreevy as poet, art historian, and curator, but even so, this is a different and more interdisciplinary kind of book as compared, for example, with the tightly-argued study of Denis Devlin by Alex Davis, which offers detailed readings of individual poems at every step.[6] Nevertheless, MacGreevy's poetry, chiefly from *Poems* (1934),[7] receives ample coverage in Chapters 1–3 in readings inspired by Beckett's famous review of "Recent Irish Poetry".[8] By placing Beckett and MacGreevy together alongside Devlin in Chapter 1 ("Becoming a Poet: MacGreevy and the Aftermath of the Irish Revolution"), Hutton-Williams may slightly misrepresent Beckett's view of MacGreevy as an "independent" whose acknowledgement of "the breakdown of the object" is not necessarily a given.[9] The tension between Hutton-Williams's sense of this "small group of Irish poets" (21)—Beckett, MacGreevy, and Devlin—as an "avant-garde network" (20) working together and his counterveiling sense of their separateness with "no uniformity of poetic approach" (21) leaves the precise synergies between these poets largely unresolved. As regards poetic approaches, there may have been only a superficial harmony between Beckett and MacGreevy and also between Beckett, Devlin, and Coffey (the "Irish modernists" or "Thirties modernists" epithet seems to have served more as a badge of convenience) and, although their interwar relations have been the focus of intense scholarly scrutiny, there remains much to discuss.[10] Seán Kennedy has revised the critical consensus about Beckett's reviews of MacGreevy's poetry and he sees Beckett as only offering "tactful equivocation" or "veiled critique" of MacGreevy's *Poems*.[11] But Kennedy's views are not mentioned by Hutton-Williams, nor is there any detailed consideration of the confessional differences which, Kennedy argues, underpin Beckett's hesitancy. Arguably, the differences revealed by Beckett's public reservations on MacGreevy's study of Jack B. Yeats can be found in less conspicuous form in "Recent Irish Poetry" and "Humanistic Quietism," the two reviews of 1934 in which Beckett discusses MacGreevy's poetry.[12]

Where Hutton-Williams does mention the confessional disparities between the Protestant, God-haunted Beckett and the Catholic MacGreevy and their consequences for their mutual appreciation of each other's work, it is a somewhat truncated discussion that neglects a good deal of potential theological complexity. Hutton-Williams suggests that MacGreevy's poetry overcomes the "no-man's land, Hellespont or vacuum" between subject and object hypothesized by Beckett in "Recent Irish Poetry"[13] and adopts a "'Thomistic' imperative to face the world head on" (38), thereby attaining "a fundamental and necessary relationship with civic life" (38). This reading comes up against Beckett's ambivalent sense of his friend's work as exhibiting "humility" of a quietistic kind more inclined to "prayer" than to direct engagement with the world,[14] and it elides potential non-Thomistic readings such as the one advanced by James Matthew Wilson in his persuasive essay "The Augustinian Imagination of Thomas MacGreevy." Wilson's Augustinian reading provides a theological account of the same engagement sensed by Hutton-Williams but from a different perspective, which reads MacGreevy's poetry as an expression of how "art and nation alike are but means to a still higher end, that of showing forth the City of God."[15] This Augustinian nuance justifies the "Yet" which concludes MacGreevy's powerful war poem "De Civitate Hominum" and signals, one feels, a broader theological "hope"[16] above and beyond the "civic life" (38) alluded to by Hutton-Williams. In this context, the brief invocation of Thomism in Chapter 1 of the present study would benefit from further development.[17]

Brian Coffey (1905–1995) was a professional philosopher who completed his doctoral studies on Thomas Aquinas at the Institut Catholique, Paris in 1947 . A correspondent of Thomist philosopher Jacques Maritain, it was Coffey whose philosophical training, Catholic convictions, and loyalty to Ireland are perhaps most closely aligned with MacGreevy's interests. Indeed, it was Coffey who plangently wrote to MacGreevy after the early death of their mutual friend Denis Devlin (1908–1959) to lament over "the accidents that scattered us" when "we could have been more 'useful' at home."[18] This Thomistic sense of *praxis* would have bolstered Hutton-Williams's arguments by demonstrating Coffey's sympathy with MacGreevy's endeavors "at home"—sympathies not necessarily shared by Beckett or Devlin. This letter and others from Coffey are arguably more relevant to MacGreevy's sense of civic and national commitment than the very brief excerpt from Coffey's "Missouri Sequence" cited in Chapter 1 (30).

The happenstance of Beckett/MacGreevy/Devlin as a trio in the book's consideration of the poetry they published in the 1930s is most readily apparent in its truncated account of crucial exchanges between Beckett/Devlin and Beckett/Coffey around the time of the publication of Beckett's novel *Murphy* in March 1938. Echoing Ruby Cohn's suggestion in *Disjecta*,[19] Hutton-Williams argues that Beckett's 1938 unpublished French article "Les Deux Besoins" ("The Two Needs") was written as part of "his defence of Devlin" (23), whose *Intercessions* (1937) Beckett had reviewed in *transition*.[20] An alternative viewpoint is advanced by J. C. C. Mays in his exposition of Coffey's review of Beckett's *Murphy*, "completed in Paris in March 1938" but unpublished at that time.[21] Mays argues that "Les Deux Besoins" makes "equal if not more sense as a response to the ideas contained" in Coffey's unpublished review, noting that Beckett and Coffey were in close correspondence at this time and insisting that it was Coffey who best understood the philosophical issues at stake in *Murphy* and who served as "a sounding board for [Beckett's] essay, *Les Deux besoins*."[22]

Hutton-Williams agrees with Mays in as far as he maintains that "Beckett was still working out" his aesthetics during this period (23). The language of Beckett's review of Devlin, which invokes "one kind of need, and art" and "another kind,"[23] in the contrapuntal manner of "Recent Irish Poetry," allows Hutton-Williams to draw a line of continuity between the 1934 and 1938 reviews. The "profounder self-awareness" (22–23) Beckett saw in the poetry of *Intercessions* in 1938 compares unfavorably with the "flight from self-awareness" of the "leading twilighters" who Beckett had excoriated in his 1934 polemic.[24] The circumstantial evidence linking "The Two Needs" essay to the *Intercessions* review seems convincing and, at the rhetorical level, irresistible given Beckett's repetition of phrases of need ("terms of need, not of opinion," "an escape from need"[25]) in his appraisal of *Intercessions*. But the dichotomies and needs of *Murphy* and of its eponymous hero are also compelling and lend credence to Mays's argument as to Coffey's influence on Beckett's thinking at this time. The hero loves and loathes his partner, Celia. He recognizes himself in Mr Endon, who doesn't seem to recognize him. He is alive in the mind but fettered to the body. Mays's suggestion that the conflictual needs within *Murphy* emerge from his dialogue with Coffey (and also prompted "Les Deux Besoins") merits fuller consideration in Hutton-Williams's study. Indeed, Hutton-Williams's astute sense of the divergences between Beckett's *Echo's Bones* (1935), Devlin's *Intercessions* (1937), and MacGreevy's *Poems* (1934) in terms of how the poems articulate "a sense of division from society" and adopt variegated stances towards "the social world" (38) evokes the same philosophical and social tug-of-war that *Murphy* grapples with, and so the relatively cursory mention of Beckett's early masterpiece in the present study (23), and the occlusion of Brian Coffey's input, leaves at least some stones unturned.

Hutton-Williams succeeds in bringing poetry and painting into well-calibrated alignment in Chapter 3 where Beckett's insights prove their worth in a lucid discussion of "MacGreevy and Postimpressionism." Here Beckett's "breakdown of the object," and his ludic declaration that "At the centre there is no theme,"[26] provide a firm basis by which to elucidate MacGreevy's defense of Mainie Jellett's "geometrical" (63) and Cubist paintings. Hutton-Williams reminds us that Jellett's work provides "new infusions of traditional Irish material" (66). MacGreevy's expertise in Celtic and Byzantine art enabled him to discern, in Beckett's words, "the old thing that has happened again"[27] and, just as importantly, to defend it before the Irish public. The painterly dimensions of MacGreevy's poetry are then explored in further readings of the "postimpressionist aesthetics" of *Poems* (67). Chapter 3 might be said to contain *in nuce* and in fluid equilibrium the three main strands of the book: MacGreevy's poetry, his art criticism, and his public/professional roles. Indeed, Hutton-Williams is largely successful in achieving a synthesis of these broad areas in MacGreevy's life, thus overcoming in close analysis the disjunctures of MacGreevy's career.

Indeed, whereas Susan Schreibman's path-breaking essay collection *The Life and Work of Thomas MacGreevy: A Critical Reappraisal* (2013) is divided into discrete sections to treat different aspects of MacGreevy's career—"MacGreevy as Poet," "MacGreevy as Critic," "Cities of MacGreevy," "MacGreevy and Friends," "MacGreevy Remembered"—Hutton-Williams's book is a critical synthesis of all of these, with additional consideration of MacGreevy's influence on the public domain of Irish cultural life. If Beckett confessed to finding himself "wishing" MacGreevy "were writing more" for himself and "less for Ireland,"[28] Hutton-Williams convincingly demonstrates that, for MacGreevy, these two activities were not mutually exclusive. A further strength of the book is its inclusion of splendid color plates which greatly enhance the discussion in Chapter 5 of MacGreevy's study of Jack B. Yeats.[29]

Citing Daniel Corkery's *Synge and Anglo-Irish Literature* (1931) in his epigraph to Chapter 4 "Reconstructing the National Painter", Hutton-Williams presents MacGreevy as "one of the wild geese of the pen" (75), MacGreevy who is also ambitious for "cultural reform" in his own country (61). The bringing together of home and abroad, Dublin via Paris, in a probing discussion of Irish modernist painting is where Hutton-Williams's study comes into its own. By reading MacGreevy's expatriate identity alongside the "Irish selves" (66) of painters whose work he supported (among them Mainie Jellett, Norah McGuinness, and Nano Reid), Hutton-Williams reorientates our sense of Ireland's insularity at a particular cultural moment. Chapters 3–5 affirm in sophisticated terms the essential Irishness that MacGreevy claimed for himself and for the experimental painters he most admired. Paris and London were but a "step on the way home," as he wrote to George Russell (*AE*) in March 1927 (41) in a quote Hutton-Williams uses an epigraph for Chapter 2 "MacGreevy as Parisian *Littérateur*, 1927-33." On his return to Ireland in 1941, MacGreevy would add a Gaelic "a" to his baptismal surname "McGreevy" and devote his career to Ireland's cultural life. His later work as Director of the National Gallery of Ireland is given full credit in the book's final chapter "The National Gallery Revisited, 1950–63," and the plural "value" (1) of MacGreevy's contributions to Irish culture are thus validated by this timely consideration of his underappreciated public service.

For W. B. Yeats the poet, revisiting the Municipal Gallery "Where my friends' portraits hang" was akin to entering a sacred or "hallowed place" (*CW1*, 328). MacGreevy's efforts at "revitalising the public's relationship with art" (99) were less portentous but more grounded, as Hutton-Williams deftly argues. By increasing annual visitor numbers at the National Gallery of Ireland "from 37,547 in 1958 to 53,452 in 1961" (99), MacGreevy proved that (at least some of) "the People wanted Pictures" without any need to invoke Renaissance patterns of patronage as W. B. Yeats had done in his 1912 poem "To a wealthy Man who promised a second Subscription to the Dublin Municipal Gallery if it were proved the People wanted Pictures" (*CW1*, 106). Of course, both W. B. Yeats and MacGreevy made themselves "'useful' at home" (to quote again from Coffey's letter of 1959) through their tireless advocacy of "museum culture in Dublin" (98). However, W. B. Yeats's exasperation at his fellow countrymen and women perhaps bears closer comparison with Beckett's savage indignation at what he saw as the unredeemed philistinism of the Irish Free State.

Hutton-Williams's study invokes W. B. Yeats in many areas but without the extensive treatment accorded to his artist brother in Chapter 4, "Reconstructing the National Painter." Importantly, Hutton-Williams demonstrates how MacGreevy casts Ireland's "romantic national heritage" (32) in a different light from W. B. Yeats while echoing major Yeats poems in places. He notes that "Crón Tráth na nDéithe," with its heavily Eliotic structure, mood, and syntax, is at some level also "a response to Yeats's 'Easter, 1916'" (32) and he compares, briefly, W. B. Yeats's "An Irish Airman Foresees His Death" with MacGreevy's aerial war poem "De Civitate Hominum," noting the different perspectives in the two poems as they convey the airman's fatal descent.

Dealing as it does with the aftermath of the Irish revolution, Hutton-Williams's study elucidates "the split between Ireland's earlier revolutionary aspirations and its conservative artistic direction" (94) and how MacGreevy's "discursive interventions" served to "shape" the evolution of the state's cultural life in "affirmative" and progressive ways (95). The more senior poet, of course, belonged to the previous revolutionary generation and the elegiac tone of W.

B. Yeats's "The Municipal Gallery Revisited" knowingly articulates the poet's awareness of being one of "the old regime," (98) not the avant-garde.

NOTES

1 Samuel Beckett, *Murphy* (London: Faber and Faber, 2009), 22; italics in original.

2 John Banville, "Memory and Forgetting: The Ireland of de Valera and O'Faolain," *The Irish Review* 17/18 (Winter 1995), 147.

3 Quoted in Samuel Beckett, "MacGreevy on Yeats," in *Disjecta*, ed. Ruby Cohn (London: John Calder, 1983), 96.

4 Beckett, "MacGreevy on Yeats," 97.

5 Seán Kennedy, "'Too Absolute and Ireland Haunted': MacGreevy, Beckett and the Catholic Irish Nation," in *The Life and Work of Thomas MacGreevy: A Critical Reappraisal*, ed. Susan Schreibman (London: Bloomsbury, 2013), 199.

6 See Alex Davis, *A Broken Line: Denis Devlin and Irish Poetic Modernism* (Dublin: University College Dublin Press, 2000).

7 Thomas MacGreevy, *Poems* (London: William Heinemann, 1934).

8 Samuel Beckett, "Recent Irish Poetry," in *Disjecta*, ed. Ruby Cohn (London: John Calder, 1983), 70.

9 Beckett, "Recent Irish Poetry," 70.

10 See, for example three significant critical interventions by Seán Kennedy: "Beckett Reviewing MacGreevy: A Reconsideration," *Irish University Review* 35, no. 2 (Autumn/Winter 2005): 273-287; "'The Artist Who Stakes His Being is from Nowhere': Beckett and Thomas MacGreevy on the Art of Jack B. Yeats." *Samuel Beckett Today/Aujourd'hui*, 14 (2004): 61-74, and "'Too Absolute and Ireland Haunted,'" 189–202. Patricia Coughlan, "The poetry is another pair of sleeves: Beckett, Ireland and Modernist Lyric Poetry," in *Modernism and Ireland: The Poetry of the 1930s*, ed. Patricia Coughlan and Alex Davis (Cork: Cork University Press, 1995), 173–208; Benjamin Keatinge and Aengus Woods, "Introduction," in *Other Edens: The Life and Work of Brian Coffey*, ed. Keatinge and Woods (Dublin: Irish Academic Press, 2010), 1-11; Michael Smith, "Michael Smith Asks Mervyn Wall Some Questions about the Thirties" [interview with Mervyn Wall], *The Lace Curtain* 4 (1971), 79–80.

11 Seán Kennedy, "Beckett Reviewing MacGreevy: A Reconsideration," *Irish University Review* 35, no. 2 (Autumn/Winter 2005): 273, 278.

12 Beckett, "Recent Irish Poetry," 70 and Samuel Beckett, "Humanistic Quietism," in *Disjecta*, ed. Ruby Cohn (London: John Calder, 1983), 68.

13 Beckett, "Recent Irish Poetry," 70.

14 Beckett, "Humanistic Quietism," 68.

15 James Matthew Wilson, "The Augustinian Imagination of Thomas MacGreevy", in *The Life and Work of Thomas MacGreevy: A Critical Reappraisal*, ed. Susan Schreibman (London: Bloomsbury, 2013), 81.

16 Beckett, "Humanistic Quietism," 68.

17 It is worth noting that Thomism and neo-Thomism, deriving from the philosophy of St. Thomas Aquinas (c. 1225–74), have more Aristotelean and worldly aspects than Augustinian ideas deriving from St. Augustine of Hippo (354–430). *The Oxford Dictionary of Philosophy* describes Thomistic philosophy as follows: "Throughout his writings Aquinas's major concern is to defend a 'naturalistic' or Aristotelian Christianity, in opposition not only to sceptics but also to the surrounding tendency to read Christianity in Neoplatonic terms, derived largely from Augustine, and also channelled to the 13th century through

such writers as Avicenna. Aquinas takes issue with the occasionalism of the Neoplatonists, which reduces mankind to spectators of the world order in which all causality is ultimately an expression of God's will; like Aristotle he is concerned to protect the notion of a genuine human agent who is the responsible author of his or her own actions." Simon Blackburn, *The Oxford Dictionary of Philosophy* (Oxford: Oxford University Press, 2008). Accessed January 26, 2021, https://www-oxfordreference-com.elib.tcd.ie/view/10.1093/acref/9780199541430.001.0001/acref-9780199541430-e-229.

18 Brian Coffey to Thomas MacGreevy, September 10, 1959. Quoted in Benjamin Keatinge, "'Missouri Sequence' and the Search for a Habitat," in *Other Edens: The Life and Work of Brian Coffey*, ed. Keatinge and Woods (Dublin: Irish Academic Press, 2010), 107.

19 Ruby Cohn, "Notes," in *Disjecta*, ed. Ruby Cohn (London: John Calder, 1983), 174.

20 Samuel Beckett, "*Intercessions* by Denis Devlin," in Disjecta, ed. Ruby Cohn (London: John Calder, 1983), 91–94. Original review published in *transition* 27 (April–May 1938), 289–94.

21 J. C. C. Mays, "Brian Coffey's Review of Beckett's *Murphy*: 'Take warning while you praise,'" in *Other Edens: The Life and Work of Brian Coffey*, ed. Keatinge and Woods (Dublin: Irish Academic Press, 2010), 85.

22 Mays, "Brian Coffey's Review of Beckett's *Murphy*," 95.

23 Beckett, "*Intercessions* by Denis Devlin," 91.

24 Beckett, "Recent Irish Poetry," 71.

25 Beckett, "*Intercessions* by Denis Devlin," 91.

26 Beckett, "Recent Irish Poetry," 70–71.

27 Beckett, "Recent Irish Poetry," 70.

28 Samuel Beckett to Thomas MacGreevy, March 18, 1948. Quoted in Kennedy, "'Too Absolute and Ireland Haunted,'" 190.

29 Thomas MacGreevy, *Jack B. Yeats: An Appreciation and an Interpretation* (Dublin: Victor Waddington, 1945).

Making the Impossible Possible, A Review of *Dance and Modernism in Irish and German Literature and Culture: Connections in Motion*

Sabine Egger, Catherine E. Foley, and Margaret Mills Harper, eds. *Dance and Modernism in Irish and German Literature and Culture: Connections in Motion* (Lanham, MD: Lexington Books, 2019), hardcover and eBook, pp. 261, ISBN 978-1-4985-9426-4.

Reviewed by Melinda Szűts

The collection *Dance and Modernism in Irish and German Literature and Culture: Connections in Motion* is a delightful endeavor to make the "impossible possible": it provides a panoramic overview on the influence of dance on its sister arts and on the creative processes of artists of Irish and German cultural heritage from the 1920s to the present (158). The challenges of the project lie first and foremost in its far-reaching, international, and interdisciplinary scope—integrating new research from the fields of dance, literature, drama, ethnochoreology, and architecture—and in the acknowledged difficulty in the definition and interpretation of its main subject. As most authors in the volume point out, dance in all of its manifestations is on the "periphery of comprehensibility," which is a quality that derives from its essential dynamism and ability for constant change (176). What positions dance at the forefront of critical attention today is exactly its changeability and self-renewing energy, which make it not only a subject but also a prevailing agent of transformation and discovery. It is this creative power of movement, corporeality, and choreographic expression that provided the main theme of the interdisciplinary conference held at the University of Limerick in 2016, from which the present volume of essays emerged. The collection, edited by Sabine Egger, Catherine E. Foley, and Margaret Mills Harper, includes essays by academics and researcher-practitioners alike, which provides an illuminating double perspective on its chosen subject. The volume is divided into two main sections. In the first group of essays, contributors discuss dance as a tool for cultural exchange and national identification, by presenting significant "connections in motion" through artistic engagements between Ireland and the German-speaking world in the past century (2). The second part of the volume comprises studies of Modernist and contemporary literature, drama, and architecture, focusing on works both by German and Irish authors and practitioners, in the light of their "intermedial encounters" with dance (2). The shared aim of these discussions is to illuminate the importance of corporeality and physical expression in all means of artistic creation, and to highlight the validity and vital need of its inclusion into the fields of academic research and education.

The volume opens with discourses on cross-cultural exchanges and important transformations in the Irish cultural scene through dance and art education. In her study on Modernism, migration, and Irish-German connections in the 1930s and 1940s, Gisela Holfter discusses the life and work of three German-speaking dance artists (Erina Brady, Kurt Jooss, and Helen Lewis) and how dance education and performance stimulated important changes in twentieth-century Irish society and in the nation's cultural aesthetics. All three artists lived or performed in Ireland as political refugees, and brought new performance styles and training techniques of Modernist dance from the Continent, which were welcomed with "considerable interest" by Irish audiences and practitioners (11). In contrast to the common presentations of Ireland in the interwar period as an isolated territory resistant to change and the influences of Modernism, Holfter's examples provide evidence for the claim that the country was, in fact, a "safe haven" for refugee artists, and became a fertile ground for the forward-looking ideas introduced by "the agents of change" (10). Similar views are presented by Deirdre Mulrooney and Ruth Fleischmann, who elaborate on the foundational contributions of European artist-educators of mixed cultural heritage to the Irish artistic scene, focusing on the life achievements of modern dance pioneer Erina Brady, dancer-choreographer and classical ballet teacher Joan Moriarty, and composer-scholar Aloys Fleischmann. Brady laid the groundwork got teaching modern dance on the island in an attempt to transplant the techniques of the German *Ausdrucktanz*, while Moriarty and Fleischmann introduced and developed structured training for professional ballet and classical music in the country, respectively. All three authors emphasize the fact that the significant contributions of these renowned artist-educators to Irish cultural heritage were, in all cases, attempts for personal and collective self-definition and identity-creation. The background to this is that the artists in question either moved or returned to Ireland because of their interest in the country's cultural traditions as a result of their Irish ancestry, or settled down in Éire to rediscover their national identities, away from their home countries. The personal journeys of these artists thus not only helped them reformulate their relationship to the traditions of their nations, but also stimulated the Irish cultural scene to shape, to express, and to redefine its very own national values.

(Re)definitions and representations of national identity and cultural belonging are recurring themes in subsequent chapters as well, many of which present these most complex issues from a more personal perspective. From the thirteen contributors, three (Catherine E. Foley, Marguerite Donlon, and Finola Cronin) elaborate exclusively on their own embodied experiences of identity formation through dance, which could be considered as keys to the reception and appropriation of the volume, for at least two important reasons. Firstly, they serve as justifications and authentic examples for Lucia Ruprecht's argument, in which she claims that contemporary writings on movement and dance (let it be creative or academic) predominantly derive from the authors' own experience, which leads to a more "subjective, biographical focus" in discourses on dance in performance and in literature (175). Secondly, they provide an important toolkit for the reader to obtain a deeper understanding of the artistic processes described and analyzed in the other chapters of the collection, in which authors apply more objective approaches.

In their personal accounts, Irish dancer-choreographers Donlon and Cronin present how they "found" Ireland in their own creative processes while working on international projects away from home, and how the outcomes of these projects were received as cultural signifiers of Irishness by foreign audiences (112). Donlon's narrative begins with the recollection of her training in Irish step-dance, in which she emphasizes her disappointment in not being able to use her arms (85). The partial restriction of the body's movement led to Donlon's growing interest in classical ballet, which later brought her international fame and acknowledgement. The focus of the analysis is on her creative process in adapting a poem by the Irish poet Brendan Kennelly to the stage of the Stuttgart Ballet, in which Donlon was seeking to reach back to her Irish roots. By incorporating elements of traditional Irish step-dance into the stylistic frames of modern dance and classical ballet, Donlon redefined her Irishness by means of choreographic expression—in a creative process which she situated "somewhere between remembering and forgetting" (85). Cronin's essay reflects on similar processes of self-definition: her analysis presents a fascinating insight to her work with iconic dancer-choreographer Pina Bausch, and gives a detailed account of her contributions to Bausch's rehearsal processes. Cronin describes how she was required to trace, research, and perform her own Irishness in response to a set of tasks called the *Aufgaben* as part of Bausch's rehearsal methodology, which was an approach that demanded dancers' personal engagement with their own cultural heritage. In her creative reflection to the theme "A Dance from Your Country," Cronin presented a choreography that relied largely on elements of Irish step-dance, in which, she later acknowledged, she had no formal training, and only recalled some steps from her early childhood (110).

These two essays point towards two interesting directions of thought. Firstly, considering that the most important element of the process of discovery "for Cronin was 'spending time' with memory," her narrative, similarly to Donlon's account, emphasizes the importance of remembrance and the recollection of embodied experience in identity formation. This presupposes the necessity of a certain distance in creative self-reflection, even in cases when the discovery is made through the most subjective engagement with time, triggered by the physical involvement of the body. Secondly, both Cronin's and Donlon's performative statements on their Irish cultural belonging provide examples for "inauthentic" renditions of a style of dance that is internationally labelled as Ireland's cultural trademark. Although neither of the authors aspired to authenticity in these performances, both refer to their works (and many of their subsequent projects on international platforms) being received as "typically Irish," which brings us to the questions of national stereotypes, simplifications, misunderstandings, and misinterpretations (97). In relation to this, Cronin quotes Ninette de Valois, who claimed herself, alongside other internationally acclaimed artists with an Irish background, "a hoarder of matters Irish," pointing to the oversimplified labeling that is an inevitable part of the reception of productions that are engaged with its performers' national identity and cultural traditions (112).

Beside their commentary on the creative processes of self-definition, the aforementioned discussions provide useful examples for "embodied research"—a practice-based research approach that involves the researcher's personal and corporeal engagement with the studied material (108). Possible methodologies for this type of research are most comprehensibly described by Foley, whose chapter discusses the author's own method of "preserving the intangible cultural heritage" of Irish traditional step-dance (67). In her study, Foley summarizes her personal journey of collecting dances from elderly step dancers of the Kerry region to preserve performance styles that were on the decline due to the influences of modernity (74). In her investigations, she relied largely on her own embodied experience in learning these dances, which she later amended by applying a method of dance notation (Labanotation) that she mastered as part of her professional training in Laban Studies in London (75).

Foley's chapter brings to light two important aspects of the possible uses of dance, both of which provide interesting starting points for further critical thought and discussion. The first observation stems from the apparent similarity between Foley's case and the examples by Donlon and Cronin, concerning how authors' international connections affected their relationship to the traditions of their native cultures. In all three projects, it was the multinational context (manifested in international productions or studies) that triggered and facilitated the performers' reevaluation of their country's national values, therefore demonstrating the importance of intercultural "connections in motion" in processes of identity formation (2). The second point that requires further attention is that, despite its similarities with uses of dance described in earlier chapters, Foley's approach is contrastive to the previous examples in terms of its motivation and practical aim. Whereas all of the other practitioners exploited the possibilities of movement and choreographic expression to stimulate cultural change in forms of personal and collective discoveries, Foley applied it as a tool *against* change and transformation, and relied on corporeality as an aid for the preservation and protection of national cultural inheritances. This contrastive yet complementary juxtaposition of the uses of dance in the thread of presented examples points out the multitude of possibilities this form of expression carries, which is one of the most revealing arguments of the volume.

The collection concludes with essays discussing how dance transformed individual artists' experiences in their modes of expression, and how it became an "agent of change" in their body of work. Most of the chapters in this section focus on literature: among others, Susan Jones writes about the influence of modern dance on the style of Samuel Beckett's prose and drama, Siobhán Purcell discusses the performative aspects of the works of James Joyce and Beckett as inspired by the figure and art of modernist dancer Lucia Joyce (whose talent as an illustrator and important contributions to her father's works the chapter highlights), and Margaret Mills Harper analyses dance and the role of the dancer in W. B. Yeats's poetry. Harper's chapter, besides providing insightful reinterpretations of several of Yeats's most well-known poems with regard to their appropriations of the figure of the dancer, highlights how the poet's interest in corporeality and bodies in motion affected his logic and creative thought. The central argument of the paper is that Yeats's professional engagements with dance and Modernist dancers led him towards reformulating the "ideational structures" of his works (both creative and philosophical), which was a change inseparable from his experiments in occult practices (4). Harper defines this shift as a move for Yeats from being a "binary thinker"—understanding the working mechanism of the universe in terms of antinomies and oppositional qualities—to envisioning the driving force of life as being derived from the constantly changing relationship between these polarities (163). In other words, in Yeats's thought, "art and life" were reimagined as oppositions *in motion* (163). In addition to reinforcing the influence of dance on the poet's oeuvre, this thought provides new insight to the interpretation of the structure and dramaturgy of Yeats's later poetry and plays as inherently dynamic and dance-like. Another important statement Harper makes is that in Yeats's vision, movement not only constitutes the core of powerful life, but also always points towards something unreachable and unfathomable—to an "unsettled territory" that seeks to be, but never could be, conquered (161). With this claim, the essay turns back to the idea of considering literary representations and academic discourses on movement as essentially open-ended and thus "impossible," yet at the same time encourages and justifies the validity of these dialogues taking place (158).

The final piece in the volume, by Jan Frohburg and Tanja Poppelreuter, is a refreshing exception among discussions on literature, as it elaborates on the interplay of choreographic expression with music, performance, and architecture, presented through the work of German-American architect, Ludwig Mies van der Rohe. This closing chapter not only provides a fascinating overview of Mies van der Rohe's achievements as a pioneer of Modernist architecture, but gives a holistic overview of the manifold links between different art forms at the turn of the century, which nicely encapsulates the scope and primary aim of the volume.

The joint conclusion of the discussions in the collection is that dance has always been a means to find new possibilities, both for the creative individual and, through performance, education, and research, for the larger community as well. In the kaleidoscopic vision of the present volume of essays, these possibilities unfold in most engaging ways, through the accounts of personal and shared "connections in motion" (2).

A Review of *Viral Modernism: The Influenza Pandemic and Interwar Literature*

Elizabeth Outka. *Viral Modernism: The Influenza Pandemic and Interwar Literature* (New York: Columbia University Press, 2020), xii + 326 pp., ISBN 978-0-231-1875-2.

Reviewed by Maria Rita Drumond Viana

When George Yeats took to bed with the so-called Spanish Flu on November 18, 1918,[1] W. B. Yeats relayed his wife's desire to have his sister Lily by her side—but only in case she did not feel better soon. This tentative request was made not because of a lack of proximity between the two new sisters-in-law but because Lily was already making preparations to be rushed to another bedside: that of her own father, John B. Yeats, then in New York City and also stricken with pneumonia. The two competing demands for Lily Yeats's attention, from family members on both sides of the Atlantic, perfectly illustrate the global impact of the 1918 influenza pandemic on populations around the world: the three main waves (May–July 1918, September–December 1918, and January–May 1919) hit parts of every continent almost simultaneously, with the more serious cases (such as the Yeatses') and the highest number of deaths being concentrated in the twelve terrible weeks that surrounded the Armistice in Europe. Yeats's plans to relocate the growing family to Oxford had to be put off and, with Thoor Ballylee closed for the winter, even a move to the comfortable surroundings of Coole Park became impossible, as the flu was also rampant in the country, with nearby Gort crowded "with hearses and funerals," in Lady Gregory's words.[2]

While these events have long featured with some prominence in the biographies of all three Yeatses, they are more often discussed of in the context of the early years of W. B. and George Yeats's marriage, a period in which the couple invited in some (real) ghosts while attempting to banish (metaphorical) others. It is certainly one of the many ironies that mark W. B. Yeats's concomitant and continuing entanglement with the Gonnes since his serial proposals beginning in the summer of 1916 that, after the long renovation of Thoor Ballylee as their symbolic family home, the Yeatses would find themselves at 73 St. Stephen's Green. This was the house on which Maud Gonne had taken a lease before being sent to HM Prison Holloway in London, while Iseult Gonne, in her turn, had been forcibly removed to Yeats's bachelor lodgings at 18 Woburn Buildings.

This volatile play at domiciliary musical chairs would soon come to a dramatic, though not totally unexpected, crisis when Maud Gonne herself made her way to Dublin undercover after being given a compassionate leave from prison for health reasons. Upon arrival she demanded admittance to her house, which Yeats denied because of George's condition. In his biography Roy Foster frames these events with, on one hand, an analysis of George's role in effecting some distance between W. B. Yeats and Iseult, including a consideration of "Two Songs for a Fool" as "a poem which framed his symbolic images of George and herself [Iseult], tame and wild, as cat and hare" (*Life 2* 129), and on the other, a performative rejection by W. B. Yeats of Maud Gonne in her illness as "ghastly" and a "tragic sight." Foster then considers how the quarrel plays a role in the genesis of "On a Political Prisoner," a poem which, although ostensibly about Constance Markievicz, harkens back to the Gonnes with its white sea-bird imagery (*Life 2* 139). Ann Saddlemyer similarly presents George's illness as the storm that follows the relative calm of the spring and summer that had led to marital poems such as "Solomon to Sheba," "Solomon and the Witch," and "The Gift of Harun Al-Rashid" (*Becoming George* 188). As these two examples from biographies show, George's illness tends to be conscribed to the realm of the domestic, of interpersonal relationships, and contextualized as the moment W. B. Yeats (finally) stands up for his by-then pregnant wife and banishes the Gonnes to a more mythical realm.

By reframing Yeats's concern for George in the public context of "The Second Coming," Elizabeth Outka shines new light on both the poem and the couple's lives in her excellent *Viral Modernism*. This effect is achieved for all three main authors considered in the volume's middle section, entitled "Pandemic Modernism," in which she takes on the towering figures of Virginia Woolf, T. S. Eliot, and Yeats. These chapters are central not just because of these subjects' importance in modernist studies but also structurally, given that the book's organization examines later works first in order to do the groundwork and lay terms by which to (re)read the canonic moderns. The third part also brings one last, less weighty chapter, which considers how some of the frameworks developed for reading the more realist works in part one, and the modernists in part two, become, in their turn, metaphors for the supernatural in the popular fiction of figures such as Arthur Conan Doyle and H. P. Lovecraft. This is a methodological feat that escapes the confines of more obvious arrangements and manages to impose a very sound progression in an otherwise unwieldly mix of the canonical and the popular, with one set of texts being recalled and truly helping to illuminate the next. In this sense, it is a book to be read from cover to cover, even while some sets of chapters can work (and have worked) as author-specific studies for specialists. For this reason, before returning to the Yeatses, I must consider the buildup to Outka's central chapters and how her analysis strikes an innovative note when reading texts as widely studied as *Mrs. Dalloway*, *The Waste Land*, and, more to the scope of this journal, "The Second Coming."

The introduction opens with what the author calls a "modernist mystery"—that the 1918 influenza pandemic seems to have made few appearances in the British, Irish, and American literature of the period, a perception that classic studies of the pandemic such as John M. Barry's have helped cement when declaring that "[t]he disease has survived in memory more than in any literature".[3] The operative word, which she does not highlight here but which should jump out at the attentive reader, is seems. Part one consists of analyses of more realist works which, according to her argument, have a more overt manner of representing the pandemic because they originate at a greater geographic and temporal distance from the Great War. Written by US Americans between the years of 1922 and 1939, a novella like Katherine Anne Porter's *Pale Horse, Pale Rider* can "establish the frame we need to see the diffuse elements from the pandemic experiences in part 2" (40). This diffuseness is, in itself, characteristic of the virus, as:

> New forms of violence—an internal corruption, a miasmic enemy, an invisible weapon, a spreading contagion—become foils to the more visible violence of war. The very avoidance of the pandemic fundamentally shapes the period and thus changes how we read it: the virus becomes the ultimate form of Yeats's "mere anarchy," an invisible power without human agency and outside all control. (3)

The trope of the "miasma" is certainly the most pervasive and carries considerable explanatory power in every chapter even if, as the author recognizes, by 1918 germ theory had already replaced the explanation of "tainted air" a cause for disease—at least among medical authorities.[4] The second trope that recurs in the study is what Outka terms "viral resurrection" and is not only related to the various zombie figures of part three but to delirium states and mental-health issues caused by the virus during infection and in its sometimes lifelong after-effects with chronic conditions developed as consequences of the flu.

In bringing a "pandemic literary paradigm" to the reading of Woolf, Eliot, and Yeats, Outka does not propose a cause-and-effect model for elements of modernist style that have already been identified particularly with the war, "argu[ing] instead for a critical recognition of a symbiotic atmosphere of influence" between both pandemic and war:

> Collectively, these works [*Mrs. Dalloway*, *The Waste Land*, and "The Second Coming"] shape the sense of global menace, of a coming apocalypse or waste land that involves a form of mass death tied to—but distinct from—the more

> visible violence of war. Adjusting our framework to include the shadowy landscape of pandemic suffering requires a parallel retooling of modernist scholarship on violence and the body. (101)

This deceptively modest claim (a mere adjustment) has nevertheless shifted my own understanding of Clarissa Dalloway irrevocably. When Outka first published on the topic in *Modernism/modernity* in 2014, it read like a revelation;[5] it also led me to Jane Fisher's excellent book-length study of women's narratives of the 1918 pandemic.[6] The Yeats chapter, however, brings completely original material to her analysis and comprises far more than what the title—"Apocalyptic Pandemic: W. B. Yeats's 'The Second Coming'"—indicates.

In addition to reframing the biographical facts of George's illness, with special consideration of her status as a pregnant woman in Dublin (a reality recently fictionalized by Emma Donoghue in another great historical novel),[7] from the "internal, bodily apocalypse" to a "vast, societal breakdown" (167) of "The Second Coming," the chapter also contrasts that central poem to other poems of "Yeatsean [sic] violence" (175). Also included is the work of the third Yeats, John Butler Yeats, and his illustrations for an 1895 edition of Daniel Defoe's *A Journal of the Plague Year*.[8] Though not a Yeatsian herself, Outka deftly covers the expansive grounds of the poem's analyses (including the excision of specific allusions in drafts) and succeeds in supporting her conclusion that:

> Despite shared qualities with other works, "The Second Coming" stands as distinct in the nonhuman agency it suggests. "Easter 1916," "Nineteen Hundred and Nineteen," and "Leda and the Swan" may each offer different takes on violence, but they all concern specific people and acts, a specific history, and a human-initiated destruction, all seen from the vantage point of an outside observer who does not seem, quite, to have witnessed the violence in person [. . .]. The difference in this violence does not mean that "The Second Coming" must be about the pandemic, but it does highlight how the poem registers violence that Yeats had seen firsthand and that his wife had experienced, captured from within the immediacy of the trauma and allowing little distance from the unfolding events. (182)

Her pandemic readings add new layers to the well-known "turning and turning," "darkness drops again," and "mere anarchy is loosed," but particularly to "the ceremony of innocence is drowned," and "the blood-dimmed tide is loosed"—the very expressions whose powerful but indefinite allusiveness have made "The Second Coming" the go-to poem of crisis and turmoil among journalists and politicians, as Geraldine Higgins showed us once more in her brilliant plenary at the International Yeats Society Conference 2020.[9] The conference, hosted at the University of Łódź, Poland, was the first to take place remotely as we dealt with our own coronavirus pandemic.

Rarely does Outka fail to consider important work done on her corpus or seem to stretched her analyses too far. In the specific case of Yeats I could cite the feeble association of the "winds of winter" in "Nineteen Hundred and Nineteen" with "the terrible winter of the pandemic second wave" (178), or the casting of the titular second coming as the coming of the plague on the heels of war (182). Finally, and more locally, I was mildly irritated to see the name of the editor of this very journal, Rob Doggett, misspelt as "Dugget" on page 180 (though it was correct in the references). These are, however, minor issues in an otherwise thoroughly well-researched publication, which successfully reframes the pandemic presence for modernists and Yeatsians alike.

NOTES

1 First diagnosed as pneumonia; see Ann Saddlemyer, *Becoming George: The Life of Mrs. W. B. Yeats* (Oxford: Oxford University Press, 2002), 195. Pneumonia became a comorbidity with influenza and other acute respiratory syndromes; the the viral infection paved the way for the bacteria, making patients' prognosis worse. See, among others, David M. Morens, Jeffery K. Taubenberger, and Anthony S. Fauci, "Predominant role of bacterial pneumonia as a cause of death in pandemic influenza: Implications for pandemic influenza preparedness," *The Journal of Infectious Diseases* 198, no. 7 (2008): 962–970. The sequence of events is inverted to the more usual pattern of disease evolution in the report included in a letter to Edmund Dulac on December 13, 1918: "Two or three days after your letter came my wife developed Influenza & after that Pneumonia" (*CL InteLex* #3538).

2 Augusta Gregory to W.B. Yeats, November 27, 1918, in Saddlemyer, *Becoming George*, 195 and n151.

3 John M. Barry, *The Great Influenza: The Story of the Deadliest Pandemic in History*, revised Kindle edition (London: Penguin, 2020), 392.

4 Starting in the late seventeenth century with the development of the microscope, germ theory was greatly boosted in the 1880s after Pasteur and Koch isolated the bacilli of anthrax, tuberculosis, and cholera. However, in the general public's perception, miasmic explanations for influenza could coexist with an understanding of germ theory, according to Mark Honigsbaum, *A History of the Great Influenza Pandemics* (London: Bloomsbury, 2014), 66.

5 Elizabeth Outka, "'Wood for the Coffins Ran Out': Modernism and the Shadowed Afterlife of the Influenza Pandemic," *Modernism/modernity* 21, no. 4 (2014): 937–60.

6 Jane Fisher, *Envisioning Disease, Gender, and War: Women's Narratives of the 1918 Influenza Pandemic* (New York: Palgrave Macmillan, 2012).

7 Emma Donoghue, *The Pull of the Stars: A Novel* (London: Picador, 2020). As observed by John M. Barry, pregnant women were the most vulnerable group, with death rates reaching 71%; *The Great Influenza*, 240.

8 Daniel Defoe, *A Journal of the Plague Year*, vol. 9 of Romances and Narratives, ed. George A. Aitken, ill. John Butler Yeats (London: J. M. Dent & Co., 1895).

9 For details on the conference hosted by Wit Pietrzak and his team in Poland, see http://www.yeatsandpop.uni.lodz.pl; for the most recently published update on her ongoing "Yeats-spotting" in the news, see Geraldine Higgins, "News that Stays New: The Future Life of W.B. Yeats," *Poetry Ireland Review* 116 (2015): 183–92.

A Review of *Poetry and Uselessness: From Coleridge to Ashbery*, by Robert Archambeau

Robert Archambeau, *Poetry and Uselessness: From Coleridge to Ashbery* (New York and Abingdon: Routledge, 2020), pp. 244, ISBN: 978-0-367-20736-6 (hardcover); ISBN: 978-0-429-26317-0 (eBook).

Reviewed by Ben Grant

I'm going to begin this review with a bit of a gripe, I'm afraid. I was asked to undertake it, and enthusiastically accepted the invitation, because of my interest in the subject of uselessness. Needless to say, for me a book entitled *Poetry and Uselessness* looked like a dream come true. My eBook received, I started reading it at once, and as soon as I did so, I had a sinking feeling. No mention of uselessness in the first few paragraphs, but plenty on "aesthetic autonomy"—not the same thing at all. I decided to search the text for the word "uselessness," and found to my dismay that it occurs only three times—once in the title, once on the series page, and once on the title page. The knowledge that the word does not appear at all in the main text did, though, afford me a novel reading experience, no small thing for as hardened a reader as myself—henceforth, every time I read the phrase "aesthetic autonomy" in the introduction, its effect upon me bore a striking resemblance to a slap on the face. That said, I can see that there is a relationship between aesthetic autonomy and uselessness, so I will try to explore that through my reading of the book.

In entitling a book about poetry and aesthetic autonomy *Poetry and Uselessness*, Archambeau implies that uselessness and aesthetic autonomy are synonymous. His central thesis is that the idea of aesthetic autonomy has been put to a variety of uses by the poets he considers (Coleridge, Tennyson, Yeats, Stein, Eliot, Auden, and John Ashbery), so equating aesthetic autonomy with uselessness then makes for a neat argument: the idea of the uselessness of poetry has, in fact, proven to be an eminently useful one. This is something of a straw man argument, though, for the real focal point of Archambeau's book is not the debate between uselessness and usefulness, but that between a conception of poetry as autonomous from the social and political realm, and a conception of it as socially engaged, or politically committed. Within this debate, the dominant position of those who argue for the autonomy of literature, especially within the Anglophone tradition, has been that literature is useful in different ways than overtly political writing. The most hyperbolic expression of this is the famous concluding sentence of Percy Bysshe Shelley's *A Defence of Poetry*: "Poets are the unacknowledged legislators of the world."[1]

The fact that Archambeau equates aesthetic autonomy and uselessness means that the latter is largely repressed in this book, but it also means that it haunts the discussion of aesthetic autonomy in quite an uncanny way. I have said that the word "uselessness" does not appear in the book. However, the word "useless" does, on two (or let us say one-and-a-half) occasions. On the first of these, Archambeau writes of Coleridge: "He was certainly haunted by a sense that he was a mere imposter, a useless and weak outsider passing through a world properly belonging to people more confident, grounded, and socially integrated than himself" (34). Archambeau's approach in this book, inspired by Pierre Bourdieu, is to look at the ways in which the personal circumstances and psychologies of the poets studied intersected with ideas of aesthetic autonomy in their literary contexts to produce their unique bodies of work. A key aspect of this intersection for many of the poets is that it was their sense of displacement which led them to embrace an autonomous literary aesthetic. Thus, for instance, Eliot had to confront the loss of social status and cultural influence of the Boston Brahmin class to which he belonged; Stein had a strong sense of homelessness; and Ashbery experienced "three kinds of alienation—having to do with his sexuality, his relation to conventionally productive labor, and his status as a certain kind of poet in midcentury America" (201). Though it is only Coleridge whom Archambeau describes as feeling "useless," we might reasonably take him to suggest that these other poets also felt this way; after all, the culture to which they all belong is one which finds worth only in utility, and to be alienated from society is to be marked as useless.

Archambeau probably sees the idea of the autonomous poem as a correlative of the uselessness of the poet, but, by reopening the gap between uselessness and aesthetic autonomy, might we not instead see the latter as a kind of sublimation of the former, whereby feelings of uselessness (both individual and collective) are transformed into an eminently useful commitment to poetry? The book begins by demonstrating that the notion of aesthetic autonomy can be traced back to the eighteenth-century English philosopher Shaftesbury's philosophy of proper taste. For Shaftesbury, those who had taste were thereby placed at a remove from society and, for that very reason, able to guide it. This idea of a powerful cultured elite was developed further by Coleridge in his concept of the "clerisy," which had a strong influence on Arnold, and created the context in which Tennyson was torn between the roles of aesthete and "public moralist" (47). The late nineteenth century marked a turn from what Archambeau nicely terms "a cultured minority to a minority culture" (76), in which the idea of aesthetic autonomy served to create a sense of belonging and community within an artistic coterie, and all the later poets whom Archambeau looks at grappled in different ways with this context.

The first of these later poets considered by Archambeau is Yeats; Archambeau argues that Yeats sought, though ultimately failed, to unify aesthetic autonomy with a social role for poetry in a public form of art which could give expression to a true Irish nationalist spirit; more specifically, he dreamt that the Order of Celtic Mysteries could give "the arts a home in the world" (102). In this history of the idea of aesthetic autonomy, uselessness is indeed repressed, but if we see it as precisely that—the occluded, unconscious origin of the (as Archambeau amply demonstrates) highly useful idea of aesthetic autonomy—we might then be attentive to the ways in which it necessarily and insistently returns in unpredictable forms to undercut the historical narrative. Examples of this could include Coleridge's fixation on failure, Tennyson's enduring grief for his friend Arthur Hallam, Yeats's unrequited love for Maud Gonne, and Eliot's depression, which contributed to his most famous, and perhaps most useless, poem, *The Waste Land* (1922).

The second occurrence of the word "useless" in *Poetry and Uselessness* is not the word itself (hence the half), but its French equivalent, "inutile," which has, according to the *Oxford English Dictionary*, been adopted into English, and come back into use recently after a period of obsolescence. It appears in the course of Archambeau's discussion of the passage of Auden's poem "In Memory of W.B. Yeats" (1939) in which occurs the phrase "poetry makes nothing happen" (quoted, 197). This is a phrase which serves as something of a leitmotif in Archambeau's book: "for Auden [. . .] there is some comfort in this notion of poetry as a kind of timeless, aesthetic, inutile thing" (197). The use of the French here is entirely necessary, because "useless" simply does not belong with "timeless" and "aesthetic." When we hear that English word, we think first of all, not of timeless jewels, but of that which is without worth, if not immediately of refuse and waste. The kinds of abject emotions I have just alluded to would be embraced by this word, rather than taste, discernment, and a love of the beautiful. The fact that the French word "inutile" can be associated with the aesthetic is owing to the fact that, as Archambeau says, the connection between "aesthetic autonomy and a minority literary culture" was imported from France in the late nineteenth century into the English-speaking world, as Aestheticism (78). In using the French word instead of the English, this whole culture of French Aestheticism (or, more accurately, what it is made to stand for in the English tradition) takes the place, and thereby represses, the everyday connotations of the word "useless."

If one of these connotations is the abject, a second is purposeless play, and this is another form in which the insistent recurrence of uselessness can be traced through *Poetry and Uselessness*, most notably in the three poets whom Archambeau identifies as most strongly advocating aesthetic autonomy: Auden, Stein, and Ashbery. In the case of Auden, Archambeau finds a "deeper unity" between his claims for the aesthetic autonomy of poetry, and the political content of much of his poetry, in "camp," which he defines as "a kind of ludic and aestheticizing attitude" (163). In this light, Auden is read as a "camp dogmatist" (169), mistaken for a guru, who pokes fun at ideas which, unlike a satirist, he has some affection for, and Archambeau demonstrates that it was precisely the distance afforded by a camp attitude that gave Auden's poetry political efficacy in the ideologically-riven 1930s. In camp, therefore, uselessness and usefulness would seem to hang together in a non-binary kind of a way.

The chapter on Stein is, for me, the least satisfactory in the book, precisely because Archambeau doesn't attend to the role of play in her work. He takes her claims of genius entirely seriously as an expression of a monstrous narcissism, without considering the possibility that she might be playing (or right), and he reads in her poetry a displaced expression of her lesbianism (though it doesn't seem all that displaced to me). Archambeau thus finds in psychological and social determinants the reasons why "[Stein's] writing represents an impulse to aesthetic autonomy both purer and more radical than that of any other writer of similar stature and consequence" (109), but I would have liked to have seen a greater consideration of one of the things which makes that writing so radical, namely the free play of the signifier. Free play is certainly suggested in Archambeau's characterization of Ashbery's work as "a poetics of drift" (201), and I get the impression that Ashbery would be the most likely of any of the poets considered in this book to advocate a poetics of uselessness, for, we are told, when an interviewer "tells Ashbery he thinks Ashbery's poetry gives us 'language as a child would use it, language before it becomes useful' [. . .] Ashbery interjects 'yeah! yeah!' enthusiastically" (204). This enthusiasm for the playful uselessness of language would be in line with Ashbery's alienation from "conventionally productive labor," and when Archambeau says that his "anti-dogmatic stance [. . .] extends even to the aestheticism to which he is drawn" (202), I would conjecture that this is because for Ashbery, as for me, aesthetic autonomy and uselessness are not synonymous.

Not so much in the margins of this book, then, as somewhere beneath its surface, haunting it like an uncanny double and occasionally breaking through, most dramatically in its very title, we can indeed find the spectral presence of a book on poetry and uselessness. Perhaps this is the only way in which we can possibly approach a spirit of uselessness within a utilitarian culture in which uselessness, by definition, can have no home. Nonetheless, I would still like someone to write about the subject more directly. The title *Poetry and Uselessness* has, unfortunately, already been taken, so how about *Uselessness and Poetry*, though I know that's not the same thing at all. I'd be happy to review it.

Notes

1 Percy Bysshe Shelley, *A Defence of Poetry; or, Remarks Suggested by an Essay Entitled 'The Four Ages of Poetry'* (extracts), in *Romanticism: An Anthology*, ed. Duncan Wu, 3rd edn. (Oxford: Blackwell, 2006), 1199.

Notes on Contributors

Edward Clarke recently published a collection of poems entitled *A Book of Psalms* (Paraclete Press, 2020). He presented *Clarke's Psalter*, a documentary about writing these poems, which was broadcast on BBC Radio 4 in September 2018. He is also the author of two books of criticism, T*he Later Affluence of W. B. Yeats and Wallace Stevens* (Palgrave Macmillan, 2012) and *The Vagabond Spirit of Poetry* (Iff Books, 2014).

Matthew Fogarty is an Associate Lecturer at the School of English, Drama and Film in University College Dublin. He has published articles in the *Irish Journal of Gothic and Horror Studies and the Journal of Academic Writing*, and has an article forthcoming in *Modern Drama*. His first monograph, *Nietzschean Constellations in Irish Literary Modernism: Subjectivity and Nationhood in Yeats, Joyce, and Beckett*, is forthcoming with Liverpool University Press.

Ben Grant is a Departmental Lecturer in English Literature at the University of Oxford's Department for Continuing Education. He is the author of *Postcolonialism, Psychoanalysis, and Burton* (Routledge, 2009), and *The Aphorism and Other Short Forms* (2016). He is currently writing a book on Jenny Diski for Manchester University Press.

Sørina Higgins earned her PhD in 2021 at Baylor University, where she was a Presidential Scholar. Her dissertation, entitled *From Thaumaturgy to Dramaturgy: Staging Occult Modernism*, examined the role of ceremonial magic in modernist theatre, especially in the works of W. B. Yeats, Charles Williams, and Aleister Crowley. Sørina is a faculty member at Signum University, where she served as Chair of the Language & Literature Department from 2014–2019. Prior to her PhD, Sørina earned an MA from Middlebury College's Bread Loaf School of English. She is currently co-editing a volume on the ethical turn in speculative fiction (with Dr. Brenton Dickieson) and previously edited an academic essay collection on *The Inklings and King Arthur* (Apocryphile Press, December 2017), winner of the 2018 Mythopoeic Society Inklings Scholarship Award. Her scholarship appears or is forthcoming in *International Yeats Studies, The T. S. Eliot Studies Annual, VII: Journal of the Marion E. Wade Center, The Journal of Inklings Studies, Mythlore, and Penumbra*. Outside of academia, Sørina enjoys practicing yoga, playing with her cats, cooking, baking, gardening, dancing, and ranting about the state of the world.

Benjamin Keatinge is a Visiting Research Fellow at the School of English, Trinity College Dublin, and is editor of *Making Integral: Critical Essays on Richard Murphy* (Cork University Press, 2019).

Martin Lockerd is an Assistant Professor of English at Schreiner University in the beautiful Texas Hill Country, where he lives with his wife and three daughters. He received his Ph.D. in English from The University of Texas at Austin. His scholarship has appeared in the *Journal of Modern Literature, Modern Fiction Studies, the Yeats/Eliot Review*, and *Logos*. His monograph, Decadent Catholicism and the Making of Modernism, was published in 2020 by Bloomsbury.

Neil Mann Neil Mann has written extensively on Yeats's esoteric interests and A Vision, writing articles in the Yeats Annual and elsewhere, creating the website YeatsVision.com in 2002, editing collections of essays Yeats's 'A Vision': Explications and Contexts (Clemson, 2012), with Matthew Gibson and Claire Nally, and Yeats, Philosophy, and the Occult (Clemson, 2016) with Matthew Gibson. His book A Reader's Guide to Yeats's 'A Vision' (Clemson) came out in 2019. He also helped with text for the National Library of Ireland's long-running exhibition on Yeats, including transcriptions of Rapallo Notebook D and the PIAL Notebook for interactive display.

Ragina Mohite is Assistant Professor at FLAME University, India and the author of *Modern Writers, Transnational Literatures: Rabindranath Tagore and W. B. Yeats* (Clemson University Press, 2021). She received her PhD from the University of Leeds and works on global modernisms and transnationalism. She has works published or forthcoming in *Sculpture Journal*, *Stand* magazine, *South Asian Review*, *South Asian Diaspora*, the *Hong Kong Review of Books*, and other edited collections.

Kaori Nagai is a Lecturer in Victorian Literature at the University of Kent. She is the author of *Empire of Analogies: Kipling, India and Ireland* (Cork University Press, 2006). She has edited Rudyard Kipling's *Plain Tales from the Hills* and *The Jungle Books* for Penguin Classics, and is the co-editor of *Kipling and Beyond: Patriotism, Globalisation and Postcolonialism* (Palgrave Macmillan, 2010), and *Cosmopolitan Animals* (Palgrave Macmillan, 2015). Her new monograph, *Imperial Beast Fables: Animals, Cosmopolitanism, and the British Empire*, was published in 2020 by Palgrave Macmillan.

Melinda Szűts is an IRC Government of Ireland Postgraduate Scholar at the O'Donoghue Centre for Drama, Theatre and Performance, NUI Galway.

She is a graduate of Eötvös Loránd University, Budapest (BA in English and Film Studies, MA in English Literature). Melinda has worked in the theater as an actor, director, and dramaturge, mostly in the field of physical theater. Her most recent productions include Yeats's *The Only Jealousy of Emer* (2018, Galway Theatre Festival) and The Dreaming of the Bones (2019), both with DancePlayers Company. Her PhD project is entitled "Yeats the Dramaturge: Space Dramaturgy in *Four Plays for Dancers*." Melinda is founding member and acting head of the Hungarian Yeats Society.

YUKI TANAKA is an Assistant Professor of English at Hosei University, Japan. He has written on Virginia Woolf, Elizabeth Bishop, Seamus Heaney, and most recently on contemporary American poet Henri Cole. His poetry chapbook, *Séance in Daylight* (Bull City Press), was the winner of the 2018 Frost Place Chapbook Contest.

MARIA RITA DRUMOND VIANA is a Lecturer and Researcher in the Department of Foreign Languages and Literatures at the Universidade Federal de Santa Catarina (UFSC) in Brazil, where she works on life writing, Irish Studies, and translation. She received her PhD in English from the Universidade de São Paulo, which included a scholarship to conduct research at the Oxford Centre for Life Writing, and she was elected a Visiting Doctoral Student and member of Wolfson College. She defended her thesis on W. B. Yeats's use of public letters to editors in nineteenth-century periodicals in 2015. During 2019 she was on an academic sabbatical at the University of Toronto to conduct research on Virginia Woolf as part of a larger project on writers' correspondences.

FEARGAL WHELAN is a Postdoctoral Research Associate at the Trinity Centre for Beckett Studies, Trinity College Dublin (TCD). He has published and presented widely on Samuel Beckett and on twentieth-century Irish drama. He is a co-director of the Samuel Beckett Summer School at TCD and is a regular collaborator with Mouth on Fire Theatre Company on its annual *Beckett in Foxrock* performances. His publications include chapters in *Staging Beckett in Ireland and Northern Ireland* (Bloomsbury, 2016), *Beckett and Modernism* (Palgrave, 2018), *The Gate Theatre Dublin: Inspiration and Craft* (Peter Laing, 2018), and *Beckett and Politics* (Palgrave Macmillan, 2020), as well as articles in *Estudios Irlandeses* (2018, 2019) and *Journal of Beckett Studies* (Spring 2020). His monograph *Beckett and the Irish Protestant Imagination* was published in November 2021 with ibidem-Verlag. He is a board member of the Samuel Beckett Society and is the editor of its magazine, *The Beckett Circle*.

www.ingramcontent.com/pod-product-compliance
Lightning Source LLC
Chambersburg PA
CBHW031435160426
43195CB00010BB/734
* 9 7 8 1 6 3 8 0 4 1 2 2 1 *